# Sex and Gender in Historical Perspective

**Selections from *Quaderni Storici***

Edited by Edward Muir and Guido Ruggiero

# Sex and Gender in Historical Perspective

*Edited by Edward Muir and Guido Ruggiero*

*Translated by Margaret A. Gallucci*
*with Mary M. Gallucci and Carole C. Gallucci*



The Johns Hopkins University Press
Baltimore and London

Printed in the United States of America

The Johns Hopkins University Press
701 West 40th Street
Baltimore, Maryland 21211
The Johns Hopkins Press Ltd., London

∞ The paper used in this book meets the minimum requirements
of American National Standard for Information Sciences—
Permanence of Paper for Printed Library Materials, ANSI Z39.48-1984.

**Library of Congress Cataloging-in-Publication Data**

Sex and gender in historical perspective / edited by Edward Muir and
Guido Ruggiero ; translated by Margaret A. Gallucci with Mary M. Gallucci and
Carole C. Gallucci
p. cm. — (Selections from Quaderni storici)
Includes bibliographical references.
ISBN 0-8018-3991-2 (alk. paper). — ISBN 0-8018-4072-4 (pbk. alk. paper)
1. Sex customs—Italy—History. 2. Sex customs—Europe—History.
3. Women—Italy—History. 4. Women—Europe—History. 5. Sex role—Italy—
History. 6. Sex role—Europe—History. I. Muir, Edward, 1946– . II. Ruggiero,
Guido, 1944– . III. Gallucci, Margaret A. IV. Gallucci, Mary M. V. Gallucci,
Carole C. VI. Series.
HQ18.I8S49 1990
305.3′094—dc20 90-31730 CIP

# Contents

# Introduction

*by Guido Ruggiero*

The current fascination with the history of gender and sexuality has many ramifications. One may hope that it will continue to open and enrich perspectives on the past as it has over the past two decades, and, although it may be unduly optimistic, that with such a base the pace and quality of change are merely beginning to accelerate into a new stage of particularly important work. While the English-speaking world has clearly been a leader in these developments, scholarship in other languages has also been significant—the broad-ranging contributions of French scholars come immediately to mind. Unfortunately for the growth of a truly cosmopolitan approach to such issues, the important work that is being done in other less widely read languages remains largely unknown beyond a fairly small group of specialists. As a result, one of the primary goals in presenting the innovative and avante garde articles of *Quaderni Storici* to an English-reading audience is to make available some of the more interesting essays on sex and gender in historical perspective that have been published there over the last decade.

Perhaps because the political debate is so much more varied in Italy than in most of the rest of Europe and the West, ranging as it does from various forms of Marxism (including everything from "orthodox" Leninist Marxism to Gramsci's more cultural and nationalistic vision to the eclectic spin-offs of the late sixties and seventies) at one end of the spectrum to anarchists with their own strong tradition, who are at least formally at the other end, the debate over the correct role of women in society has been extremely rich there, both in theory and in practice. The historical debate, however, on the closely related issues of the history of gender and sexuality has to a certain degree been held back by the lack of interest demonstrated by more traditional scholarly journals. As in other areas, *Quaderni Storici* provided a forum for approaching these nontraditional concerns. Providing that forum allowed the intellectual ferment engendered by the intense debates on feminist issues to aid in the rapid development of a highly significant historical discourse in the pages of that journal and also to give prominence to an exciting group of younger women historians. In turn, the journal's tradition of open and experimental historical debate, especially its emphasis on finding new sources and new approaches to older ones, plus its predilection for the individual and the personal, added important dimensions to that developing discourse.

It has often been observed that the issues of gender and sexuality are significant for history because they offer the opportunity to rethink the past and perhaps to move beyond a view of history as merely the public affairs (and only selected affairs at that) of a small elite largely from a perspective created by them to idealize and defend their position on top. But it may be that this agenda has even more profound implications that in the scholarly world reach well beyond history. For while both gender and sex have been extremely important for the living of life in the past, neither has been effectively incorporated into the modern intellectual discourse in ways that move much beyond ideology. The great theoretical debates of the modern world have turned on class, nation, reason, progress, and the question of how inclusive the scientific method should be; perhaps with the exception of Freudian perspectives, gender and sexuality have played only an ancillary role in these disputes. And even for Freudians it might be argued that concerns with gender and sexuality have incorporated rather than analyzed a culturally specific view of both. Of course, some scholars are diligently trying to integrate gender and sex within the conceptual framework of Marx or are attempting to incorporate both more sensitively within the vision of Freud and others.

But the ever-clever Foucault seemed to be one of the first to realize that the unformed nature of our intellectual constructs of gender and sexuality (even though gender and sex were widely discussed in the modern world) provided important opportunities for rethinking the past and the present. This largely unformed discourse (or, to be more accurate, unformed outside the realm of ideology) allowed one to move beyond the mainstream and highly structured traditional range of modern discourse in ways not so much revolutionary as perhaps literally deconstructive. Those who feel that such an opening is a positive change on the path to a postmodern society may see that there is considerable potential in this area simply because it has been excluded to such an extent from modern discourse. And, of course, those who feel that the modern tradition is already pluralistic and open will in turn attempt to show how it can incorporate this wider discourse within its elastic parameters. If this is, in fact, the course that the debate on gender and sexuality follows, there can hardly be a loser. Of course, there are many other possible scenarios with much less optimistic outcomes, but simply rethinking our vision of gender and sexuality is a significant and surprisingly new project with implications that obviously move well beyond the future of scholarly discourse.

In an important article with a deceptively modest title, "Gender: A Useful Category of Historical Analysis" (published in 1986 in the *American Historical Review*), Joan W. Scott reviewed the recent literature in this area, primarily American, English, and French, and charted a program for the future. Significantly, her program, which still seems one of the most thoughtful and promising, in many ways had been anticipated in the pages of *Quaderni Storici*. This, of course, takes nothing away from the importance of Scott's vision, which remains ground-breaking: it is one thing to do innovative history; it is another to see how such work fits into a wider program that might form the basis for a new, broader, and ultimately more satisfying historical discourse, as Scott has done. Yet, as this volume was being compiled, that essay was often in my mind, and I was repeatedly struck by the significance of having some answers to and some testing of her program already in place in pioneering articles to a great extent unknown in the English-speaking world.

In a way, then, Scott's call in 1986 to pursue the meaning of gender and sexuality in a historical perspective sums up the work translated in these pages and originally published in Italian in a flurry of intellectual excitement between 1979 and 1984 in *Quaderni Storici.* Scott stated that

> to pursue meaning, we need to deal with the individual subject as well as social organization and to articulate the nature of their interrelationships, for both are crucial to understanding how gender works, how change occurs. Finally, we need to replace the notion that social power is unified, coherent, and centralized with something like Foucault's concept of power as dispersed constellations of

> unequal relationships, discursively constituted in social "fields of force." Within these processes and structures, there is room for a concept of human agency as the attempt (at least partially rational) to construct an identity, a life, a set of relationships, a society with certain limits and with language—conceptual language that at once sets boundaries and contains the possibility for negation, resistance, reinterpretation, the play of metaphoric invention and imagination.[1]

Obviously, the essays collected here do not fulfill Scott's vision so much as anticipate it in a number of suggestive ways that provide meaning, texture, and at times challenges to it.

A statement is perhaps in order on the use of the terms *gender* and *sexuality* in the title of this volume. *Gender* is a term that has not found its way widely as yet into the scholarly vocabulary or the political discourse of Italy. Yet even a cursory reading of these essays reveals that although the term is lacking, one of the central concerns of these authors is the question of how the perceptions of sexual divisions in particular historical contexts have been culturally and socially constructed; that is, most of these essays turn on the very issue for which the term has been adopted in current English usage. In this perspective, *gender* is essentially a technical term, but an extremely useful and fruitful one. *Sexuality,* in contrast, is a much less clearly defined term because it comes from common parlance, where I suppose one could say with only slight irony that it covers a host of sins. This makes it both rich with implications and fraught with methodological difficulties, perhaps the most extreme being the debate about whether sex even existed before the modern period. In trying to avoid that debate, as seems wise given its intensity and still rapidly changing parameters, sexuality is used here primarily in the limited sense of those things that particular societies have associated with the carnal pleasures of the body. Much work, clearly, is necessary to refine this concept and others associated with it; this volume, it is hoped, will contribute to that endeavor, especially with its close analysis of how even the body was constructed in particular historical and cultural contexts. From that base we may begin to consider more effectively what it really entails to discuss the history of the pleasures of the body or sexuality.

"'Menstruum Quasi Monstruum': Monstrous Births and Menstrual Taboo in the Sixteenth Century" begins the volume fittingly with the female body and the broad-ranging social and cultural constructions that surrounded menstruation, "untimely" and "passionate" sexual intercourse, and ultimately birth itself. The reader is quickly guided to a complex past where the physical body and its biological "realities" turn out to be little more than blank pages upon which a series of complex and evolving cultural codes have been written. That menstruation would have been considered monstrous in the sixteenth century, while troubling, might not seem surprising given the well-known Western tradition of viewing menstruation as unclean, but Ottavia Niccoli takes us well beyond the disconcerting to a much richer world that begins to show how this vision fit into a complex discourse on the nature of the female body and reproduction and sexuality. In the end, of course, her view is still troubling, as we see how intricate, and socially and sexually perverse, the taboos on menstruation and the female body itself had become—how much the intellectual world of early modern Europe could build upon the imagined connections between a woman's body, menstruation, and the monstrous.

Anna Foa takes us from the body and the view of its normal functioning as abnormal and as ultimately engendering monsters to the virtually monstrous infestation of the body itself with her consideration of how Europe encountered and integrated into its cultural world the new and highly disturbing disease of syphilis in "The New and the Old: The Spread of Syphilis (1494–1530)." And again the body is a point of reference for complex cultural constructs that mix the new and the old in a way that allows syphilis to be incorporated into the early modern world with surprising speed and little apparent stress—a situation that has always seemed unusual, given the virulent and sexual nature of the disease and that seems even more surprising today, given the new sexual diseases that surround and at times seem to overwhelm a supposedly much more sophisticated modern world.

Foa attempts to explain this in part by arguing that syphilis, even as its "newness" was being debated, took over many of the cultural codes that had been used to understand the earlier scourge of medieval Europe, leprosy, just at the moment when the latter had to a great extent receded from the fears of society. The transfer was complex and obviously not perfect, but ultimately it made the new and threatening familiar and relatively comfortable. Foa's thesis is clever and bold, and it explains much about the ready assimilation of this disease and opens broader perspectives on the social perception and construction of diseases associated with sexuality, perspectives applicable not just to the past.

Disease also takes us with disarming ease beyond women's bodies to the bodies of others who have troubled the European consciousness and perhaps the unconscious as well—the Jew as eternal Other for Christian society and the Indian as the new Other (with all the danger that that term implied for a world that saw the new as dangerous at every level from the theological to the practical). Both were seen in ways again rich with troubling resonances as having been the source of the disease and the cause of its spread.

While the body and its diseases may have had a much more profound influence on society, culture, and institutions than traditionally realized, all the authors in this volume are acutely aware of the dialectical nature of the relationship of body and society. Lucia Ferrante, in "Women in the Casa del Soccorso di San Paolo in Sixteenth-Century Bologna," begins on the other and more traditional side of the dialectic with the institutions that early modern Bologna used to attempt to control what were defined as errant female bodies. Quickly she sketches an impressively broad range of institutions typical of the early modern cityscape, at least in Italy and many areas of France, that aimed to enclose and discipline female bodies that did not fit within the accepted parameters for women—family and convent. Especially noteworthy in this context is the ease with which the perceptions of woman as independent and woman as sinner overlapped in early modern Bologna and in turn how elastic the label *prostitute* could be in that society. But these are not Ferrante's primary concerns; she employs the institutional frame mainly to look at how institutions intersected with the lives of individual women who were interned there.

Here we begin to encounter one of the more aesthetically pleasing and methodologically interesting tendencies of the new social history as practiced by many of the authors published by *Quaderni Storici:* the use of the individual to elucidate broader structures. At its best, this approach seems to promise a method that will help overcome the depersonalization and abstractness of social history without losing its insights on the broader structural factors that condition events. At the least, by portraying how individuals respond to and make decisions in the face of such factors as they perceive them in a concrete historical situation, this perspective provides an important caution on the too easy spinning of the web of modern theory back into the past. The theoretical issues implicit in this methodology are so significant that the second volume of this series of translations, *Microhistory and the*

*Lost Peoples of Europe*, will be dedicated to articles that exemplify and discuss the implications of this approach to history.

Ferrante's article focuses on narratives that reveal how individual women and men interacted with a set of institutions designed to discipline and control their lives and bodies, especially the Casa del Soccorso. But by turning to the concept of honor, with all its disciplinary potential for early modern society, the author significantly expands the problem of discipline and the analytical range of her discussion by moving out from the institutional to the social and at the same time moving inward to the personal. Not surprisingly, the dynamics of control in this context become much more complex, rich, and revealing about the lives of people moving within and at times beyond these complex parameters. Tellingly, while Ferrante's analysis of honor owes much to anthropological theory, she, like many of her compatriots in *Quaderni Storici,* uses that theory as a point of departure, constantly testing it against her sources and fine-tuning it to the historical situation of the sixteenth and seventeenth centuries with highly suggestive results not just for history but perhaps also for anthropological theory. Thus, theory, rather than being the measure of her work, is returned to being primarily a tool of that work. And in turn this frees her to posit some extremely interesting ideas about the exchange of honor in the Casa del Soccorso: her analysis eventually integrates chastity, money, family, social hierarchy, patronage, and obligation in a complex web of public interrelationships involved in maintaining or regaining a woman's honor.

Honor and its intimate relationship with woman's body continues as a central theme in Sandra Cavallo and Simona Cerutti's article, "Female Honor and the Social Control of Reproduction in Piedmont between 1600 and 1800." Working with the rich materials collected by ecclesiastical judges involved in marital disputes, the authors have focused on unkept promises of marriage and the testimony that grew out of them to develop a highly significant perspective on the crucial dialectic between woman's body and woman's honor. As is well known, in many premodern European communities, especially rural ones, a promise of marriage was enough to initiate sexual intercourse. Cavallo and Cerutti start at that point and examine the gender-specific exchange of honor involved in the promise of marriage and the initiation of sexual intercourse that followed, arguing that at that moment the woman exchanged her present honor for a future greater one in the eyes of society (marriage) in return for the word of the male that he would marry her. Even in a society that still valued the word highly, this was clearly a dangerous proposition for the woman, as is revealed by the very existence of the documentation used for this article. Most of the cases considered began when males failed to keep their word. Extremely dangerous for the woman was the concept of the *beffa,* or trick: this was the basis of many claims that the marriage promise had not been a serious one, but it often turned on other issues such as a difference in status that tended to make the community unsure that a true promise of marriage rather than a *beffa* had been given. Still, peer and community pressure, along with the higher value placed on the word of an individual, made the system one that functioned, that controlled in revealing ways both courtship and premarital sexuality in the rural communities of Piedmont. Again, the authors demonstrate this by examining how the system operated at the personal level of people embroiled in trying to make it work when it broke down. Of course, honor systems based in part upon such pressures and the public evaluation of behavior and words have a tendency not to function as well when the scale of social interaction becomes larger and more fluid; thus, when the authors transfer their analysis to the urban context of Turin, they find, not surprisingly, that the system of rural Piedmont no longer worked so well and that women were much more exposed to the unkept word of males and the now voyeuristic rather than protective surveillance of their neighbors.

But the honor system that had governed the promise of marriage was under attack in that period from another quarter: the Church's drive to control more directly that central institution of society—the family—by controlling the moment that created it—marriage. The authors argue cogently that the path to marriage governed by this honor system allowed the community to control and tailor to individual needs the honorable steps to matrimony and creation of a family. The Church, however, opted to replace this individualized communal approach to discipline, which it had neither the ability nor, I would suggest, the will to control, with a more bureaucratic one. Following the Council of Trent, the key became the marriage ceremony. Essentially the Church attempted to wrest control of marriage from the local community by denying the significance of the promise of marriage in the formation of a married couple and the initiation of sexual intercourse, replacing that tradition with the marriage ceremony now more closely monitored by the Church and conducted by a priest. While this battle was not easily won, at least in rural Piedmont, it had dramatic effects in the long run on the evaluation of women's honor, the practice of premarital sex, and the nature of community. Some of Cavallo and Cerutti's perspectives are troubling, especially what might be seen as a dangerous tendency to underevaluate the significance of accusations of rape, but again their analysis is subtle and they are not reluctant to arrive at difficult conclusions.

Shifting to the other side of Italy, the Friuli, Luisa Accati returns the discussion of sexuality to one of its bases, the body, in "The Spirit of Fornication: Virtue of the Soul and Virtue of the Body in Friuli, 1600–1800." In a way, she shares the perspective of Niccoli and Foa in that she looks at the rich complex of powers that the peasant culture of Friuli had bestowed upon the female body and its sexuality, but she does so within the methodological framework of Ferrante and of Cavallo and Cerutti in that she builds her analysis upon individual case histories that she has reconstructed from court documents gathered by the Inquisition in Friuli. By the seventeenth century, Accati argues, the conflicts between popular culture and the Church, fought out in inquisitional investigations and trials, had considerably attenuated. As a result, the people brought before the Inquisition were not as fearful of the procedure and its outcome, and the inquisitors themselves were not as aggressive in trying to uncover evidence to support their preconceived notions of dangerous popular practices. Instead, some inquisitors operated in a virtually ethnographic fashion to discover how that culture actually worked and what it meant, although they perhaps were still ultimately motivated by the desire to perfect controls already in place.

The first major issue considered by Accati is the distinction between female and male magical practices: Accati posits that female magic was the product of a women's culture that empowered the female body in ways that reveal gender values and stereotypes. Male magic, in contrast, was based more upon learned traditions and techniques. Rich with powerful and suggestive insights and argued in a prose that is compellingly clever in Italian, Accati's analysis cannot be adequately conveyed by a quick summary. For example, playing upon the relative scarcity of images of the male body in early modern culture, which was supposedly dominated by the male and male values, she sums up the contrast between the rich, magical fecundity of the female body and the virtual emptiness of the male body: "Of the Dionysian splendors of the phallus, there remained only a weak trace: the comb used to make the sign of the cross on the breasts in the spell against swollen breasts." In Accati's vision, the female body as the boundary between life and death, as the carnal power that balances and competes with the priest's spiritual power, as the continuing medieval grotesque body of Bakhtin alive with the potentiality of this world, leaves the pale, unimpressive carnality of the male body far behind.

While the sweep of the analysis may at times be disconcerting, there are also many insights into the complex, darker corners of misogyny at levels from the theological to the popular. And again, because Accati moves between the general and the particular stories of individuals, her broad generalizations are often exemplified in the particular lives of peasant women of the Friuli. Returning to a close analysis of other relationships between the clerics who ran the Inquisition and the women who were brought before the tribunal, Accati concludes her essay by suggesting that there was a shift in the dialectic between witch and priest late in the early modern period. Once more, female honor and power are seen as the key. Together they led to a strange reversal of roles, with the witch empowering the priest in the community, especially among other women, with her confession of guilt; in turn, the priest in accepting that empowerment repaid it by reintegrating the witch into the Church and ultimately into the honor dynamic of the community. However, it was an uneven exchange, as Accati cleverly notes, for the priest never gained control of the female body and its powers. In a way, his very spirituality left him estranged from the virtue of the body, and the spirit of fornication eluded him. The response, one of the few available to the Church, was an attack on the body and its sexuality, which Accati sees as characterizing the later early modern period. Without attempting to reconstruct that attack in detail, Accati offers some telling examples on the level of individual women of what may have been the results of that campaign. But the female body, even if redefined as hysterical and neurotic, still retained a richer past, as the unhappy Domenica of Faedis seemed unable to deny (even as she tried desperately to do so) in her last self-effacing and destructive confession: "I ask pardon of God, and this Holy Tribunal and of Your Most Reverend Father and I pray that for the love of God, you will pardon my many sins, and free *if not my body at least my soul from the hands of the demon.*" Domenica's body, although battered and rendered sinful, still eluded the Church's control.

In "One Saint Less: The Story of Angela Mellini, a Bolognese

Seamstress (1667–17[?]),” Luisa Ciammitti continues the theme of the encounter between individual women and the disciplining drive of the Church, but carries it in a different direction by opening up another relatively overlooked area of documentation—Church records evaluating claims of sanctity. Because of the Church's growing concern with such claims in the early modern period, these records often contain detailed reconstructions of individual lives. Moreover, as female sanctity entailed so many gender-specific characteristics, especially in regard to the body and its perceived sexual nature, many of the details are particularly pertinent to the history of gender and sexual values.

“One Saint Less” tells the story of Angela Mellini, who, caught up in the reforming zeal and new spiritual techniques of her time, attempted to lead a saintlike life with the help of her male spiritual advisers. In that quest she learned to read and write, attempted to avoid and overcome internal and external pressures to conform to more standard gender expectations, and eventually developed an extremely complex and revealing set of relationships with her spiritual advisers and Christ himself. Mellini's story reveals the particularly intense spiritual world of a woman profoundly affected by the renewed spirituality of the Catholic Church. This allows Ciammitti to expand our understanding of gender stereotypes in a specific historic context at a moment that particularly tests an individual—Angela's encounter with God. Mellini's god-lover is at once sensitive and cruel, a male who gives pleasure but pain as well, a man who rewards with grace but also demands service and subservience, a male who loves but destroys. The imagery of sexual relations between God and a woman is especially powerful and perhaps perverse; but even without value judgments (and Ciammitti is careful to let the story speak for itself), Mellini's case suggests another valuable type of source for the history of sexuality.

Equally suggestive is the account of Mellini's relationship with her spiritual advisers, especially with her confessor, Giovanni Battista Ruggieri. In this case, the relationship is significantly different from Mellini's relationship with Christ. Although the temptations of sexuality were not entirely avoided, the sexual was ultimately reserved for Christ, while the relationship with Ruggieri was eventually perceived by both Mellini and her confessor as maternal. Thus, in what is argued was a fairly common reversal, Angela paradoxically became the spiritual mother and guide of her spiritual father; he in turn became her spiritual son, even in Angela's reveries, drawing spiritual sustenance from her breast as a baby would have drawn milk. As a result, having rejected marriage and maternity (in essence, what standard gender expectations required women to accept in the name of family and society), Angela Mellini found that her own and contemporary spiritual expectations required her to re-create those very same sexual and maternal roles.

Interestingly, although Ciammitti does not stress the point, it appears that both the Church and Angela herself were not unaware of the ambiguities of her maternal and sexual spirituality. Of course, as Ciammitti shows, intense relationships with Christ had a long tradition that made Mellini's less troubling to Church authorities, even if they were becoming more concerned that women might be fooled by the devil or his minions into believing that they were relating to Christ. But maternal feeling for a priest who was supposed to be a spiritual father was more clearly a dangerous redrawing of the gendered relationships between the clergy and women (even if it too had its tradition), and this was where the Church made its primary attack on Angela Mellini and Father Ruggieri, rendering their story as told by Ciammitti a tragedy and leaving us ultimately with one saint less.

Flaviana Zanolla, in "Mothers-in-law, Daughters-in-law, and Sisters-in-law at the Beginning of the Twentieth Century in P. of Friuli," takes us from early modern times and questions of saintliness to the modern period and questions of power within the context of family in the agrarian world of rural Friuli. But while it may seem a long temporal and conceptual leap, maternity and the female body remain at the heart of the discourse, even as both are reconstructed within new social and cultural dynamics. Family is divested of many of the quasi-mythical trappings that have so often distorted and made atemporal our understanding of the changing emotional and power structures that underlie this seemingly unchanging building block of society. Of course, family structures have recently received close attention from several disciplinary perspectives, and some have begun to look carefully at issues like love and affection in marriage or notions of childhood, adolescence, and maturity that stand behind those structures and have historically been most significant for their shaping. But even if we recognize its broad structural transformations, the enduring family, much like enduring gender stereotypes, masks deeper and perhaps more significant variations and meanings.

Using the fruitful concept of networks, Zanolla has analyzed interviews with peasant women to reconstruct the power dynamics of peasant families at the turn of this century. Behind what might be labeled a patrilinear extended family structure, a different pattern emerges as Zanolla moves from traditional theory to women's strategies for power within the formal structures of the family. The picture that emerges of life for women is not particularly attractive; in fact, in many ways this is the most troubling essay in the volume, because the author sees women's networks as often constructed in such a manner as to keep power out of the hands of other women—frequently aligning women with their sons or manipulating husbands to marginalize other women. Yet by closely focusing on the individual, the author is able to take what could have become a traditional and ultimately misogynistic perspective and reveal instead a much more subtle and ultimately useful picture of a world where women and men created and sustained largely unrecognized dynamics of power and, more importantly, also learned to survive and make the most of the situation in which they found themselves. Not only does one come away with a much clearer understanding of a particular set of at times destructive power dynamics that operated within the family in rural Friuli (a family, incidentally, structured similarly to the one idealized by certain ideologies), one gains a much more nuanced view of the possibilities for understanding how society functions by understanding how the broad range of power strategies available within the family worked, not merely how the family was supposed to work, given its formal structure and current theory.

Childbirth is central to Zanolla's analysis. While marriage brought a woman formally into the family in rural Friuli, in fact it was only with childbirth that she began to gain status and the possibility of building networks of power within a family. Thus, pregnancy and childbirth were important periods of tension, conflict, and ultimately reformulation of power dynamics within the family. As a result, women's networks tended not to support women in childbirth but to impede or, at the least, to isolate young women about to give birth. In turn, while giving birth was significant in itself, it also empowered young women and provided a significant range of new possibilities for their building networks of power.

The networks were both vertical and horizontal: vertical in that the mother used her children (or, to be more accurate, her sons) to create a network that allowed her, first, more power within the family and, ultimately, as her children grew older, to transcend the formal limitations placed on women. They were horizontal in that once children were born, the woman, with her evolving power within the family, came to have increasing power over her husband, who tended to operate beyond the family and thus was not able or perhaps willing to dominate its internal dynamics. Thus, what seems at first glance to have been a hopeless situation dominated by the injunction "work and suffer" imposed by a ruthless mother-in-law and indifferent sisters-in-law, one at best mitigated by an ideally largely nonexistent husband ("a truly 'good' husband was equal to no husband at all"), in the end became a situation in which women were able to construct for themselves meaningful networks of power. Of course, these networks were formed (or, perhaps more accurately, deformed) and restricted by the broader realities of power and family in society; but the point that emerges from this essay is that the complex networks of power that people are capable of constructing in the interstices of more formal and recognized power dynamics can be significant.

The final essay concerns not only the modern world, but a world much more familiar on the surface at least: the life of women in U.S. factories in the early years of this century. Giulia Calvi, in "Women in the Factory: Women's Networks and Female Social Life in America (1900–1915)," also uses women's networks as a central conceptual tool in her analysis but this time for women largely beyond the family or at least perceived and often feared to be beyond the family and on their own. For many reasons, this is currently an area of intense and fruitful research for scholars of gender. Perhaps the most salient are the richness of the documentation, the perception that industrialization and its impact on society have been central to the formation of the modern world, and the view that women, traditionally seen as formed and disciplined within the family, have in these cases been socialized beyond its confines. The result is a set of significant theoretical and methodological implications.

Because of the intensity of work in this area, Calvi's essay may not seem as innovative today as when it was first published in *Quaderni Storici* in 1982. Yet it remains current and addresses issues that are central to the discussion of women in the factory. It has another attribute, however, that also warrants its inclusion in this anthology: the richness and fresh perspective that an outsider's eye can bring to American history. Fortunately, in Italian as in other non-English-language scholarship, there is a growing body of methodologically sophisticated work on American history that breaks through many of the virtually unseen parameters of U.S. scholarship; unfortunately, too little of it is read to have the impact that it might. Perhaps publishing articles like Calvi's in this series will whet the appetite of Americanists for more. Most interesting, perhaps, is her emphasis on the way that working women created a different factory environment and built new social identities involving nontraditional perceptions of friendship, time, space, and money. Fittingly, this essay brings home the methodological innovations and new insights of this volume, literally as well as figuratively, by tying them to the recent history of the United States and using these insights to expand the current debates on the impact of changing gender roles on the modern work force and society.

## A Note on the Translation

Although *Quaderni Storici* had as one of its goals a simpler and less rhetorical style than is common in most Italian scholarly journals, in Italian there seems to be a style even for writing without style. Most of these essays are written in the first person and largely in what might be labeled a historical present tense rich in wordplay and suggestive layers of meaning very difficult to render in English. And in fact when the authors have come closest to writing in the lean, journalistic style that was to be the ideal of the periodical, the result in English is so chopped and terse as to be barely readable. Thus, these translations have been fairly extensively edited to cut some of the flowery prose; to eliminate a bit of the personal (especially in transitions where it seemed to be largely a rhetorical device); and to make the arguments flow as smoothly as possible in English without sacrificing their careful distinctions. We hope we have been successful in providing a readable and scholarly text without unduly eliminating the individual styles of the authors translated.

It has also been very difficult to render in English some of the quotes in early modern dialects. Few translators are masters of the wide range of dialects used in Italy with their often quite different vocabularies and grammars. In fact, the reader will note that at times the authors themselves are not sure what their entire texts meant or even how they read; once again we find ourselves here in the "notebook" context of *Quaderni.* A special word of thanks, however, is due to Laura Giannetti, who used her own extensive knowledge of the dialect of Friuli and her networks of contacts in the area to help solve many translation problems for that especially difficult dialect. And, of course, very special thanks are in order to the translators of this volume, Carole, Mary, and especially Margaret Gallucci. Not only did each provide thoughtful and accurate literal translations of the articles, they read each with a critical and informed eye that helped a great deal in the editorial process of drawing out meaning and cutting without, it is hoped, doing undue violence to the texts. In the end, of course, the errors remain mine, but those errors are far fewer because of their help.

## Note

1. Joan W. Scott, "Gender: A Useful Category of Historical Analysis," *American Historical Review* 91 (1986): 1067.

Sex and Gender in Historical Perspective

# 1 ❧ "Menstruum Quasi Monstruum": Monstrous Births and Menstrual Taboo in the Sixteenth Century

*by Ottavia Niccoli*

In 1560 the Italian translation of *Occulta naturae miracula,* by the Flemish physician Lievin Lemnes, was published with the *Magia naturale* of Giovan Battista della Porta by the Venetian printer Lodovico Avanzi.[1] Chapter 8 was dedicated to "monstrous births"; and, next to the title in the copy of the work held today by the University of Bologna, a sixteenth-century hand had written a warning, "For crazy and dirty married people."[2]

The sixteenth-century reader was underscoring, harshly, one of the arguments contained in the pages of Lemnes; namely, that those spouses, especially wives, who wished "to gratify their hardly honest desires" without abiding by the appropriate time constraints should be censured: "To these deviant acts I know Flemish women to be much given, and especially those women who live near the seashore, who in the carnal act are restless, wild, and not very considerate, so that they will impose upon the embryo a coarse and ugly form."[3]

But what could the relationship between carnal frenzy and imperfect births have been?

> This occurs [Lemnes responded] because their husbands, being seamen, are far away for long stretches of time; they [the women] running with joy to embrace them, and the men, without regard for whether it is a good time or bad, that is whether the women are having their periods or not, have relations with them: which is very dangerous and harmful because at that time the human seed cannot

"'Menstruum quasi monstruum': Parti mostruosi e tabù mestruali nel '500," *Quaderni Storici,* no. 44 (1980): 402–28. Translated by Mary M. Gallucci.

> grow, nor can it cleanly unite itself with the blood of the women. Wherefore it happens either that the seed comes out or, instead, adhering [to the womb] it cannot receive the perfect form, since human nature cannot be formed easily at that time. . . . Obviously, the matter is corrupt and filthy, and unfit to take on a beautiful and complete form. Indeed it seems to me that Moses by divine precept taught very well in the Law that a man ought not to meddle with a woman who was having her period. Clearly, one cannot imagine how many difficulties and infirmities a woman causes for one of her children when in that condition she wants to gratify her dishonest desires. As that contagion little by little occupies all of the members of the body and then causes it to be filled with leprosy and scabies . . . it is not surprising that so many are born monsters, so many people deformed, maimed, scabby, full of boils and inflammations in diverse parts of the body. And as far as the soul is concerned, are foolish, forgetful, lunatic, and crazy.[4]

These lines, at first seeming merely bizarre, were based upon texts and influences from diverse cultures: from Aristotelian theories of generation—which, taken up during the Middle Ages, were still commonly held in the sixteenth century—to echoes of the Old Testament, surely strengthened by the Reformation ideology of the Flemish areas in which this writer lived. Out of these different visions grew a progressive tightening of sexual morals and convictions, common to many cultures, that held that menstrual blood was something "corrupt and dirty"; but the unifying factor was the necessity of having to explain monstrous births—their causes, their significance, and their place in a cosmos ordered by God. In these pages, then, I attempt to clarify both attitudes about reproduction (an issue for the history of ideas) and the complex web of cultural factors of wide provenance involving folklore and social customs surrounding birth. This is done in the context of their interrelationship in a definite historical moment—the decades from the second half of the 1500s to the early years of the 1600s.

❧ In *La nature et les prodiges*, J. Céard has revealed, without providing a complete explanation, that teratology (the classification of monsters, real or imagined) garnered far wider attention than might seem its due in the culture of the 1500s, especially after 1550.[5] But it is not the general significance of this phenomenon that I wish to consider. Rather, I begin by examining one particular aspect: the special attention given to the generation of the monstrous child, to its birth, to the behavior of its parents and of those attending its birth, and finally to the perceived causes of its abnormal conception.

Birth was undoubtedly considered the most important moment of life for the monstrous baby. Italian chronicles in the 1400s and 1500s frequently made note of monstrous births, which were enumerated among the phenomena judged as excesses of nature and thus considered to be "signs" of divine ire and omens of imminent catastrophe.[6] Cicero's opinion that "monsters therefore are called monsters, because . . . they de-monstrate something that had to appear and had to happen"[7] was revived during the 1580s by the prolific and wide-ranging writer Tommaso Garzoni in *Serraglio degli stupori del mondo*,[8] and later by Ulisse Aldrovandi.[9] Garzoni also referred to Isidore of Seville, who even affirmed that monsters die immediately after birth because by so doing they fulfill the role assigned to them by God, which was that of warning men of His anger and of admonishing them.[10]

Some years earlier the German physician Martin Weinrich, in *De ortu monstrorum* (which Garzoni also knew, although he did not cite the text here referred to), had reported a passage of Theophrastus, which held that "monsters born of human beings rarely live, and the more they are strange and terrible the more quickly they die; so much so that the majority of them do not reach their third day of life among humans, unless they are hidden in secret places and separated from the sight of people."[11] Weinrich bitterly criticized Theophrastus's opinion, judging it to be "entirely without reason"; but by having done so, he publicized its controversial nature and contributed to its diffusion.

The idea of the "terribleness" of monstrous birth had its origins in the unadmitted but widespread habit of killing immediately after birth the deformed child who did not die spontaneously. Midwives were the ministers of this deadly rite, as can be seen from manuals of midwifery, as well as from the decisions of post-Tridentine diocesan synods, which attempted to give them some notion of whether or not to baptize monsters and stillborns.[12] They probably also needed advice on when it was lawful to kill such creatures, at least those who had not been baptized because they were not judged to be human.[13] Lemnes provided an account of a deformed baby "who had a long and round neck, a beaked and misshapen muzzle, terrifying glowing eyes, a pointed tail, and the fastest feet," born with a twin. Immediately after birth the two were separated and the monstrous one was suffocated by the midwives, who, "grabbing the pillows and throwing them on him, smothered him,"[14] in this following a common method of infanticide.[15] The mother, however, did not appear in any way involved in the incident, remaining a passive spectator. Lemnes reported only that when he approached her bedside he found her "tired and fatigued"; after having treated her, he left her still "all feeble and sluggish."[16]

Nor is this by any means the only such case for which we have testimony. In Passau in 1590 there was born to a certain Margareta Heckelin a monstrous baby who was killed immediately by the women present. The later description that these women provided of the baby was highly unusual; as in the case of the monster described by Lemnes, it has no relation at all to anomalies actually reported by modern embryology. The newborn reportedly had the head of a cat, thirty eyes, six feet, four arms, hands like the hooves of a calf, a bovine tail, and goat's hooves.[17] These fantastic deformities evidently served to define the nonhumanity of the creature and thus justified, even authorized, its murder. When the animal or diabolical nature of the newborn could not be determined, an accident (which had a good probability of being deliberate) often resolved the situation, as happened to a certain baby girl with two heads, born in Milan, whose neck, "by mistake," was wrung by the midwife.[18]

That the custom of killing monsters was widespread can also be deduced from the pages that Martin Weinrich dedicated to the problem "Is it lawful to kill monsters?"[19] His first response was that divine law prohibited it (although Weinrich observed, significantly, that for monsters death was preferable to life); but then this general rule was qualified by so many exceptions, each furnished with examples, that they undermined, even overturned, its sense. The arguments of the German doctor were in essence to kill all those born whom one did not hold it opportune to baptize because they were deemed "inhuman." Thus, those babies could be killed who were believed to be the result of sexual intercourse between humans and beasts; those who, even only in fantasy, "bordered on the bestial," like the Flemish monster and that of Passau; those who were feared to be of diabolical origin, like the baby who was not satisfied by the milk of its mother or of many wet nurses and who, therefore, "was drowned."[20] Cases of diabolical conception—like that of bestial conception—at times implicated the mother as well, who was often burned alive with her child, as happened in 1543 in Avignon,[21] at the end of the century at Messina,[22] and in 1618 at Basilea.[23]

The monster who escaped the double risk of the birth itself and the terror and horror of the bystanders did not escape the singular destiny of being shown by its parents for money. The relevant testimonies are so numerous[24] that one can be certain about the continuity and frequency of the phenomenon, notwithstanding the fact that there were many who, like Weinrich, maintained that it was necessary to forbid absolutely "that poor parents make money by showing such monsters."[25] Display for gain guaranteed survival, but only briefly. A newborn already deformed, put through the trauma of continual movement and changes in temperature, lacking appropriate care, quiet, or rest, could not live long;[26] and no one, in effect, wanted it to. It is noteworthy that doctors, theologians, and jurists who spoke of monsters did not bother to consider the problems of their survival, their eventual social placement, or even their relationships with family and society. The birth of a gravely deformed baby represents—today, as in the sixteenth century—a trauma for the parents, one so difficult that it is often resolved by killing the newborn or by indirectly causing its death. For the mother, the emotional trauma could not help but be complicated by the physiological reality of the extreme abnormality of the birth. Yet, in works on teratology the mother was consistently ignored, and no mention was made of her emotional reactions. This might well reflect a lesser affective identification with newborns, common in an epoch of very high infant mortality, but it also points to the overall lack of consideration by medical science for the woman and for any problems that faced her that were not strictly physical. The female body and its functions were the object of investigation, but the psychological component of those functions was ignored.[27]

❧ What interested doctors, theologians, and jurists was, instead, the causes and manner of the conception of monsters. The classical tradition, from Empedocles and Democritus up to Hippocrates and Galen, identified those causes as an overabundance or scarcity of the masculine seed (the sperm) or of the feminine material (the menstrual blood), both of which converged in generation; or as springing from the inadequate state of the uterus, which could lead to malformation or to the mixture of embryos. The latter, in particular, was the opinion expressed by Aristotle in *De generatione animalium*,[28] a work that, owing to its fundamental role in the curriculum of Renaissance university studies, certainly had a basic influence upon sixteenth-century embryology.[29] In the end, along with these possible causes, others gained ever-greater support: the impact of maternal fantasy, which even today has not lost its power in popular imagination [Editor's note: this is true at least in Italy, where the mother's *voglio,* or strongly felt wish, is still believed to have a potential impact on the future baby. Birthmarks are still commonly explained in this fashion, e.g., a strawberry-like mark is attributed to a prenatal *voglio* for strawberries.]; bestial or diabolical coitus (which we have already seen used to authorize the killing of the monster); and the divinatory role of the monstrous baby—its function, that is, as a sign of divine ire and future punishments. The causes of monstrous conceptions were synthesized with great clarity by Ulisse Aldrovandi in 1581 in a document that was didactic rather than scholarly in character, his *Avvertimenti,* which he addressed on 21 August 1581 to the bishop of Bologna, Gabriele Paleotti, "on the issue of monstrous and prodigious pictures."[30] This work falls within a program of pedagogic control of the figurative arts which Paleotti conducted with great efficacy in his diocese, through both theoretical writings and concrete directives that followed the prescriptions of the Council of Trent. Paleotti's goal was to ensure that sacred art met the dual standards of the Scriptures and verisimilitude.[31] In this ideological context it was necessary that the images of monsters be detached from the grotesque fantasies of the preceding centuries in order that they conform to reality. Aldrovandi had therefore been consulted—on this as on other occasions—as an expert naturalist, and the *Avvertimenti* were his response.

In the first place, he wrote, "nature sometimes produces monsters because it is kept from being able to achieve its end": for example, if the uterus was too narrow, or too wide, nature could never produce a creature with correct measurements. To this first and general cause four others were added:

> The first type [of monster] is due to the excess and deficiency of the matter. . . . The second way in which monsters originate is through coitus between diverse species. . . . And then the third way is due to the imagination, as Levino Lemnes most learnedly shows and as Your Most Illustrious Lordship will have seen and as I have also written. . . . There is in addition the fourth way and cause which seems to me the most miraculous of all; and I can attribute it to

> none other than celestial constellations and causes superior and divine.[32]

Thus, Aldrovandi linked these "causes superior and divine" to the discussion that was being conducted with Paleotti in general on "things prodigious, which are against the habit of nature," and he concluded that "often times the great God sends these signs . . . and He uses them as instruments to admonish us to correct our impious and depraved lives."[33]

One notes that Aldrovandi did not speak of the possibility of a fertile sexual relationship between humans and demons or brutes, and he limited himself to alluding, in a vague and prudent manner, to "coitus between diverse species." Apart from this, his *Avvertimenti,* given their finality, evidently represent a collection of the ideas commonly accepted on the subject; and it is significant that this discussion of the possible origins of monsters closed by highlighting the sins of humans, "our impious and depraved lives."

Along with theories of the causes of deformed births that appear to have been derived from theological treatises or from the scientific debate on classical embryology, at midcentury other ideas expressed a sense of sin (in general in indirect and vague forms) but often understood these births as resulting from transgressing the sexual ethic. Earlier the author of *De secretis mulierum,* a short work wrongly attributed to Albertus Magnus, which had been widely read since the 1400s, wrote, "Immoderate coitus is a factor in many monstrosities."[34] And the commentator noted forcefully: "Above all it is necessary to particularly avoid disorderly and violent copulation . . . so that the seed will not be badly attached to the womb. And beware that as a result coitus while standing up goes against nature (even if the ignorant will not pay attention to this) because the seed thus emitted cannot be properly attached, as it should be."[35]

In the second half of the sixteenth century these texts reappeared, fortified with a moral perspective. Thus, in *De conceptu et generatione hominis,* printed for the first time in 1554, the Zurich doctor Jacob Rueff affirmed that intercourse which generated monsters was not only unwise but blameworthy: "It is necessary to know first of all . . . that occurrences of this type are often permitted in the context of the just judgment [of God] in order to punish and warn men. We hold then as accused the excessive search for pleasure, which is such that the human seed becomes too weak and imperfect, and as a necessary result the child born is also weak and imperfect."[36]

For Tommaso Garzoni, who wrote in the 1580s, monsters were "births of an incorrect nature due to sin, and what is more, not only do we know these things happen because of sin in general, but also at times because of particular sin."[37] Garzoni supported this affirmation by citing a passage from Paré, discussed later, which considered the responsibility of parents who unite "without manner, without law, in either desirous or evil concupiscence."[38] Even the hermaphrodite, according to Lemnes, "sometimes is born from the sinister and not customary joining of man and woman, as when the woman is on top, and the man below."[39] Finally, Gaspard Bauhin, in his diligently compiled "Demonstrating the Causes of Monstrous Births," still noted in 1614, among other causes, the "joining in the manner of brutes" and "excessive libido."[40]

Not a lack of reason, but a disorder of the senses and an excessive search for pleasure, then, generated monsters. It is difficult, of course, to label these positions gleaned from authors of different countries and almost certainly of different religious beliefs as the same; yet, they do cite each other extensively, and one can certainly speak of the circulation of their ideas across Europe. Furthermore, it should be remembered that a definite tightening of sexual morals was, in the second half of the sixteenth century, a fact common to both Catholic and Calvinist countries, and it undoubtedly reinforced the insistence, seen in the passages cited, that there was a relationship between "excess libido" and monstrous births. In fact, this is the context in which we can more appropriately understand the passage from Lemnes about Flemish women, cited at the beginning of this essay, who were "in the carnal act . . . restless, wild, and hardly considerate." They, then, more than their husbands, were culpable in giving birth to monsters. In this context also belongs the warning that the Italian reader of the *Occulti miracoli della natura* added in the margin about "crazy and dirty married people."

❧ It seems clear that the belief which Lemnes formulated, namely, that copulation during menstruation generated monsters, is but one aspect of a menstrual taboo that, with diverse characteristics and nuances, was common to times and traditions otherwise very different from one another. Even in times and cultures closer to us, the menstruating woman was held to be maximally impure, and relations with her were damaging: at her touch flowers withered, the strings of musical instruments snapped, beer went sour, sauces boiled over. In other cultures, seclusion, especially at menarche, was compulsory and severe.[41] If every contact with this impure creature was perilous and to be avoided, it was natural that the primary and most resolute prohibition struck at the most intimate and profound of contacts, sexual relations.

The belief in the menstrual conception of monsters could still be found in the medical-anthropological literature of the nineteenth and twentieth centuries, a traditional folkloric given torn from historical context. "The belief, from the most ancient traditions, that coitus during menstruation leads to the birth of monsters was at times quite widespread . . . and it is not completely dead today," wrote R. Crawfurd in 1915;[42] and P. Mantegazza observed in *Igiene dell'amore,* published for the first time in 1877, that "some people have still today the prejudice that intercourse with a menstruating woman can produce monstrous and insane children. These are reflections of the terror with which menstruation is discussed in the Bible."[43] According to F. Loux, this belief is still alive today in the French countryside, where the prevailing belief is that creatures are born with red skin from menstrual conceptions.[44] It is evident that scholars (albeit not many) of anthropology and of popular medicine who have touched incidentally upon this theme in their research have consistently assumed that it had to do with an unchanging taboo and, for people of the Judeo-Christian tradition, that it was largely derived from the proscriptions for the menstruating woman found in Leviticus.

But it may not be that simple. Turning to Leviticus, in the midst of pages and pages of proscriptions concerning the impurity of the woman after childbirth, of lepers, of the male who has emitted sperm, and finally of the menstruating woman, we find only three short passages concerning sexual relations during menstruation:

"If a man dares to lie with her, he contracts her impurity and shall be unclean for seven days; every bed on which he then lies also becomes unclean" (Lev. 15:24).

"You shall not approach a woman to uncover her nakedness while she is unclean from menstruation" (Lev. 18:19).

"If a man lies in sexual intercourse with a woman during her menstrual period, and uncovers her nakedness, he has made naked her flow, and she has uncovered the flow of her blood; both of them shall be cut off from among the people" (Lev. 20:18).

There is no sign here of the possibility that monstrous children will be conceived; nor are they alluded to in other canonical books of the Bible. One trace of this concept is found instead in one of the canons of the first Nicene Council, which, however, was probably written after A.D. 325. It affirmed that "for husbands it is not allowed that they approach their wives during menstruation, so that their bodies and their children will not manifest the effects of elephantiasis and leprosy; in fact that type of blood corrupts both the body of the parents as well as that of their children."[45] Menstrual blood contaminates, then, as does the leprous sore of which Leviticus speaks shortly before citing impurities of sexual origin, and this also affects the unborn children. But this still does not explain monstrosity.

Rupert of Deutz, in the twelfth century, was evidently inspired by this passage in his commentary on Leviticus: "It is said that fetuses conceived at that time suffer from the corruption of their seed, such that from such a conception are born lepers and people with elephantiasis."[46]

In the same period Michael Scotus, in part echoing Pliny, wrote: "Of menstrual blood we say that if a dog eats it he indeed becomes rabid, if a flourishing plant is splashed by it, it dries up. . . . It makes the man to whom it is administered lose his good sense and it renders him a leper."[47]

The *De secretis mulierum* warned directly that "overall one must avoid coitus with menstruating women, because the man can become a leper."[48] Leprosy was the great terror of the Middle Ages, and it was normal for it to appear as the worst threat in order to discourage violations of menstrual impurity. By the middle of the fifteenth century, however, it was no longer the most frightening disease and thus was no longer a deterrent to menstrual contact (in the second half of the following century, the relationship between periods and leprosy would actually be numbered among "popular errors").[49] Thus, in the great *Practica maior* of Michele Savonarola, completed in 1440 but not printed until 1479, leprosy was no longer spoken of as the result of menstrual conception. Instead, another incurable disease, judged just as terrible, and also laden with meanings that transcended the merely medical, took its place—epilepsy, the "sacred disease": "If one is conceived at the time of menstruation, or by impure sperm or by parents who are epileptics, and contracts epilepsy, then it does not seem that it may be cured . . . however much the men may abstain from relationships with menstruating women."[50]

As negative as such a vision was, the effects of a menstrual conception did not as yet include a monstrous birth. Nevertheless, a bit later, speaking of menstrual blood itself, Michele Savonarola, citing Aristotle but relying in reality on Pliny, used a singular play on words, which does not provide information on the specific problem with which we are concerned but certainly contributes to clarifying its cultural background: "It is said *menstruum quasi monstruum;* for it is alleged by Aristotle that it has extraordinary properties."[51]

❧ These, then, were the positions of official medicine at the beginning of the modern era. A profoundly new idea insinuated itself, however, among the ideas about menstrual conception around the middle of the sixteenth century. In 1559 there was published at Anversa, as mentioned previously, the original Latin edition of Lemnes's *Occulta naturae miracula;* and "Lennio," as he was called in Italian, spoke explicitly, at length and in dark tones, of the role of menstrual conceptions in monstrous births. He began with the Aristotelian doctrine expounded in *De generatione animalium,* which held that in the act of generation man provided the formative seed and woman, in the form of menstrual blood, the material that each month had to be renewed. The sense of Lemnes's argument was that, since menstrual blood at the moment of the flow is "matter . . . corrupt and dirty and unsuitable to receive a beautiful and well shaped form," the masculine seed is not strong enough to dominate it and form it suitably; thus, "through these filthy embraces and joinings outside of the time . . . the corruption of the seed of the parents spreads itself to the children."[52] From this he moved on to the activities of Flemish women noted earlier.

The foundations of Lemnes's argument, beyond his own experience and Aristotle, Pliny, and Leviticus, were these: "Pliny and many others . . . say that this [menstrual] blood is naturally most pernicious and monstrous. . . . I know to what extent such blood is a filthy thing, and that it makes nutriment [for the fetus], and that not without reason Moses commanded that a man should not join with a woman who has this evil."[53]

Thus, it appears that it was not until Lemnes that a cause-and-effect relationship between menstrual conception and monstrous births was affirmed. No longer were epilepsy and leprosy the consequences of violating the menstrual taboo, but rather the birth of monsters. It is clear that this development was linked to the great popularity that the theme of monstrous births enjoyed in European culture especially after 1550. To Lemnes's arguments—which certainly had a major impact as the *Occulta miracula naturae* was rapidly translated into Italian, French, and German[54]—it is necessary to add another, a new element, which seems to have gained wide attention in the teratological treatises of the following decades. The first, and perhaps most famous among these classifications of monsters, was *Des monstres et prodiges* by the French surgeon Ambroise Paré, which enjoyed a particularly wide audience because Paré, scandalizing his colleagues, composed it in the vernacular. In the first pages of *Des monstres,* issued in 1573, one reads, "It is certain that most often these monstrous and prodigious creatures are a result of the judgment of God, who permits fathers and mothers to produce such abominations through the disorder that they create in copulating like brute beasts, whence their appetite drives them, without respecting the time or the other laws ordained by God and Nature."

Up to this point, nothing is new: monsters are a result of God's castigating wayward humans "for the disorder . . . in copulating." Paré probably had in hand the previously cited passage by Lemnes (an author he certainly knew),[55] as also seems likely, given the lines that follow immediately. These apparently echo Lemnes's discussion of the "nutritive" theory, which argued that the baby conceived during menstruation is nourished by corrupt blood and thus cannot receive a beautiful form and included a list of sicknesses to which the newborn might fall victim. But the passage continues, introducing an element that does not appear in Lemnes:

> Without respecting the time or the other laws ordained by God and Nature as is written in Ezra the prophet, the woman soiled by menstrual blood will engender monsters. Equally Moses prohibits such unions in Leviticus, chap. 16. The ancients, too, have observed from long experience that the woman who has conceived during her period will engender leprous babies or ones subject to a thousand illnesses, since the infant conceived during the menstrual flow takes nourishment and grows while in the uterus of the mother, from vilified blood, filthy and corrupt. With time having rooted its infection, it manifests and makes appear its malignancy: some will be scabby, others gouty, others leprous, others will have smallpox or rubella, and others an infinity of other maladies. In conclusion, it is a filthy and brutal thing to have contact with a woman during the time she is purging herself.[56]

First, it should be noted that here Paré seems blatantly to contradict what he had affirmed in his book *De la generation,* published with *Des monstres.* There he limited himself to observing, somewhat blandly, that if conception occurred during the menstrual flow, the fetus "might" have some mark on its body, especially if the woman was not in good health; but if the woman was healthy, her blood would also be healthy, and she would not transmit illnesses to the baby.[57] At work here is undoubtedly the distinction between the medical and the theological, which permitted the simultaneous espousal of extremely contradictory opinions. But the most striking element in this passage, and one that was actually new, was the citation of the prophet Ezra. This unified the different parts of the argument—and upon it, in fact, depended the affirmations concerning divine justice against such disorderly copulation and its consequences. This would seem to contradict the earlier affirmation that in the Bible a relationship between monstrous births and menstrual conceptions was never posited.

One who today opens any modern edition of the Bible and searches for this text in the book of Ezra, between Chronicles and Nehemia, will be disappointed: the passage is not there. The Ezra alluded to is the so-called 4 Ezra, one of the apocryphal books of the Old Testament, definitively expelled from the canon of the authentic books of the Bible with the Council of Trent. It was a compilation written down between the first and third centuries after Christ. The central and oldest part, which contains the passage that interests us, includes chapters 3 to 14, and is apocalyptic in its seven visions; it was composed by an unknown Jewish writer in Aramaic. Subsequently, it was translated into Greek, and from Greek into Latin. The Aramaic text is, however, completely lost, as is most of the Greek.[58] There remains the Latin version, where, at the beginning of chapter 5, verse 8, we find the words "menstruating women give birth to monsters."

Here, then, is the text upon which Paré based his argument, and which will return many times in the treatises on teratology as support for the theory of the menstrual conception of monsters. In reality, and it is disconcerting to point it out, the words cited above contain a copyist's error. The oldest Latin manuscripts that we possess, dating back to the ninth century, read "mulieres parient menstruatae monstra"; but the equivalent of the word *menstruatae* does not exist in the Arabic version, nor in the Armenian, nor in the Ethiopian, nor in the Syrian, all derived, like that of the Latin, from the Greek translation of the text.[59] One is actually speaking, then, of a later addition to the only Latin version, the error of an unknown scribe, which occurred sometime between the second and ninth centuries. The original Hebrew said only that "women will give birth to monsters" as one of the signs of the approaching end of time. The copyist's lapse seems significant as an involuntary admission of a fear of menstruation which was certainly present in the tradition of late Latinity and was most likely derived from Pliny's *Historia naturalis.* The origin of the error (*menstrua* as a duplicate of *monstra*) might actually be explained by hypothesizing the copyist's knowledge of Pliny's words "nihil facile reperiatur mulierum profluvium magis monstrificum" (one will not easily find anything more stupefying, more anomalous, than women's periods). The evocation of the word *monstra* next to *mulieres* in the passage from Ezra perhaps provoked an involuntary and irresistible connection in the mind of the copyist: what more than menstruation could be connected with the female and with the monstrous?

Paré based his conclusions, then, on a corrupt passage from an apocryphal text. It might seem strange that the French surgeon—who did not even know Latin—came to cite this work, today unknown, and to give such prominence and authority to it. Yet, in the sixteenth century, 4 Ezra actually was widely diffused and very notorious, in part owing to the extensive use Saint Ambrose had made of it in *De bono mortis* (continued indirectly today in the Catholic funeral liturgy)[60] and, more importantly, to its frequent appearance in numerous Bibles of the sixteenth and seventeenth centuries, vulgar or Latin, Catholic or reform (especially Calvinist), printed in Italy, France, Switzerland, Holland, and England, before and after the Council of Trent. From a rapid survey of approximately forty different editions of the Bible, reinforced by the data offered by various standard bibliographies, it appears that the Apocrypha was included in the majority of the Bibles edited in the second half of the sixteenth century.[61]

Fourth Ezra was a part, then, of the common patrimony of Christian Europe between the 1500s and 1600s, particularly in the countries that were predominantly Catholic or Calvinist (Luther's distrust of 4 Ezra and his refusal to translate it made the situation different in Lutheran territories). Moreover, the steady increase in editions of the Scriptures, which in the second half of the 1500s accelerated, especially in the Reformed countries, may have accentuated this assimilation in those decades. In fact, we also find 4 Ezra being used in the same period in a different manner: thus, the humanist Conrad

Wolfhart (Lycostenes) cited it in an apocalyptic sense in the dedicatory epistle of *Prodigiorum ac ostentorum chronicon,* published in Basel in 1557.[62]

❧ The citation of 4 Ezra would become, for a few decades, a consistent element in the debate on the menstrual conception of monsters. It was frequently found in the vernacular, in one or another form, reflecting the different editions of the Bible used by authors who, from Paré on, participated in that debate.

The arguments of the French surgeon were taken up again some years later by Martin Weinrich, in the already cited treatise *De ortu monstrorum.* Weinrich listed the supernatural among the causes of monsters—following Paré's logic, whom nevertheless he does not cite—using a complex argument that in the end tended to negate the value of what he himself had earlier maintained. "Si queras ex theologo"; if one reasons from the theological point of view, Weinrich admitted, everything proceeds from God, and just as diseases proceed from sin, so too monsters are the penalties for sin.

> But in the book commonly called IV Ezra, chap. 5, there also appears in a more explicit manner: women suffering from their monthlies will give birth to monsters. . . . In fact at that time are conceived cripples, blind, lame and lepers, because the sin of those parents who were not ashamed to join themselves furtively is punished in their children in a way that is public and notorious to everyone; doctors however deny that at that time one can conceive.[63]

The argument, as one sees, follows Paré's, although with greater complexity: monsters can be the punishment sent by God for the sins of men, and in particular for copulation during the prohibited time. The babies then conceived can be crippled, blind, leprous, and also monstrous, because deformed children are a public reprimand for the sins of the parents.

This last element was lacking in Paré, and thus would seem to render Weinrich's position even more harsh if he had not added the qualification—which denied the whole argument—that conception during menstruation was not possible. The theological level and the medical one contradicted each other, as in Paré, but Weinrich made his choice, adopting, for the most part, the latter.

Nevertheless, Weinrich's long and ordered exposition of the theory of the menstrual conception of monsters rested on the citation of 4

Ezra, as was the case for Paré ("mulieres mensibus laborantes parient monstra"). Weinrich, however, had not merely copied the text from the French surgeon. He had personally checked the Latin version of the Apocrypha published by François Du Jon in 1579, in the appendix to the great edition of the Bible edited by Emmanuel Tremellio,[64] which was gaining ever greater credit among the reformers and especially among the Calvinists. Du Jon's edition could be defined by how much less liberal it was. The text of 4 Ezra, as noted earlier, was available only in Latin; thus, it was impossible to translate it into the same language. But Du Jon tried hard to render it in a more elegant form, thus altering the original *menstruatae,* judged too crude, into the more euphemistic *mensibus laborantes.* Paré instead had based his work either on the Bible edited in 1535 in Neuchâtel, which was the French version of Lefèvre d'Etaples revised by Robert Olivetan and by Calvin, or on the translation edited in 1546 by the Catholic theologians of Louvain, commissioned by Charles the Fifth.[65] Both of these editions, in fact, made use of expressions similar to those used by Paré, "les femmes souillées de sang menstruel engendront des monstres" (women soiled with menstrual blood will engender monsters).

The theory that monsters originate in sinful sexual intercourse during menstruation, even though questioned, thus gained wider notoriety. And it seemed plausible because it was based on a book of the Bible whose authority different Christian churches did not refute, even when they denied its authenticity; and there were numerous Bibles, among them the very widely circulated edition of Louvain, perhaps used by Paré, which did not make it clear that 4 Ezra was not one of the approved books of the Bible. The relationship among menstruation, monstrous fetuses, and guilt-ridden sexual disorder therefore was undisputed in European medical and teratological treatises for several decades, for example, in the works of Luis de Mercado, Spanish doctor to Philip the Second and Philip the Third; the Portuguese Roderigo da Castro; the Scotsman Duncan Liddel; and the Swiss Gaspard Bauhin.[66] By that time it had become a commonplace, as was the quote from 4 Ezra, which often accompanied these texts.

In Italy, this relationship was not directly argued. Rather, it was presented in terms of citations of Paré; even he had been rendered authoritative with an opportune Latin translation of his works, which appeared in 1582. Tommaso Garzoni depended upon this translation, in *Serraglio degli stupori del mondo,* published posthumously in

1613,[67] as did Fortunio Liceto with greater insistence in *De monstrorum causis,* published in 1616.[68] Liceto, in fact, examined in depth the theme of the relationship between menstrual conception and monstrosity, trying hard to account for it more from the medical than the theological standpoint. He pointed out how in such circumstances the menstrual blood, which ought to have been destined to nourish the fetus, was mixed with that which should have formed the fetus itself, "and from that confusion there cannot be born anything but a shameless monster."[69]

The works of Bauhin and Liceto represented, chronologically, the end point of the unquestioned acceptance of the relationship between menstruation and monsters. In the following decades that relationship seems, in numerous teratological treatises, to have become less certain, though there was no lack of mention of it. But 4 Ezra was no longer cited. Thus, Grozio, commenting on the story in John (9:2) of the man born blind, responded to the Pharisees' question, "Who sinned? He or his parents?" by observing, "In what manner? Rendering themselves guilty against the law of Leviticus 20:18; since this sin is placed among those grave ones by Ezechiel, 18:6. From such a relationship imperfect births usually come about, since feminine nature, bounded by those [menstrual] pains, cannot give to the fruit of conception the correct form."[70]

The biblical quotations used were taken from the canonical books of the Reformed Bible and were clearly innocuous. The commentary also blurred monstrous births into imperfect ones, among which can be found a man blind from birth. What a distance from the terrible fruits of the "filthy embraces and couplings outside of their time" of those Flemish women!

Still, thirty years later, in 1674, the German Michael Heiland printed his own *Historia infantis monstrosi* in which, among the possible causes of the conception of monsters, he hinted at the menstrual one: "If conception happens during menstruation . . . without any other cause intervening, monsters can be generated, as Roderigo da Castro, Duncan Liddel and others testify."[71]

One is dealing, however, with an outdated idea: references to the "causes superior and divine" had disappeared as the basis of theory. Embryological science had distanced itself, by then definitively, from theology. We can also see the progressive advance of the "new science," which would make it impossible to maintain the mental construct that was the basis of the theory of the menstrual conception of monsters. Strikingly, by the middle of the seventeenth century even the memory of the theory was completely lost. In the letter *Della natura dei mostri,* sent in 1747 by Dr. Giambattista Sormani to Ranieri Bonaparte, "public professor of medicine at the University of Pisa," there was an accurate review of what "so many so learned and venerable masters," that is Aristotle, Galen, Albertus Magnus, Fortunio Liceto, "the immortal Pareo [Paré]," and others had written on the subject, and of their theories of the causes of monstrous births. Conception during menstruation was not even mentioned.[72]

Although the theory had disappeared from the educated strata of society, it reappeared at the end of the nineteenth century as a "folkloric" belief. We can therefore hypothesize that (much as in the region of Carso, where water emerges suddenly from beneath the ground only to quickly disappear again and then reappear farther on) the theory of the menstrual conception of monsters, whose foundations undoubtedly belong in the anthropological sphere of the menstrual taboo articulated and given form at the level of learned culture, subsequently disappeared from that culture only to reappear among those things that at one time were called "popular superstitions." This provides yet another confirmation of the dialectical nature of the relationship between "high" and "low" culture. A sign of this passage can perhaps be found in a *canard* (one of those popular tracts of a few pages which, between the sixteenth and seventeenth centuries, were widely disseminated in Europe) that was issued in different editions in various French-speaking cities in 1609, entitled, *Miracle which happened in the city of Geneva in this year of 1609. About a woman who gave birth to a calf, because of disdain for the power of God and of milady Saint Marguerite. Women soiled by blood will bear monsters: Ezra, chap. 5.*[73]

Certainly the public for this pamphlet was wider and more varied than that for the treatises of Lemnes, Paré, or Weinrich. No longer did the theory of the menstrual conception of monsters circulate only among doctors and theologians—indeed, they shortly would refute it—but among artisans, shopkeepers, and women of modest social status; among those who were, in sum, the public for the popular "press." I do not assert that the *canard* in its various editions was the starting point for the passage of theory from the learned sphere to the popular one; it is, however, undoubtedly a sign of this passage.

❧ Let me try, then, to pull together the threads of my argument. The belief that conception during menstruation led to the birth of monsters was not an immemorial folkloric given (even if developed upon an anthropological base) but a precise historical fact, born in a specific moment: that is, in the second half of the sixteenth century under the pressure of a concomitant series of cultural and religious factors. One of these factors was of long standing, that is, the interdiction which, as far as we know, fell upon the menstruating woman in almost every culture. Other factors, however, had briefer moments of success. The fascination with monsters, already present, became more concrete in the latter half of the sixteenth century, as we have seen, in the great flourishing of teratological literature. No longer did people speak of monstrous species, nor even so much of single imaginary monsters, but of the real babies, gravely deformed, whose existence doctors and obstetricians acknowledged. The medieval "monstrous fantastic" disappeared to be replaced by the "monstrous realistic" in order to provide what Paleotti sought in Aldrovandi.[74]

Often, in these decades, teratology was strictly tied to obstetric and embryological discussions, as in the works of Paré and Rueff. The problem of monstrous births involved the problem of birth in general; this, in turn, focused attention on how the monster was conceived and its birth. And the moment of birth involved an immediate theological-judicial problem, the dilemma of whether to baptize the monster or to kill it. As we have seen, the manuals for midwives and the diocesan synods that were held after the Council of Trent put forth specific norms to guide obstetricians on the issue of the baptism of monsters and aborted fetuses.

At the same time, new editions of the Scriptures were proliferating in Europe. A large number of them included the apocryphal book called 4 Ezra, which contained a passage that was the essential connection between theological and embryological learning.[75] The fact that the verse from Ezra reflected a corrupt tradition of the text is of no import, or more accurately it is significant only inasmuch as the copyist's lapse appears to have been based upon the same horror of menstruation that contributed to the text's spread. S. Timpanaro, criticizing Freud's *Psychopathology of Everyday Life*, has in particular attacked the psychoanalytic interpretations of the lapses of copyists,[76] but the events that I have described suggest how reductive were Timpanaro's critiques. It is clear that the copyist's error was not an isolated event but was frequently associated with wordplays on the verbal pairing menstruous/monstrous—*menstruo/mostro*. (One example of this wordplay was Michele Savonarola's, which I chose as the title of this essay.) Even on its own, it relates to the logic proposed by Freud. It is at least justified in this case to posit that the copyist's error was not a fact analyzable by exclusively philological criteria.

The increasing severity of sexual morality in a large portion of Europe during the second half of the 1500s probably favored the interaction between the two levels, theological and embryological, since the menstrual conception of monsters was insistently proposed as divine punishment for those spouses, and especially for women, who did not know how to discipline their immoderate sexual desires. The bodily disorder of the monstrous child thus became in a certain way the visible expression of the disorder of the senses of those who had generated it. When in the first decades of the 1600s the link between theology and embryology first became more tenuous and then vanished under the pressure of new anatomical discoveries (especially because of the new scientific method), the relationship between menstruation and monsters also disappeared, at least from medical culture. Instead, the connection remained in popular culture, where it may still be present. The history of a medical-theological hypothesis, transformed into a commonplace and then in turn into "popular superstition," concludes by returning to the anthropological sphere from which it arose. Yet, it remains exemplary; present in the cultural context of Europe at the beginning of the modern era, it was a symptom of one way of conceptualizing woman and her genital functions as the source of impurity and corruption.

## Notes

1. L. Lemnes, *De gli occulti miracoli, et varii ammaestramenti delle cose della natura . . .* (Venice, 1560).

2. Ibid., col. 21v (Bibl. Univ. di Bologna, A.IV.F.XI.49). The same hand seems to have written the note of ownership on the frontispiece, "Cesaris Egnatti"; on Egnazio, see A. Tarducci, *Dizionarietto biografico cagliese* (Cagli, 1909), p. 86.

3. Lemnes, *De gli occulti miracoli,* col. 22r.

4. Ibid., cols. 22r–23v.

5. J. Céard, *La nature et les prodiges: L'insolite au XVIe siècle en France* (Geneva, 1977). Interest in the significance of monsters in sixteenth-century culture is growing. See, for example *Mostri e immagine,* in AA.VV., *La scienza a corte: Collezionismo eclettico, natura e immagine a Mantova tra Rinascimento e Manierismo* (Rome, 1979), pp. 101–15; C. Gentili, "I Musei Aldrovandi e Cospi e la loro sistemazione nell'Istituto," in *I materiali dell'Istituto delle Scienze* (Bologna: Università degli Studi di Bologna, 1979), esp. p. 96.

6. On "signs," see O. Niccoli, "Profezie in Piazza: Note sul profetismo popolare nell'Italia del primo Cinquecento," *Quaderni Storici,* no. 41 (1979): 506–7.

7. *De divinatione,* 1.42.

8. T. Garzoni, *Il serraglio de gli stupori del mondo . . . diviso in diece appartamenti, cioè di mostri, prodigii, prestigii, sorti, oracoli, sibille, sogni, curiosità astrologica, miracoli in genere e meraviglie in spetie* (Venice, 1613), p. 175. The work was published posthumously (Garzoni died in 1589).

9. U. Aldrovandi, *Monstrorum historia* (Bologna, 1642), p. 378. The book was extensively reworked by Bartolomeo Ambrosini, so the part taken from Aldrovandi must date before 1605, the year of his death.

10. Isidorus Hispalensis, *Etymologiarum* 1.11.3 (*PL* 82, col. 420).

11. M. Weinrich, *De ortu monstrorum commentarius, in quo essentia, differentiae, causae et affectiones mirabilium animalium explicantur* (n.p., 1595), col. 31r. I was unable to consult earlier editions of the work, which must have been known before 1589, the date of the death of Garzoni, who used it.

12. P. Stella and G. Da Molin, "Offensiva rigoristica e comportamento demografico in Italia (1600–1860): Natalità e mortalità infantile," in *Salesianum* 40 (1978): 31; *Mostri e immagini,* p. 113; S. Mercurio, *La commare o raccoglitrice . . . divisa in tre libri* (Verona, 1652), p. 216; F. E. Cangiamila, *Embriologia sacra, overo dell'uffizio de' sacerdoti, medici e superiori circa l'eterna salute de' bambini racchiusi nell'utero* (Palermo, 1745), pp. 75, 94; Diodato da Cuneo, *Notizie fisico-storico-morali conducenti alla salvezza de' bambini nonnati, abortivi e projetti* (Venice, 1760), pp. 211–12, 265–69, 288–91. The problem was discussed earlier; for example, when in 1531 a female obstetrician from Casalmaggiore noticed during a birth that the baby being born was gravely deformed, she had it baptized immediately without even waiting for it to emerge completely from the birth canal: "The arm with two hands came out first, and it moved in such a way that the obstetrician baptized it *according to their custom.*" Alessandro Valleneri to Francesco II Sforza, Casalmaggiore 15 Nov. 1531, in *Mostruosità fetale inedita osservata nel secolo XVI: Documento per servire alla storia della teratologia,* ed. C. Decio (Milan, 1897), p. 31. See also Bernardino da Siena, *Prediche volgari,* vol. 2, ed. C. Cannarozzi (Pistoia, 1934), p. 135.

13. Diodato da Cuneo felt it to be opportune, in 1760, to warn midwives and parents that monsters "cannot be killed on private authority, one must await the judgment of Superiors" (*Notizie fisico-storico-morali,* p. 368).

14. Lemnes, *De gli occulti miracoli,* col. 24v.

15. Examples from a different context are offered by R. W. Malcolmson, "Infanticide in the Eighteenth Century," in *Crime in England, 1550–1800,* ed. J. S. Cockburn (London, 1977), p. 192.

16. Lemnes, *De gli occulti miracoli,* col. 25r.

17. I. G. Schenk, *Monstrorum historia memorabilis, monstrosa humanorum partuum miracula . . .* (Frankfurt, 1609), p. 87.

18. Ibid., p. 19.

19. Weinrich, *De ortu monstrorum,* cols. 51v–56v.

20. Ibid., col. 56r.

21. G. Maggi, *Variarum lectionum seu miscellaneorum libri,* vol. 4 (Venice, 1564), p. 61.

22. *Discours prodigieux et veritable d'une fille de chambre laquelle a produict un monstre après avoir eu la compagnie d'un singe en la ville de Messine: En ce discours sont recitées les paroles que la dite fille profera etant au supplice et les prières qu'elle fit ensemble le jour qu'elle fut brulée avec le monstre et le singe* (Paris, n.d. [c.1600]).

23. I. Rhodii, *Observationum medicinalium centuriae tres* (Padua, 1657), p. 178. The practice of killing monstrous births was still widespread in the 1800s: in 1825, a

baby born with a malformed head in Aggira, Sicily, was thrown by her terrified parents down a dry well, although since 1751 an edict from the viceroy had prohibited such actions (F. Scavone, "Relazione d'un feto mostruoso," in *Atti dell'Accademia Gioenia,* vol. 2 [1827], p. 15; Stella and Da Molin, *Offensiva rigoristica,* p. 10); and, according to testimony dated 1875, in Calabria "monstrous fetuses are left to die of starvation" (in C. Taruffi, *Storia della teratologia,* pt. 1, vol. 1 [Bologna, 1881], p. 111).

24. See, for example, C. Lycostenes, *Prodigiorum ac ostentorum chronicon* (Basilea, 1557), pp. 490, 565; A. Allegretti, *Diari senesi, R.I.S.,* vol. 23, p. 775; J. Rainieri, *Diario bolognese (1535–1549),* ed. O. Guerrini and C. Ricci (Bologna, 1887), p. 29; Schenk, *Monstrorum historia,* p. 61.

25. Weinrich, *De ortu monstrorum,* col. 56v.

26. The description of the journeys of two coupled fetuses of unclear sex born near Pavia on June 16, 1748, cannot help but arouse sympathy: within twelve days of birth the two creatures were brought to Milan to be examined; subsequently, "in order to satisfy the public's curiosity, these infants were transported to various cities in Lombardy, Pavia, Milan, Lodi, Cremona, Piacenza, Tortona and Alexandria." G. B. Bianchi, *Storia del mostro con due corpi che nacque sul Pavese in giugno 1748* (Turin, n.d. [1749/50]), p. 11. The two babies died in Alexandria on July 28, in part because of the maltreatment involved in being continually undressed and handled by whoever wished to see them naked. Perhaps the Piemontese priest Diodato da Cuneo was thinking of them when about ten years after this episode he wrote, "It should also be forbidden to the parents of such monstrous babies, to bring them hither and yon in order to have them seen by the curious crowds; while, besides the risk of startling the imagination of some pregnant woman curious to see such a monster, its death will be the price of the wretch's greed for money, with his transporting it from one city to another, and exposing it frequently out in the open to the eyes of anyone, when it would have been infinitely better to have concealed it from everyone" (*Notizie fisico-storico-morali,* p. 368). He does not seem to agree with Stella (*Offensiva rigoristica,* p. 10), who maintained that there was a progression from murdering monsters to showing them for money: it seems more probable that there was a social distinction between those who adopted the two behaviors, given that the babies exposed also came, for the most part, from peasant families (see, for example, Lycostenes, *Prodigiorum ac ostentorum chronicon,* p. 490; Schenk, *Monstrorum historia,* p. 59).

27. See J. Revel and J. P. Peter, "Le corps: L'homme malade et son histoire," in *Faire de l'histoire,* vol. 3, ed. J. Le Goff and P. Nora (Paris, 1974), p. 176.

28. Aristotle, *De generatione animalium,* 50.4.4.

29. On the fortunes of *De generatione animalium* in the sixteenth century, see Aristotle, *Opere biologiche,* ed. S. Lanza and M. Vegetti (Turin, 1971), p. 780, and Ch. B. Schmitt, "Thomas Linacre and Italy," in *Linacre Studies: Essays on the Life and Work of Thomas Linacre,* ed. F. Maddison, M. Pelling, and C. Webster (Oxford, 1977), p. 50.

30. *Avvertimenti del Dottore Aldrovandi sopra le pitture mostrifiche et prodigiose all'Ill.mo et Rev.mo Mons: Il Cardinal Paleotti, Sig.r et Patron suo colendissimo* (Bibl. Univ. di Bologna, MS. Aldrovandi, 6, II, cols. 129–37). The text will be cited as published in the edition of G. Olmi, *Osservazione della natura e raffigurazione in Ulisse Aldrovandi (1522–1605),* Annali dell'Ist. storico italo-germanico in Trento, vol. 3 (1977), pp. 177–80.

31. See P. Prodi, "Ricerche sulle arti figurative nella riforma cattolica," in *Archivio italiano per la storia della pietà* 4 (1965): 121–212.

32. *Avvertimenti del Dottore Aldrovandi,* pp. 179–80.

33. Ibid., p. 180.

34. Alberti Magni, *De secretis mulierum libellus scholiis auctus . . .* (Léon, 1598), p. 101.

35. Ibid., p. 102.

36. I. Rueff, *De conceptu et generatione hominis* (Frankfurt, 1587), col. 42r. On Rueff's embryologico-moral positions, see Céard, *La nature et les prodiges,* p. 294.

37. *Garzoni, Il Serraglio de gli stupori del mondo,* p. 178.

38. Garzoni cites Paré's work in its Latin version, which appeared in 1582 for the first time: A. Paré, *Opera chirurgica* (Frankfurt, 1594), p. 718. This helps to establish limits for the date of the composition of the *Serraglio degli stupori del mondo,* written evidently between 1582 and 1589, the year of Garzoni's death.

39. Lemnes, *De gli occulti miracoli,* col. 29r.

40. G. Bauhin, *De hermaphroditorum monstrorumque partuum natura ex theologorum . . . sententia libri duo* (Oppenheim, 1614), p. 59.

41. There exists an ample set of sources. See, however, R. Crawfurd, "Notes on the Superstitions of Menstruation," *Lancet,* no. 4816 (18 Dec. 1915): 1331–36; F. Vosselmann, *La menstruation: Légendes, coutumes, et superstitions* (Paris, 1936); P. C. Racamier, "Mythologie de la grossesse et de la menstruation," *Evolution psychiatrique* 20, no. 2 (1955): 285–97; M. Douglas, *Purezza et pericolo; Un'analisi dei concetti di contaminazione e tabù* (Bologna, 1976), pp. 151, 187, 206, 211, 215, 218, 223, 228 (*Purity and Danger: An Analysis of Concepts of Pollution and Taboo* [New York, 1966]); I. Magli, *La donna, un problema aperto: Guida alla ricerca antropologica* (Florence, 1978), pp. 53–62. I have been unable to consult K. Delaney, M. J. Lupton, and E. Toth, *The Curse: A Cultural History of Menstruation* (New York, 1977).

42. Crawfurd, "Notes on the Superstitions," p. 1335.

43. P. Mantegazza, *Igiene dell'amore* (Florence, 1908), p. 381.

44. F. Loux, *Le jeune enfant et son corps dans la médecine traditionnelle* (Paris, 1978), p. 73.

45. P. Labb and J. D. Mansi, *Sacrorum Conciliorum nova et amplissima collectio,* vol. 2 (Florence, 1759), col. 1038.

46. Rupert de Deutz, *In Leviticum* 1.2, *PL* 167, col. 818.

47. M. Scoti, *De secretis naturae,* in Alberti Magni, *De secretis mulierum,* p. 253.

48. Ibid., p. 56. The idea that coitus with a menstruating woman rendered the male a leper had also penetrated into Arabic medicine; it can be found in particular in Averroës, according to Gerolamo Mercuriale in the fourth book of *De morbis muliebribus:* "Averr. 3 Collec. cap. 7 dicebat, coitum cum menstruata lepram inducere" (*Gynaeciorum sive de mulierum tum communibus, tum gravidarum, parientium, et puerperarum affectibus et morbis libri graecorum, arabum, latinorum* [Strasbourg, 1597], p. 257). It is difficult to specify the relationships of reciprocal dependence in these texts.

49. L. Gioberti, [Laurent Joubert], *La prima parte de gli errori popolari . . . nella quale si contiene l'eccellenza della medicina, et de' medici, della concettione et generatione; della gravidezza, del parto, et delle donne di parto; et del latte, et del nutrire i bambini* (Florence, 1592), p. 67.

50. G. M. Savonarola, *Practica maior* (Venice, 1560), col. 69r.

51. Ibid., col. 251r. See Pliny, *Natualis historia,* 7.15.

52. Lemnes, *De gli occulti miracoli,* cols. 23r–v.

53. Ibid., col. 30r.

54. L. Thorndike, *A History of Magic and Experimental Science,* vol. 6 (New York, 1941), p. 393.

55. A. Paré, *Des monstres et prodiges,* ed. J. Céard (Geneva, 1971), pp. 60, 170.

56. "Il est certain que le plus souvent ces creatures monstrueuses et prodigieuses procedent du jugement de Dieu, lequel permet que les peres et meres produisent telles

abominations au desordre qu'ils font en la copulation comme bestes brutes, où leur appetit les guide, sans respecter le temps ou autre loix ordonnees de Dieu et de Nature, comme il est escrit en Esdras le Prophete, que les femmes souillees de sang menstruel engendront des monstres. Pareillement Moyse defend telle conjonction au Levitique chap. 16. Aussi les anciens ont observé par longues experiences que la femme qui aura conceu durant ses fleurs engendrera enfans lepreux ou soujets à mille maladies, d'autant que l'enfant conceu durant le flux menstruel prend nourriture et accroissement estant au ventre de la mere, d'un sang vicieux, salle et corrompu, lequel avec le temps ayant enraciné son infection se manifeste et fait apparoistre sa malignité: aucuns seront tigneux, autres goutteux, autres lepreux, autres auront la petite verolle ou rougeolle, et autres infinitez de maladie. Conclusion, c'est une chose salle et brutale d'avoir affaire à une femme pendant qu'elle se purge" (ibid., p. 6).

57. I have been able to consult only a recent Italian translation of *De la generation:* A. Paré, *L'opera ostetrico-ginecologica,* ed. V. Pedote (Bologna, 1966), pp. 147–48.

58. On 4 Ezra, see R. L. Bensley and M. R. James, *The Fourth Book of Ezra: The Latin Version Edited from Mss.* (Cambridge, 1895); B. Violet, *Die Esra-Apokalypse (IV. Esra),* pt. 1, *Die Überlieferung* (Leipzig, 1910); *Apocrypha and Pseudoepigrapha of the Old Testament,* ed. R. H. Charles, vol. 2 (Oxford, 1913); A. M. Denis, *Introduction aux pseudépigraphes grecs d'Ancien Testament* (Leiden, 1970). From these works are taken the notes that appear in the text.

59. *Die Esra-Apokalypse,* pp. 55–57.

60. Ibid., p. 433. A prayer for the dead that still appears widely in common religious practice derives from 4 Ezra 2:355: "Give eternal repose to them, O Lord. Cover them in perpetual light, and may they rest in peace."

61. *The Cambridge History of the Bible,* vol. 3 (Cambridge, 1963), passim; W. J. van Eys, *Bibliographie des Bibles et des Nouveaux Testaments en langue française des XVme et XVIme siècles,* pt. 1, *Bibles* (Geneva, 1900–1901). Fourth Ezra appears in numerous Latin Bibles at least until 1480 (Venice, F. de Heilbrun, 1480; Venice, L. Wild, 1481); in the 1508 edition, glossed by Nicholas of Lyre (*Biblia sacra cum glossa et postilla,* vol. 2 (n.p., 1508)—Italian version by Santi Marmochino (Venice, Sons of L. Giunta, 1538), not in that of Nicolò Malermi—and in that of Antonio Brucioli (Venice, F. Bindoni and M. Pasini, 1538); in the French edition edited by the theologians of Louvain (Louvain, B. de Grave, A. M. Bergagne, and J. Waen, 1550); in the Reform Bible of Neuchâtel (Wingel, 1535, on which see van Eys, *Bibliographie des Bibles,* pp. 45–49), and in the Geneva edition of Calvin, in which the Apocrypha appear from 1551 on; in the French version of Théodore Bèze (Geneva, J. Crespin, 1551); in the Latin version of Emmanuele Tremellio and François Du Jon; and in many others that were less widely diffused.

62. Lycostenes, *Prodigiorum ac ostentorum chronicon,* epist. nuncupat.

63. Weinrich, *De ortu monstrorum,* pp. 79v–80v.

64. The volume containing the Apocrypha bore the title *Libri apocryphi sive Appendix Testamenti Veteris ad canonem priscae Ecclesiae latinaque recens et graece sermone facta et notis brevibus illustrata per Franciscum Junium* (Frankfurt, 1579).

65. See n. 61.

66. Roderici da Castro, *De universa muliebrum morborum medicina, novo et antehac a nemine tentato opus absolutissimum . . . ,* 2d ed. (Hamburg, 1617 [1603]), p. 398; L. de Mercado, *De mulierum affectione,* in *Gynaeciorum,* p. 1012; G. Bauhin, *De hermaphroditorum,* p. 65; D. Liddel, *Ars medica succincte et perspicue explicata* (Hamburg, 1617[2a]), p. 531.

67. Garzoni, *Il serraglio de gli stupori del mondo,* p. 178.

68. F. Liceto, *De monstrorum causis* (Padua, 1633[2a]), pp. 147, 204–5.

69. Ibid., p. 148.

70. U. Grozio, *Operum theologicarum*, vol. 2, pt. 1, *Annotationes in quattuor Evangelia et Acta Apostolorum* (Amsterdam, 1679), p. 523. The work was written in 1642.

71. M. Heiland, *Historia infantis monstrosi* (Leiden, 1674), pp. 21–22.

72. *Della natura de'mostri: Lettera del dottore Giambattista Sormani all'Illustrissimo Signore Ranieri Buonaparte Pubblico Professore di Medicina nell'Università di Pisa* (Lucca, 1747).

73. This was identified as produced "in Paris, from the copy printed in Tonon, near the city called Geneva, 1609." Two other editions are cited in J. P. Seguin, *L'information en France avant le périodique: 517 canards imprimés entre 1529 et 1631* (Paris, 1964), p. 123, nn. 480–81. Seguin has identified in the period twenty works about monsters (pp. 121–23, nn. 464–83).

74. One could even observe that from the iconographic point of view the representation of the monstrous body permitted the fulfillment of two contrasting figurative tendencies, both present in the Renaissance, the grotesque and the natural phenomenon.

75. The close relationship between theological and embryological discussions in the middle of the 1500s is also examined by J. Irwin in "Embryology and the Incarnation: A Sixteenth Century Debate," *Sixteenth Century Journal* 9 (1978): 93–104.

76. S. Timpanaro, *Il Lapsus freudiano: Psicanalisi e critica testuale* (Florence, 1974).

# 2 ꙮ The New and the Old: The Spread of Syphilis (1494–1530)

*by Anna Foa*

> ***Quae lues unquam pari celeritate percurrit singulas Europae, Africae Asiaque patres? Quae penitius sese inferit venis ac visceribus. Quae tenacius haeret aut pervicacius repugnat arti curae medicorum? Quae faciliore contagio transilit in alterum? Quae crudeliores habet cruciatus?***
>
> —*Lingua per Desiderum Erasmum Roterodamum . . . Epist. Nuncupatoria* (Coloniae, 1530), p. 3v

The illness[1] that Girolamo Fracastoro would much later call syphilis appeared in Italy around 1494 and, within a few months, spread quickly to all of Europe in an extremely virulent form, with the character of a pandemic. The disease did not have a single name as yet; as Tritemio wrote, it was a disease "that one could not define with any usual medical term."[2] Yet, while waiting to find a cure, it was necessary to provide a name: the most widespread was the one immediately given to it in Italy, attributing its origin to the army of Charles VIII—*mal francese.* But before long, the disease had many other names virtually paralleling its spread across space, from *mal napoletano,* which the French called it, to *male dei cristiani,* as the Turks labeled it.

One thing is immediately clear: syphilis was always a disease/evil (*male*) that came from the outside—from a neighboring country or, better yet, from the country of the enemy. Moreover, it was a new disease, an unknown one. Learned discussions would develop on this issue, in which doctors would analyze their own knowledge, comparing the symptoms of the disease with those already codified for other diseases, especially leprosy. These discussions, all rigidly "medical" and extremely important from the perspective of the history of medicine, were not devoid of other important implications that fall outside scientific parameters. And beyond those parameters they derived essential ways of understanding how the disease should be viewed, of

---

"Il nuovo e il vecchio: L'insorge della sifilide (1494–1530)," *Quaderni Storici,* no. 55 (1984): 11–34. Translated by Carole C. Gallucci.

what space was reserved for it in the consciousness of the period; in short, of how it would be incorporated into the medical and nonmedical vision of the Renaissance. As the new disease rapidly found its place within that vision, coordinates were developed to define it. It was accepted as well as explained. And it is this development that I attempt to explain in this essay.

Even earlier than doctors, chroniclers began to emphasize the newness of the disease, its exceptionality, its calamitous character. As witnesses of a certain vision, one not quite popular but in any case widespread and not the exclusive property of the erudite, chroniclers immediately revealed the other characteristic of the new disease: that it was a venereal disease which attacked a person through sexual intercourse, and which first attacked the genitals. "This disease struck women as well as men and the great majority got this evil from coitus and only slowly did they recover so that they were free from it."[3]

For centuries, the Christian world had questioned itself about the sicknesses/evils (*mali*) that afflicted it. For centuries, a religious preoccupation had intertwined in myriad ways with scientific knowledge: the diseases of humans, of the individual as well as of the community, had been attributed time and again to the movement of the stars, to the change of humors, to witchcraft, to the fumes of the air. Yet one explanation had always underlain the others and had justified the sickness/evil by turning it against the sinner and comforting the just with the hope of immunity. Illness was a punishment from God for the sins of humanity and could strike either the individual sinner or entire communities in order to make them expiate the sins of the world. Thus, sin always appeared just below the surface of sickness. And, of all the sins of humanity, one was especially troublesome because it was the origin of life and therefore the origin of death; because it was the sin of the body and hence required that the body be punished by disease—the sin of the flesh, sexuality. Thus, for centuries, the shadow of carnal sin touched, more or less intimately, the illnesses of humanity.

Christianity had its own venereal sickness/evil, the true one. Yet it is a fact that even in the most acute phase of syphilis, at the beginning of the sixteenth century, European society did not activate its customary mechanism to preserve itself from mental disintegration in the face of calamity: it did not seek out opportune scapegoats. Certainly, there were attempts of this kind, such as Maximilian's edict against blasphemers, but they were rare. In spite of the fact that the means of transmission of the disease and its venereal character had been immediately recognized, the sexual act did not become particularly negatively charged. Also, repression of prostitutes constituted a sporadic and limited response. It is possible that strict attempts to limit the spread of homosexuality in Renaissance society were related. But in short, syphilis did not introduce mechanisms of metaphor[4] on the part of European society in the sixteenth century.

Through two mechanisms in particular, European society succeeded at the outset in integrating this disastrous illness without excessive trauma: projections onto the Other and the use of reassuring *topoi.* Focusing on its relationship with leprosy (a disease that maintained a powerful form of metaphor based on physical and moral sickness/evil),[5] the stereotypes associated with syphilis tended to tame the new and to exorcise its potential for fomenting social disintegration. The mechanisms that projected blame on others at first spontaneously, then by direction, transferred responsibility: the sin remained, of course, but was concrete, real, and controllable, and thus fear was attenuated.

Where did syphilis come from? The answer to this question was not neutral but involved important questions of a moral and religious as well as a scientific nature. Through the debate on its origin, one can reconstruct the path traced by the disease through the culture of the time: the path traveled by European society at the end of the fifteenth century and in the first half of the sixteenth in successfully assimilating the new illness. The first interpretation of syphilis at the level of general opinion was that it was an absolutely new and unknown disease. All the reports of the chroniclers categorically agreed in this regard and leave no doubt about the wonder that swept society at the first appearance of the illness.[6] Even if obviously conditioned by general opinion and by the scarcity of efficacious remedies, doctors, more cautious, quickly began a debate that saw one group argue in favor of the novelty of the disease, while the other attempted to identify the illness with other sicknesses known in the ancient world.

This latter approach had indisputable advantages, because it eliminated the danger of the new and made use of preexisting patterns: in short, it reinserted this punishment in a more reassuring frame, helping in a certain sense to exorcise fear. It was much less reassuring to argue the newness of the disease, even if this was the general opinion. Moreover, doctors were not especially inclined to break away too definitively from the classical and Arabic medical traditions. Thus, the work of Niccolò Leoniceno, written just after the outbreak of syphilis in 1497, began by systematically demolishing its tentative identification with other known illnesses, but nevertheless decisively rejected the idea that it was a new disease:

> The fact that there was not only uncertainty regarding the name of the disease but also disagreement regarding its nature, led many to hypothesize that this illness was new, that the ancients had never known it, and that for these reasons the Greek and Arabic doctors had never spoken of it. In my opinion, as I do not agree with those who have given different names to the disease that do not correspond at all to its nature; when I consider that humanity has the same nature, is born under the same sky, grows up under the same stars, I must conclude that we have always been subjected to the same illnesses, and I absolutely cannot believe that this illness is born suddenly only now and has infected only our epoch and none of the preceding. And if someone thinks differently, I will clear up this point: Is one dealing with a revenge of the gods? In fact, if one considers natural causes, the same conditions repeat themselves thousands of times from the beginning of the world. And so we feel it is necessary to affirm that a similar illness, deriving from similar causes, has also infected preceding epochs.[7]

❧ This essay is not focused as much on the solution that Leoniceno provided for the problem of the origins of syphilis (although this is very important from a scientific perspective for its analogies with the mixed theories that have appeared in our own century) as in how it was possible to overturn such a strong affirmation of the principle that rejected the possibility of new diseases. In spite of Leoniceno's openness (and one thinks of the ease with which he dismissed the hypothesis that syphilis was a divine punishment), what was new had no right of citizenship in his universe. A significant mental leap was required to overcome this fundamental principle. In those same years, the European conscience was already facing another novelty that had disrupted conceptions of the world, created a crisis for the very words of Sacred Scripture, and posed problems difficult to resolve within the old structures of thought: the discovery of a New World, as well as millions of people neither foreseen nor touched by Revelation. There is a direct analogy between the protective mechanisms and mental paths which the learned European mind used to accept the idea of the New World and those mechanisms used to integrate the terrible *mal francese* without trauma into the culture.[8] The new was becoming overbearingly evident, and whoever had accepted that there was a New World could also believe that in their own world, so changed, there were new illnesses. This was made easier by the fact that fairly quickly syphilis was related back to the unknown territories discovered by Columbus, to the American Indians who had not known the Word of Christ.

Quickly, the idea of the novelty of the disease was also affirmed on the medical level. Actually, Leoniceno had lain the foundations for this by demolishing with great precision and timeliness possible identifications with past diseases that, if they had been accepted, would have greatly compromised scientific advances.[9] With such possible identifications rejected, doctors also confronted the problem of a name. While geographic names remained the most widespread and popular, and while there were only two names tied to the protector saints (*mal di San Giobbe* and *mal di San Mento*),[10] doctors invented many erudite names for the disease. Among these, only Fracastoro's *syphilis* had a future.

The general recognition of the novelty of this disease constituted a notable qualitative leap forward in the collective mentality. On the medical level it represented a position linked to an empirical and experimental vision of medicine which saw the disease, as did Fracastoro, as contagious. It therefore saw the epidemic of syphilis as "the trial by fire of the new medicine."[11] With the idea of contagion, the complex web of medical and religious considerations, which had characterized medicine until then, disentangled. In fact, this idea permitted a fundamental shift of focus from concern with primary causes to the ways in which the disease was transmitted and, therefore, a secularization of the theories about it. It was no accident that in those diseases in which the question of contagion was largely overlooked, as for example with the plague, a confusion of discourse continued up through the seventeenth century. Yet the two positions were still not well defined, and the supporters of the theory that the disease was new included even those who sustained *tout court* that the illness was due, not to contagion, but to divine punishment for the lasciviousness and immorality of the times. Such an interpretation, however, tended to minimize or directly deny the newness of the disease, precisely because it underlined the value of divine punishment for the traditional and enduring inclination of humanity to sins of the flesh. Among the supporters of the endogenous origin of syphilis (that is, among those who were opposed to the idea of contagion), there were some who, more attuned to a natural vision of cause, considered syphilis a spontaneous consequence of sexual misconduct.[12]

Undoubtedly, accepting the idea of contagion, which turned attention from causes to the form of transmission, permitted the elimination, at least in part, of the problem of blame. In fact, the idea of contagion, with its totally natural means of transmission, tended to eliminate an essential aspect of blaming: the aura of mystery that always surrounded it. Blame, however, was not completely removed but only moved back to its distant origins, to an indefinite time and space.

Two of these assignments of blame, however, interest us here, because they concerned the primary Others of Christian society at that time: first, the internal Other, the witness of the Christian world—the Jew; second, the absolute Other unrelated to Christianity, who still had not been placed in the cultural context of the time—the Indian. If we focus on the ideas that syphilis originated in the newly discovered Americas of Columbus or came from the Jews driven out of Spain in that same year, we will see the implications of similar projections of blame that went well beyond any rational investigation of the disease's origin that was attempted at the time.

❧ Attributing the origin of syphilis to the Indians won out only in the 1530s, although it had already been proposed at the beginning of the century. Initial support for this position came from people associated in one way or another with the Discovery and the Conquest: Pietro Martire d'Anghiera,[13] Gomara,[14] Fernandez de Oviedo, and doctor Roderico de Isla, who had taken care of Columbus's sailors in Spain.[15] Analysis of their accounts has primarily been focused on proving their veracity in a debate essentially still open on the possible American origin of syphilis. Actually, the fact that these accounts were given later or were subsequent reelaborations of direct testimonies has often been noted.[16] But my goal is to explain the cultural factors that caused the diffusion of the thesis of the American origin of the disease, the way in which it became a dominant explanation, and the intellectual points of reference that were required. Moreover, because the blame for the new disease could be placed on the Indians, it was necessary that a stereotype of the lascivious Indian be formed. Amerigo Vespucci, without alluding directly to syphilis, wrote, "They have as many wives as they desire; they live in promiscuity without regard to blood relations; mothers lie with sons, brothers with sisters; they satisfy their desires as they occur to their libidos as beasts do."[17] Fernandez de Oviedo gave a similar account, which frequently emphasized the libidinous habits of the women of the Americas, so much so that "few Christians who carnally lie with Indian women of these places are saved from this disgraceful sickness/evil."[18] Oviedo had no doubts about the origin of syphilis: "I have laughed many times hearing the Italians name it the *mal Francese* and the French call it the *malo di Napoli,* and in effect they would have guessed its true name if they had called it the *male dell'Indie.*"[19] Guicciardini adopted the American thesis in a passage from *The History of Italy:*

> After the narration of other things, it does not seem inappropriate to mention that . . . an illness began that was called the *male di Napoli* by the French but which was commonly called *the blisters* or the *male francese* by the Italians because, having broken out among them [the French invaders] while they were in Naples, it was spread by them throughout all of Italy as they returned to France. This illness, either totally new or completely unknown in our hemisphere until this age, if not in its most remote and distant parts, was for many years such a grave calamity that it deserves mention. . . . But this ignominious name should be removed from the French because it was shown later that such an illness had been transported from Spain to Naples. And it was not really from that nation but brought there from those islands which . . . began to be known in our hemisphere because of the voyages of the Genovese Christopher Columbus, almost in these same years.[20]

The perception of the gravity of the disease and its newness is evident in this account. Two other important aspects of the vision of the disease are also revealed: first, the projection onto the French; second, its later attribution to the Americas, which the historian believed but which in reality re-created an analogous mechanism of projection (and this was the trap of the text itself).

The Indians continued to be blamed for syphilis for two fundamental reasons: first, the diffusion of a cure containing guaiac wood found in the Antilles, which made contemporaries think by analogy that because the remedy had been found beyond the ocean, the sickness had also originated there; second, the elaboration already completed of the *topos* of the Indian as Other. In 1494, no one would have thought to attribute the origin of the new disease that was raging in

Europe to the few Indians brought to Europe by Columbus as a spectacle for the king of Spain. Thirty years later, the Indian was the Other whose nature had been extensively written about and who had been the subject of important maneuvers in both the political and the cultural arena. It was not by chance that Fernandez de Oviedo was one of the cruelest butchers in history, hotly criticized by Las Casas because he promoted the thesis that the Indians were useful only as slaves and was very inclined to portray their customs in a negative light. It appears that a stereotype had somehow developed, for even with the limited credibility of people like Oviedo such ideas could be advanced. The savage world discovered by Columbus had become the mystery that created a crisis for the hypothesis of a universal Church, that (in the words of Guicciardini) had with its discovery created "some anxiety" for the interpreters of Sacred Scripture,[21] and had with the Conquest effectively defined the image of the Indian as Other.[22]

To attribute the origin of syphilis to the Indians was clearly not an innocent act. It meant searching for the origin of a sickness/evil of this kind, a sickness/evil tied to sexual excess and located as far from oneself as possible in the absolute Other, the person who had never known Christianity. This was an extreme projection: the disease was thrown back onto the "nonhuman," onto the totally alien. To attribute it to a people outside of the Revelation of Christ served to attenuate the impact of the debates on blame and divine punishment which had been encouraged by endogenous theories of the origin as the result of lasciviousness. In turn, the reassuring value of this projection of the disease onto the myth of the "lustful savage" is obvious, just as it is obvious that this process of alienation took so long that it was not to be among the first answers to the epidemic.

There is a direct analogy between the attitude of those who immediately defined the disease as the *mal francese* and those who later searched for its origins in the New World, as Guicciardini seemed to sense when he emphasized that those who attributed the disease to the French were doing so in order to place on their shoulders the blame for Italian misfortunes. All the earliest texts effectively linked the disease to the invasion of the French, and this projection only later changed direction. It is as if the already popular projection that blamed the enemy who had descended into Italy for the new and obscure disease (which the preachers attributed to lust and the doctors attributed to the stars or to floods) had been redirected in the scholarly and ecclesiastical milieu to the most useful scapegoats, the Indians and the Jews. The complex picture thus became more homogeneous: the Other, whether external or internal, was opposed to Christian society and its order, representing symbolically, in the illness, disorder—an enemy of every rule and every hierarchy.

❧ Astruc, the most authoritative eighteenth-century supporter of the American thesis, would attempt more than two centuries later to answer the questions "Why the Indians? Why the Americas?" He held that syphilis among the Indians was endemic and was provoked by internal causes, not by contagion, as was the case in Western Europe and the rest of the world. This thesis raised the question of causation. The explanation of divine punishment for the lust of the Indians could not satisfy an eighteenth-century doctor. If there had to be an internal cause, then it had to be a natural one, and Astruc, relying upon evidence from Ovid and suggestions from the Bible and from Pliny, characterized it as a result of the combined effect of the extremely heavy menstrual flow of the women and the particularly torrid climate. An old *topos,* holding that there were grave dangers in having sexual intercourse with menstruating women, reappeared in this analysis; but here the danger was not in conceiving monstrous or leprous children but in contracting venereal diseases.[23] Attributing this particular effect to the torrid climate gave a scientific coloring to the old stereotype. Only in this way could Astruc completely support the idea of syphilis as an external disease generated in the Americas and could he reaffirm the possibility of an indigenous endemic in the torrid zones caused by questionable customs. Without the voyage of Columbus and the infection of his sailors, the mild climate of Europe, if not its customs, would have preserved it from the sickness/evil.

If the Indian was the external Other, Christian society also knew an internal Other, the Jew, who already had a well-defined role, in contrast to the still undetermined role of the inhabitants of the Indies.[24] For centuries the Jew had been the witness of the promise of Christ's return, the reverse image of the Christian, the one against whom Christians were able to define themselves. But then the politics of progressive elimination of this Other had begun: they were ordered to convert, to assimilate—to be the Other no longer or to disappear. In the same year that Columbus landed in the Indies, the Jews in Spain were converted by force or driven out. Arriving in Italy, the exiled Spanish Jews briefly stopped at the gates of Rome but were unable to enter the city. There, in this new Diaspora, they were decimated by epidemics that, in spite of the precautions of the authorities, soon spread to the entire city. In 1492, as the *Chronicon* of J. Naucler reported, "During their trek, 30,000 Jews driven out of Spain died of the plague."[25] "The plague entered the city and great numbers died contaminated by the pestilence brought by the so-called *Marrani*," wrote Stefano Infessura in his *Diario*, describing the camps of the Jews along the Via Appia in 1493.[26]

These are the bare facts as they were reported in the chronicles: the passage of masses of fleeing people decimated by illnesses (here the term *plague* [*pestis*] assumes a totally generic meaning, even if perhaps not devoid of symbolic overtones: *pestis iudaeorum*, *pestis marrana*). Yet, something quite different was constructed from these facts. The diseases that were decimating the Jews encamped at the gates of Rome were reinterpreted precisely because it was the children of Israel who passed before the gates of Rome. Quickly, the epidemic that was destroying the Jews and spreading throughout the city of Rome was identified as syphilis. Paolo Giovio, writing as if conveying general opinion, stated, "There were those who believed that this disease came from the newly discovered world to the west, and had been carried to Italy and to the rest of the world by the Jews, driven out in that moment from Spain at the time when Charles V dominated all of Italy."[27] Here the Jews had an evident role as intermediary: the two theses, that of the American origin and that of the origin in the new Diaspora, merged. Leone Africano identified this same role for the Jews in North Africa: "The inhabitants of Africa did not even know the name of this illness before the time in which Ferdinand, King of Spain, drove all the Jews out of Spain."[28] In their journey to Africa, Jewish women had transmitted the disease to the population, which from that time gave syphilis the name *male spagnolo*. In this work, which is also interesting because it was written by a man who had lived a life analogous to that of the Jews whom he described (born in Granada, converted to Christianity, he traveled to Africa where he returned to Islam), he deduced among other things that at least for the populations of the Maghreb, the Spanish origin referred more to the Jews driven out of Spain than to the actual Spanish themselves.

But the report that linked syphilis to the Jews, not on the basis of coincidental facts of time or place, but on the basis of an internal connection between the two terms Jew (*ebreo*) and Gallic disease (*morbo gallico*), was that of an ecclesiastical chronicler, Sigismondo de' Conti da Foligno, who wrote as a contemporary sometime before 1512:

> While the French found themselves in Naples, a terrible illness exploded in Italy . . . and this illness, although it had been called the Gallic disease by the French, did not derive from them but from the *Marrani*, who had been driven out of Spain and gathered by Ferdinand in Naples. In fact, the Jews, because they abstain from pork, are subject to leprosy more than other peoples, and this is the reason why, according to the most authoritative Cornelius Tacitus, they were driven out of Egypt. More significantly, Sacred Scripture, in which one must believe, makes clear that leprosy was a sign that revealed an even more vile incontinence: in fact, it began to manifest itself in the genitals.[29]

The chronicler noted two expulsions of the Jews in this text. The first was the one recorded in Sacred Scripture, the Exodus. Sigismondo de' Conti returned here explicitly to an excursus of Tacitus, marginal to his account of the Judaic War,[30] where he repeated a historiographic tradition born in Hellenistic Egypt and fed by Alexandrian anti-Judaism, which held that the Jews driven out of Egypt had been none other than leprous Egyptians expelled from their land. In the chronicler's text there was an explicit parallel between the expulsion of the Jews from Egypt and that of the *Marrani* (in reality, Jews) from Spain: as the Jews driven out of Egypt brought leprosy with them, so their descendants in the West, driven out of Spain, brought syphilis to the rest of Europe. It was inconsequential that Sigismondi de' Conti did not bother to explain how on earth the Jews, before the expulsion, had avoided infecting the rest of Spain, for his explanation worked on another level. This is made clear by comparing the implications of Tacitus's text with those of the chronicler's regarding the Jewish taboo against eating pork. Tacitus wrote, "These people abstain from pork in remembrance of the leprosy that had once contaminated them, and of which this animal is subject."[31] The relationship between leprosy and the Jews was, then, in Tacitus as in the tradition that he reflects, an episodic relation, remote in time, not necessarily repeatable. The abstention from pork was motivated by the ignominious memory of the leprosy that drove them out of Egypt: in fact, the pig was considered an animal subject to leprosy.[32]

Although maintaining Tacitus's terms *pig*, *leprosy*, and *Jew*, Sigismondo de' Conti modified their internal relationship. It was of little importance that the pig was subject to leprosy; for Christian culture, it was already a symbol full of ambiguity. The Jews abstained from pork, but to no effect because they were *by nature* subject to leprosy, which made the relationship between the Jew and leprosy eternal. Finding pork repugnant not only did not diminish the impurity of the Jew: it actually accentuated it. It was because the Jew was seen as by nature impure that to an even greater extent a Jew had to abstain from pork. The real connection was the one between the Jew and impurity, and the pig served as a catalyst, even more so because it was the symbol of lasciviousness. Abstaining from pork was not enough; the Jews still remained more subject to leprosy than others.[33]

The reason for the relation between Jews and leprosy was that they were sexually intemperate. This explanation, then, was derived from this fourth term introduced on the basis of Sacred Scripture: lasciviousness. The symbolic path from this point to an explanation of syphilis was short, even if untraversable in reality, turning on the stereotype of the infected Jew. Similar to the wandering Jew, the infected Jew also crossed the Western tradition but was an even older theme. As noted earlier, the first traces of the stereotype of the infected Jew are found in the distortions of Exodus created in the Hellenistic age. "Jew" and "leper" remained linked together even in the Christian Middle Ages: according to accusations made in France in 1321, the lepers poisoned wells as, according to legend, did the Jews, thus widening their persecution. In a tragic interchange of terms and roles, the lepers and the Jews were considered responsible for the plague of 1348 and were exterminated in the pogroms that followed the path of the Black Death.

Physical and moral infection were therefore closely intertwined in the Jew, who was subject to leprosy because of sins of the flesh. In fact, in the culture and the imagination of the time, leprosy was closely linked to sin, particularly with lasciviousness. Once again, the link with the pig appears relevant. In ecclesiastical symbolism, the pig represented both the throat and lasciviousness: the theme of the *Judensau,* found in German art from the thirteenth to the eighteenth centuries,[34] placed before the eyes of all the faithful a tight connection between the Jew and this symbol of lasciviousness: the Jew sucking the udder of a sow.

In the Middle Ages, leprosy assumed an extremely strong symbolic valence: it was the sign of sin, it was the most feared disease, it became the central metaphor of sickness/evil. The complex ritual of separating the leper from the world with a kind of symbolic burial represented the total alienation necessary to force the leper away from the Christian community. The powerful symbolism of leprosy and the strict tie that literature, ecclesiastical tradition, and the popular imagination created between this disease and lasciviousness did not end with the almost total disappearance of the disease in the fifteenth century.[35] When syphilis appeared as a sickness/evil tied to sexual intercourse, its symbolic and metaphoric weight was almost nonexistent; it was as if Christian society had already dealt with its fear of sex by symbolizing it in leprosy. Society, then, had virtually used up its metaphorical capacities. Leprosy, even if it had disappeared, remained the obscure shadow of sickness/evil that filled the symbolic possibilities to overflowing. Syphilis, specifically tied to sexual intercourse with Renaissance prostitutes, never assumed the symbolic status of a sickness/evil at the same level as leprosy—the punishment of embraces only dreamed and feared.

This is supported by noting the relative lack of an iconography for syphilis and its dependence on that of leprosy. The images that revealed the signs of leprosy, as well as the deformed beggars of Breughel and Grünewald, have been widely discussed by critics and doctors. I shall focus, instead, on the symbolism of the leper, the type of leper who was painted in a tradition that ranged from the representations hailed by Christ to those of Job. There we find the same iconographic forms that would be used to represent the syphilitic, from the celebrated Dürer woodcut in 1496 to the image taken from the work of Grünpeck, where two sick women covered by pustules invoked, on their knees, the protection of the Virgin.[36] The iconography of syphilis was, in this way, channeled without great change into paths already followed by leprosy, with the distinction that it was represented only in the woodcuts that accompanied medical works. Painting per se was not affected in any way by the new disease. The absence of an original iconography of syphilis and its dependence on the forms of leprosy seem to confirm that the primary place in the symbolism of sickness/evil always went to the primary disease of evil, leprosy. Even the patron saints of one were transferred to the other. In particular Saint Job, the biblical Job who had been transformed into a saint and was already patron of the leprous, became protector of the syphilitics.

Between the decline of leprosy and the rise of syphilis there was, in effect, great confusion fostered not only by doctors who supported the antiquity of the Gallic disease and attempted to identify it with leprosy or with other related illnesses, but above all by the persistence of several *topoi* from the mythology of leprosy. This confusion allowed a sort of mitigation of the very difficult mental adaptation that would have been required by having to face a completely new disease without mediations of any kind. Thus, while the idea that the disease was a novelty permitted great strides forward in medical science through the expansion of the concept of contagion to areas less well defined, there remained a tradition of stereotypes and ways of thinking that had, to a great extent, leprosy at their center.

Because they are important indications of this tradition, let us consider what the eighteenth-century physician Astruc labeled *fabulae* (tales) concerning the origin of syphilis. Among these, Astruc included the theses that linked the illness to astrological influences or to a humid climate, both of which were tied to a particular tradition of Renaissance science. But more important for my analysis were the *fabulae* contained in later works, those tied to the idea of contagion as a means of transmitting the sickness/evil, which were backed by the most famous and unquestionable authorities at that time.[37]

Several of the *fabulae* were concerned with the relationship between leprosy and syphilis. For Pietro Mainardi, who wrote in 1525, the origin of syphilis was to be found in the union of a Spanish prostitute and a leper: the prostitute had then infected many of Charles VIII's soldiers. Mainardi attributed this *fabula* to "earlier beliefs and the greater part of the reports."[38] Pietro Andrea Mattioli told a similar story of coitus with leprous women and was above all vague about his sources (which he claimed "no report would contradict").[39] Paracelsus believed that syphilis came from the sexual intercourse of a leprous Frenchman and a prostitute suffering from venereal sores.[40] The origin of the disease, according to Brasavola, who wrote around 1551, was attributable to a prostitute affected by a uterine abscess.[41] Syphilis, for Falloppio, who wrote in 1560, had a *manufactured* origin: it originated from poison that Spanish soldiers had put in the wells during the War of Naples.[42] This citation lacked a direct tie to leprosy, but the stereotype of poisoned wells was itself linked to the Jews and the leprous. The connection was made specific in the reelaboration written by Andrea Cesalpino in 1601, where it was no longer wells that were poisoned, but wine with the blood of the leprous.[43] Another group of tales linked syphilis to cannibalism and bestiality: thus,

Leonardo Fioravanti, in *Capricci medicinali,* attributed the origin of the disease to the fact that, during the war between Angevins and Aragon in 1456, soldiers had unknowingly eaten human flesh.[44] An analogous story was reported by Francis Bacon.[45] Finally, Jean Baptiste van Helmont narrated a dreamlike story of bestiality.[46]

These *fabulae,* then, focused on three themes: the relationship between leprosy and syphilis, the origin of syphilis, and bestiality and cannibalism. The links between these themes were extremely close. In fact, they are really variations on one theme: syphilis, the disease derived from a monstrous relation, whether sexual or sexuality transposed as cannibalism. Just as a disordered and monstrous relation generated monsters and lepers, a disordered and monstrous relation between lepers and prostitutes or between animals and humans generated syphilis. Even the ingestion of human flesh could be considered a form of relationship that at once destroyed society and created monstrosity; moreover, there was an account of cannibalism in the Caribbean, which Bacon explicitly linked to the origin of syphilis in the Americas. At the same time, the very sexuality of the leper, the originator of syphilis, was viewed as in itself monstrous. It was not a pure and simple excess, but the very mark of monstrosity.[47]

Another common element in these *fabulae* was that the disease developed from a single, unrepeatable act that, once completed, created an unstoppable mechanism whose consequences involved the whole of society. The relationship between the disease and the act that created it was placed in a historical context (thus, the necessity of testimonies), but in reality it was metahistorical. In fact, these *fabulae* were not able to explain reality but only to reestablish it. In the end they were myths, whether drawn from oral or written tradition or invented from whole cloth. As such, they were simply placed in a historical time to make them appear objective and to give them a false precision. But this did not change the *fabulae*'s mythical nature. This process of mythmaking for syphilis did little beyond proposing mechanisms already used for leprosy, and at least in part for calamities, even if new times and new needs prevented their full utilization. Syphilis was stamped onto leprosy, it was molded over it in a process of reproduction in which the new based itself on the old, the expected, the foreseen, but then was forced to reproduce its features.

Those who wrote these myths knew very well that leprosy and syphilis were not the same thing, but the generic relationship that they tried to establish was nothing other than the reproduction of a twin.

To do this, it was necessary to use what seemed the simpler and more immediate means of diffusion, the prostitute, with all her implications and her valences. An example is the story of the infected prostitute, yet another doubling of leprosy, syphilis, and a not very precise venereal sore, that represented the internal rottenness of woman, an old misogynist *topos.* Moreover, in a great number of these fables the female sex was represented as a pure receptacle of monstrosity, of disease. In the creative act that caused syphilis, the language was the Aristotelian language of generation: woman, a mere vessel, conceived the disease as she conceived a child, a monstrous child. Van Helmont's story was emblematic of a myth-making process still in progress. The traditional phantasm, an intellectual vision of the infected beast of burden, was reinserted in actual history (the siege of Naples) and reinterpreted in light of the old scheme of monstrous sexual relationships and the generation of monsters. There was more of an emphasis on the role of divine punishment, even if it was stressed less than in other variations, as the reference to leprosy was, itself, loaded with such connotations.

In what way do all these variations of the same myth find a place, even if it was a place softened by the distance created by attributing the story to others ("no others deny it") in the works of the most important scientists of this period? Above all, by giving up the rational in order to label; by transforming myth into an explanation, into a curiosity, into mere trifles, or, at the extreme, into dreams floating in a language without structure. In addition, by providing a powerful reassurance—the endurance of known reasons anchored in the known—even when dealing with an absolutely mythic vision. Once again, syphilis gave way in these scholarly fables to leprosy and to its constant, persistent, extremely strong symbolic value.

These fables, primarily falling later than the period examined in this essay (but was not Fracastoro's poem on the shepherd Sifilo also a fable?), reveal that the relationship between leprosy and syphilis was a complex one that remained entrusted to the symbolic realm, and that it cannot in any way be reduced to the simple confusion of symptoms of the two diseases, even if this was occasionally true. The two diseases, clearly distinguished by the doctors at an early date, with two completely different destinies, were intertwined in that no-man's-land which makes up mental representation: the symbolism and iconography are proof of this. Leprosy, which had in some way anticipated it, usurped the symbolic valence of syphilis. Even though it almost disappeared at the end of the fifteenth century, it continued to condition, through assimilation and stereotyping, the way in which syphilis came to be conceived and perceived. Therefore, in the third decade of the sixteenth century, when syphilis was attenuating and losing its virulence, it had already been exorcised from the minds of its contemporaries.

## Notes

1. The most famous sixteenth-century collection of texts on syphilis is that of L. Luisini, *De morbo gallico omnia quae extant . . . apud omnes medicos cuiuscumque nationis . . .* (Venice, 1566–67, republished, ed. H. Boerhaave [Leiden] in 1728 with the title *Aphrodisiacus sive de lue venera . . .*). Luisini's work was continued by C. G. Gruner, in *Aphrodisiacus sive de lue venera* (Jena, 1789) and in *De morbo gallico scriptores medici et historici . . .* (Jena, 1793). Also important is the collection of texts by A. Corradi, *Nuovi documenti per la storia delle malattie veneree in Italia dalla fine del Quattrocento alla metà del Cinquecento* (Milan, 1884). In 1924, K. Sudhoff edited, in the series *Monumenta medica,* directed by H. E. Sigerist, the facsimile edition of ten incunabula, *Zehn Syphilisdrucke aus den Jahren, 1495–1498* (Milan, 1924).

2. Gruner, Aphrodisiacus, p. 54.

3. *Cronica di Bologna,* called *Cronica Bianchina,* dated 1496, in Corradi, *Nuovi documenti,* p. 58. See also the *Cronaca* of Friano degli Ubaldini (in ibid., p. 59).

4. See Susan Sontag, *Illness as Metaphor* (New York, 1978).

5. On leprosy and its interpretations, see S. N. Brody, *The Disease of the Soul* (Ithaca, 1974).

6. "A strange and horrible illness which was not known by any doctor" was the perspective of the *Cronica* of Friano degli Ubaldini (in Corradi, *Nuovi documenti,* p. 59); "a cruel illness no longer heard of," *Annali di Sicilia* (in ibid., p. 61); "a kind of illness never named, just as much forgotten by the living as never heard of by our ancestors," from *Castigatissimi Annali,* by Agostino Giustiniani (in ibid., p. 77), but the examples are innumerable.

7. N. Leoniceno, *Libellus de epidemia, quam vulgo morbum Gallicum vocant* (1497), in Sudhoff, *Monumenta medica,* p. 124.

8. On the ways in which the European mind accepted the New World, see J. Lafaye, *Quetzalcòatl et Guadalupe: La formation de la conscience nationale au Mexique* (Paris, 1974) (*Quetzalcoatl and Guadalupe: The Formation of Mexican National Consciousness, 1531–1815,* trans. Benjamin Keen [Chicago, 1976]); and T. Todorov, *La conquête de l'Amérique: La question de l'autre* (Paris, 1982) (*The Conquest of America: The Question of the Other,* trans. Richard Howard [New York, 1984]).

9. Leoniceno systematically demolished the attempts that had been made to link syphilis with elephantiasis (that is, with leprosy), with lichen (that is, with any of various eruptive skin diseases), and with other diseases. On these problems, see D. Mugnai Carrara, "Fra causalità astrologica e causalità naturale: Gli interventi di Nicolo Leoniceno e della sua scuola sul morbo gallico," *Physis* 21 (1979): 37–54. Identification with leprosy was, however, the most widespread. See Pietro Mainardi, *De morbo gallico,* in Luisini, *De morbo gallico,* cols. 390–91. The Leoniceno school supported the thesis of the novelty of the disease: thus, Pietro Mainardi attempted to resolve the contradiction between the fact that the disease could be new and the fact that it was transmitted by contagion. One possible response to this contradiction was

to see the origin of syphilis in the New World, where it would have been endemic. See *Epistola II ad Michaelem Sanctannam* (1525), in Luisini, cols. 605–6. Antonio Musa Brasavola, one of Leoniceno's principal allies, also sustained the newness of syphilis in *De morbo gallico* (1555), in Luisini, col. 671).

10. On the latter saint (known variously also as Maiano, Mevenno, and Maino), see *Acta Sanctorum,* June, vol. 4, p. 100ff. From the sixth century, he founded a monastery in Bretagna, where pilgrims sick with scabies went. In fact, his prayers are said to have brought forth a miraculous spring, which had the power to cure scabies. Among his miracles, he supposedly had cured a woman of leprosy. G. Torrella writes that the identification of the new disease with the sickness of S. Mento, or S. Semento, had been the work of the Spanish (*De dolore in pudendagra dialogus,* in Luisini, *De morbo gallico,* col. 502).

11. A. Castiglioni, *Storia della medicina* (Milan, 1936), p. 405.

12. The idea of divine punishment is present in almost all medical texts, even if one is often dealing with a mere formality. We have seen the lack of interest which Leoniceno had in this; see also the position of Brasavola in Luisini, *De morbo gallico,* col. 672. See also what Jean Astruc wrote two centuries later, in *De morbis venereis* (Venice, 1760 [1793]), p. 8.

13. Pietro Martire d'Anghiera, *De Orbe Novo* (1st ed., 1500), in Gruner, *Aphrodisiacus,* p. 116.

14. Francisco Lopez de Gomara, *Historia general de las Indias* (1st ed., Saragozza, 1552), in ibid., pp. 129–30.

15. Roderigo Diaz de Isla, in *Tractado contra el mal serpentino que vulgarmente en Espana es lamado bubas,* written in 1539, half a century after the events that he narrated, held that the disease was from the New World and recalled the epidemic in Barcelona in 1493, identified as syphilis and attributed to those sailors whom the author cared for on their return to Spain (in ibid., pp. 162–63).

16. D. Thiene, *Sulla storia de' mali venerei, lettere* (Venice 1836), p. 35ff.

17. Amerigo Vespucci, in Gruner, *Aphrodisiacus,* p. 117.

18. Gonzalo Fernandez De Oviedo, *Historia general y natural de las Indias Occidentales,* in ibid., p. 133. The Italian [trad.] that Gruner cites is that published by Ramusio.

19. Ibid., p. 132.

20. F. Guicciardini, *Storia d'Italia,* ed. C. Panigada, vol. 1 (Bari, 1929), 204–5.

21. Ibid., vol. 2, p. 132.

22. See Lafaye, *Quetzalcòatl and Guadalupe,* pp. 51–77, and Todorov, *Conquête de l'Amérique.*

23. After having cited Pliny the Elder and having referred to the Jewish taboo regarding menstruating women, Astruc stated his conclusions about the origin of syphilis (Astruc, *De morbis venereis,* p. 64). Here the emphasis was shifted to blame: in the Indies, syphilis did not originate in contagion but in sexual disorder and the female libido. The emphases are the same as those from the endogenous theses on the origin of the disease, which Astruc himself refuted, in favor of the hypothesis of contagion. On the *topos* of monstrous conceptions and leprous children caused by intercourse with menstruating women, see Chapter 1 in this volume.

24. See Todorov, *Conquête de l'Amérique,* p. 54.

25. J. Naucler, *Chronicon,* in Gruner, *Aphrodisiacus,* p. 38.

26. S. Infessura, *Diarium urbis Romae,* in ibid., p. 38.

27. P. Giovio, *Historia sui temporis,* in ibid., p. 125.

28. G. Leone Africano, *De totius Africae descriptione,* in ibid., p. 125. Leone, called the African, one of the most important geographers of the sixteenth century, was taken prisoner by Christian privateers and given as a slave to Leo X, who pro-

tected him and made him convert to Christianity. After the death of the pope, he returned to Tunis, converting back to Islam.

29. Sigismondo de' Conti da Foligno, *Le storie dei suoi tempi dal 1475 al 1510,* vol. 2 (Rome, 1883), 271–72.

30. Tacitus, *Hist.* 5.1.ff.

31. Ibid., 5.4.3. It is clear that Tacitus, in the anti-Jewish excursus that he appended to his description of the final phase of the Judaic War (70 A.D.), depends, directly or indirectly, on the Alexandrian anti-Jewish tradition. However it is more difficult to determine the source of it (Appian? Lysimachus?). All that we do know of this tradition derives ultimately from the *Contra Apionem* of Flavius Josephus (1.219–2.32). In particular, we know through Flavius Josephus the position, first held by Manetheo, who said that the Jews were the lepers driven out of Egypt.

32. Plutarch dedicates one of his *Quaestiones conviviales* (4.5), a significant title, to the Jewish abstention from pork: "Is it due to veneration for the pig or due to aversion that Jews abstain from eating it?" One of the interlocutors, Lamprias, argues that the Jews had proscribed pork for fear of leprosy and scabies, contagious illnesses considered by them capable of infecting even the pig.

33. Pork does not seem to be considered the cause of leprosy in the medical tradition of the Middle Ages. In the chapter dedicated to leprosy in *De natura et proprietatibus omnium rerum* (thirteenth century), which is virtually a compendium of medical opinions on the forms of the transmission of leprosy, Bartolomeo Anglico refered to pork, but only if spoiled like other foods such as wine or other kinds of meat (Cologne, 1481), fol. 132v.

34. See I. Shacar, *The Judensau: A Medical Anti-Jewish Motif and Its History* (London, 1974). This motif, documented in sculpture, painting, and woodcuts, is iconographically linked to the theme of the ritual killing of children and shows, in its later elaborations, variations that represent the Jew not only taking milk from a sow but nourishing himself from its excrement. Luther refers to the relief representing this motif in the cathedral of Wittenburg in *Schem Hamphoras,* one of his most violent anti-Jewish libels. *Die Wunderzeitung,* a short poem composed in 1574 by the satirical poet Johann Fischart, speaks of a Jewish woman giving birth to two small pigs. It deals with the revival of an analogous story by Sebastian Brant (*Von der wuderbaren Su zü Landser jm Suntgaw des Jahrs, 1496*), which, however, links the sow, a repulsive and impure animal, to the Turks, not the Jews (on this, see F. Saxl, *Lectures,* vol. 1, *Illustrated Pamphlets of the Reformation* [London, 1957], p. 259).

35. On the relationship between leprosy, syphilis, and segregation, see Michel Foucault, *Storia della follia nell'età classica* (Milan, 1976), pp. 1–19 (*Madness and Civilization: A History of Insanity in the Age of Reason,* trans. Richard Howard [New York, 1965]).

36. See Brody, *Disease of the Soul,* p. 56. The image that I mention in the text, the illustration of Joseph Grünpeck's treatise, is reproduced in Sudhoff, *Zehn Syphilisdrucke,* p. 71. Several hurried annotations on the iconography of syphilis can be found in M. Morel, *Essai critique sur la syphilis en Espagne au temps de Renaissance* (Bourg, 1936), p. 200ff.

37. Astruc, *De morbis venereis,* pp. 46–48.

38. Mainardi, *Epistola II ad Michaelem Sanctannam,* col. 606.

39. Pietro Andrea Mattioli, *De morbo gallico opusculum* (1530), in Luisini, *De morbo gallico,* col. 247.

40. Paracelsus, *Chirurgia magna* (Strasbourg, 1573 [1536]), p. 97.

41. Antonio Musa Brasavola, *De morbo gallico,* in Luisini, *De morbo gallico,* cols. 671–72.

42. G. Falloppio, *De morbo gallico tractatus* (1560), in ibid., col. 762.

43. Andrea Cesalpino, *Speculum artis medicae Hippocraticum* . . . (Frankfurt, 1606), p. 239.

44. "Due to the exceedingly long, great war between the Spanish and the French in the said kingdom, they began to lack provisions, especially meat. As a result, the provisioners on both sides next went to the battlefield in order to get money. They secretly began to roast the flesh of those dead bodies and to make certain foods with it . . . in such a way that the armies of one, and of the other, having eaten human flesh for a long time, began to become corrupted to such an extent that there did not remain even one man who was not completely full of sores and of sharp pains." Leonardo Fioravanti, *De capricci medicinali* (Venice, 1564), fols. 51r–51v.

45. Francis Bacon, *Sylva Sylvarum sive historia naturalis* . . . (Amsterdam, 1648), pp. 17–18.

46. J. B. van Helmont, *Tumulus pestis,* in *Opera omnia* (Frankfurt, 1682), pp. 221–22.

47. The leprous Yvain says to King Mark in *Tristan* of Bèroul (vv. 1166–71): "Veez: j'ai ci compaignon cent. / Yseut nos done, s'ert comune. / Poior fin dame n'ot mais une. / Sire, en nos a si grant ardor. / Soz ciel n'a dame qui un jor / Pest soufrir nostre convers."

# 3 Honor Regained: Women in the Casa del Soccorso di San Paolo in Sixteenth-Century Bologna

*by Lucia Ferrante*

Beginning in the mid-sixteenth century, institutions for women "sinners" developed in Bologna and other Italian cities.[1] There "fallen" women became the objects of an intervention that was more articulated and precise than previously; these institutions, both religious and lay, were added to the traditional convents for repentant women and followed significantly different paths to save the "fallen."

In Bologna these institutions each had their own history, which modified over time their interrelationships: yet between the end of the sixteenth and the mid-seventeenth century, the period considered in this essay, there were not, as far as I was able to discern, significant changes in their principal characteristics.

In Pope Pius's brief of 1560, which created the Opera dei Poveri Mendicanti di Bologna, prostitution was considered the inevitable corollary of vagrancy and poverty.[2] Thus, providing shelter for those women who sought charity was implicitly presented as an action that would limit prostitution. The statutes of the Mendicanti issued after 1574 warned that women who, before their internment in the institution, had been "accustomed to the evil life" should not be sent into domestic service.[3] The charitable work of the institution was initially slightly coercive, but later it acquired a strong punitive character. As a punishment, the worst women of other institutions came to be sent to the Mendicanti.[4] Nevertheless, in the second half of the seventeenth

---

"L'onore ritrovato: Donne nella Casa del Soccorso di San Paolo a Bologna (sec. XVI-XVII)," *Quaderni Storici,* no. 53 (1983): 499–528. Translated by Margaret A. Gallucci.

century and in the eighteenth, more sections for reform of the interned than for punishment were planned.[5]

The Casa del Soccorso di San Paolo, which will provide the focus of this essay, was founded in 1589.[6] It was supposed to accept "young women [who were] poor, disreputable, and fallen" into sin, yet desirous of redeeming themselves, and who, "for the lack of a dowry," were not able to enter the convent of the Convertite.[7] Their maintenance was virtually never provided by the institution, even if some women paid a very small amount for shelter and board.[8] Reintegration in society through marriage, becoming a nun with the help of some benefactor, or some other honorable placement was its goal.[9] A certain number of women admitted to San Paolo came from the Casa della Probazione. The latter, for which we possess very little information, played a role similar to that of San Paolo, from which it was distinguished by the ease of admission.[10] In some cases of particularly bad behavior, however, women were sent to the Mendicanti.[11]

The convent of Santi Giacomo e Filippo, called the Convento delle Convertite, was founded in 1559 and was among the oldest medieval monasteries for penitents.[12] Women who wanted to withdraw from a life of sin and who possessed a dowry entered it.[13] In the first half of the seventeenth century, in addition to nuns, there were also *mondane* (prostitutes), *malmaritate* (abandoned or maltreated wives), *a educazione* (women to be educated), and *in deposito* (women left in custody).[14] The maintenance fee paid was relatively higher than that paid to the Casa di San Paolo, even if with time the difference appears to have decreased. Some of the nuns had spent a period of time in the Casa del Soccorso before entering the convent.[15]

From this brief survey, which can only suggest the complexity of the issues involved, even at the level of the ethical and cultural nature of the various organizations, we can glimpse a kind of socio-economic hierarchy of the Bolognese institutes for female sinners. Thus, a fall or rise from one institution to another, while not at all usual, was nevertheless possible. Such movement was caused by acquiring merit or demerit, changed economic conditions, or the intervention of benefactors or patrons. Catarina Merighi, who enjoyed the protection of the noblewoman Ippolita Boncompagni, for example, left the Mendicanti in 1624 to enter San Paolo and from there became a nun in the Convertite.[16] In contrast, Ippolita Bertucci, who was admitted to San Paolo in 1592, "persevering in sinful thought and for her other

**Table 1.** *Number of Women Present in San Paolo, 1589–1662*

| | |
|---|---|
| Number of women whose entrance and exit are certified | 445 |
| Number of women for whom only entrance is certified | 115 |
| Number of women who entered and exited several times | 43 |
| Total | 603 |

Note: In the documents, 26 women are named who may not have entered. There are another 63 whose request for admission was not accepted because they did not meet the requirements or whose request was not acted upon because of a changed, negative attitude toward internment.

offenses was sent away to the Mendicanti so that she would sin no more."[17]

After this brief institutional overview, I would like to consider some problems which are linked to the Casa del Soccorso di San Paolo, the median institution in the socio-economic hierarchy of institutions for sinners. The capacity of San Paolo was rather modest (rarely were there more than thirty women living there).[18] From 1589 to 1662, just under six hundred women entered, an average of fewer than ten a year. In some years, not even one woman entered (1597, 1648); in others, admissions surpassed twenty. Several factors determined this development. If the end of the sixteenth century and the year 1648 were years of exceptionally bad harvests for Bologna,[19] 1635 was instead a year of real crisis for the Casa della Probazione, which perhaps San Paolo helped overcome in part. Four years later, in 1639, there was an "extraordinary influx" of penitents due to the preaching of Father Innocenzo Salvi in San Pietro, who called for the reforming of fallen women.[20]

The women interned were subdivided into *ordinarie,* who paid three lire a month, and *straordinarie,* who paid a sum that could reach fifteen or sixteen lire a month, at least by 1627.[21] Whoever did not have a family or some benefactor who could pay the entire fee (*dozena*) had to pay by working.[22] Maddalena Rioli was accepted on the condition "that she being able with her labors to satisfy the week's obligation will do so, and not being able, her brother Giovanni Domenico is obliged to supply the payment."[23] Charity intervened in various ways in individual cases: good behavior might allow a lowering of the maintenance fee even if not admission among the *ordinarie.* But other solutions were also possible. For example, Angela Anna

Bonassoni was accepted in 1611 with the agreement that she pay "lire 3 a month when she will do the cooking and washing and lire 8 a month when she will not do it."[24] Some women who had given proof of good will and obedience were directly integrated into the government staff: Prassede Bersani, who had asked for a reduction of the maintenance fee, was allowed instead to serve "as the matron [*madonna*] in the said Casa so that she not pay for any future provisions as long as she persevered in moving from good to better in this service."[25] As often happens in such so-called total institutions, the ones who had been interned the longest ended up finding that that was the only place where they could live, and they were transformed from the watched into the watchers.[26]

In some cases, it was husbands and relatives who asked for reductions in payments.[27] We do not know if the *ordinarie* were treated differently from the *straordinarie;* if working or not working for the Casa created a hierarchy similar to that existing in the convents between nuns who did not take their vows and those who did, or, on the contrary, if it produced leaders. We also are not certain if some women were able to save money for themselves and what relationship they had with those who were able to avoid all work for pay. The sole index of a hierarchy found was the fact that some women enjoyed a single room apparently because of payment of a supplementary sum.[28]

The model of organization and communal life was conventual: a trial period, not always required, at the Casa della Probazione or at the home of some member of the congregation was followed by a regimen we could define as cloistral.[29] The women did not have the right to receive visitors without authorization of the president of the Congregation, nor could they receive letters. Any gifts received had to be divided equally among all, while the donor and the recipient had to remain unknown. The place itself was predisposed to silence, meditation, and separation from the world: even the tables of the refectory were placed in such a way that the women all sat on one side in order to allow the minimum of convivial sociability. Spaces leased contiguous to the Casa were eventually left vacant to avoid possible contact with the outside. Much time was given to preoccupations with securing the door with large chains and also to the plans to construct a new wall and a more secure entrance.[30] Singing and music were prohibited as at convents.[31] Sins, according to their gravity and the woman's condition, were to be punished with imprisonment or with expulsion.[32]

Although only women who explicitly requested entrance were

supposed to be admitted, it is possible to distinguish many problems and even rebellion within. Several escapes, allusions to irreverent and disputatious behaviors, hysterical and depressive crises ("possessed, of "melancholic humor"), and many petitions to be freed suggest doubts are in order concerning the authentic desire for expiation on the part of some of the women interned.[33] Although it is impossible to verify the degree of consensus in confinement, we can hypothesize that a more rigorous discipline than anticipated undercut many good intentions.

One concrete level on which the encounter/clash took place between the confined women and the Congregation involved the staff of the institution, which consisted of two or three matrons (*madonne*), one of whom was a doorkeeper. Guards (*custodi, sorveglianti, secondi*) were also fundamental in all institutions of this type; their role was to mediate between those enclosed and those who did the enclosing, and their effectiveness was the result of a series of delicate balances that excessive harshness or excessive familiarity could endanger. In the history of San Paolo, the problem of who would serve as guards was the source of constant preoccupation and for long periods appears to have gone unresolved.[34] Several times aides (*assonti*) were appointed to manage the confined women with the goal of "bettering them and calming them."[35] Once it was even decided to get an entirely new group of guards, "not desiring to continue with the present matrons because of the many mishaps which have occurred and been reported" (shortly before, three women had escaped). The goal was "to learn clearly the problems and disorders that occur and the disagreements between the matrons and the women of the Casa . . . realizing . . . that the principal cause of the disturbance is . . . the matron of the Casa."[36] Francesca Morandi was dismissed "for being too bossy and not being obedient to the patrons," while the matron Isabella was sent away "for being too austere and not being able to command." Others, in contrast, were dismissed for being "too affectionate."[37]

Side by side with conflict, lines of solidarity existed as well. Gentile Pulzoni encountered such solidarity or kindness when, marrying after a year and a half stay in San Paolo, she received five lire as a wedding gift from both Maddalena Campagnoli, who had already returned to her family some months earlier, and Isabella, matron of the Casa.[38] Friendship conceived within the institution was actually able to help provide the means to leave it. Margherita Pritoni, after at least ten years of internment, married Stefano Fanagaressi, father of Costanza, her companion in the Casa del Soccorso; several months after their marriage, the latter was able to leave San Paolo, entrusted to her father and her old companion, now her stepmother.[39] Long residence in the Casa could at times establish those ties that literally took one beyond the institution, assuming characteristics close to familial bonds.

Santa Manzolino, however, represented one of the rare cases where confinement was truly lengthy: twenty-one years. Entering San Paolo in 1595 after her husband had abandoned her for another woman, Santa remained until 1616, when she went to live "in the company" of Lucia Cavazzi.[40] The latter, confined for fourteen years, had decided to leave in order to go "govern" her two daughters. When she asked to have one of her young daughters enter the Casa, she received the answer that it was not wise "to introduce novelties" and that, above all, to live there would be "prejudicial" to the young girl. For "recognition of long service and obedience observed," a collection was made among the Congregation for Santa and Lucia.[41]

Throughout, the documents lamented the poverty of the Opera, which not only could not accept all the requests for admission but struggled to maintain the women already admitted.[42] Given the lack of admission registers, it is not possible to learn the actual financial situation of San Paolo: nevertheless, based upon the minutes of the Congregation and a survey of the notarial acts, we can assert that its economic situation was not strong. Real estate holdings were limited, until 1644, to the building in which the women lived and another house on the same street.[43] Testamentary bequests, never numerous, involved primarily consumption goods (grapes, grain, cords of wood) along with some wealth.[44] The inheritance of Marchesa Virginia Ruini was an exception; in 1644 she left a farm situated in the commune of Gesso, valued at about L. 3250.[45] The revenue from this bequest would have permitted, for the first time in the history of the institution, the maintenance of one woman. Earlier, however, in 1630, Isabetta Sirantoni, "kept by this Congregation at great expense" for about twenty months, had had to transfer a share of a house inherited from her brother to the institution, "in order to cover her poverty."[46]

In 1595, Lucia Piazza was accepted with her mother's promise to pay three lire a month and a promise from her husband's employer to give as much, deducted each month from his salary, until a sum equivalent to the dowry given by Lucia's family was paid.[47] Moreover, it appears that the charity of benefactors was not always timely, for in

1660 it was formally decided that "a woman is not to be accepted or introduced into the Casa of any sort whatsoever to live, unless she has been given secure pledges by a suitable and manageable person such as a merchant or shopkeeper or citizen; gentlemen or other respectable people are to be avoided, against whom it is not easy to act or from whom payment is not easily secured when it is needed."[48] It could be that it was so difficult to avoid the request of assistance that persons of an elevated status ended up promising aid they were not always able to give. The unusual case of Giacinta Bertocchi reveals a patronage relationship with an unlikely outcome.[49] Giacinta, a "good young woman," but maltreated by her husband, wanted to add the protection of noble Ferdinando Ignazio Bolognini to that she already had from the Laternese canon Don Salvatore Barozzi. Unfortunately, the intervention of these patrons "did not bear any fruit . . . because that one [her husband] was a wicked man."[50] Refuge in San Paolo appeared the best solution, and Giacinta was brought there by Bolognini himself while the canon undertook to pay the maintenance fee. The hope was that a period of separation would induce a change in her husband's attitude. But it did not work out that way: his aggressiveness proved to be stronger than every attempted remedy.

As a result, a very curious story emerged from the records of the Inquisition, where Bolognini later testified about the case. According to the nobleman's account, when Barozzi wanted "to gain relief from the burden he had to maintain the said woman in that place," he became involved in a series of spells which had the aim of "reuniting or dividing forever the two spouses." In short, lacking a reconciliation, the husband's death would have permitted them to free themselves from their obligation. This reading of the event seems problematic, but I believe that we can recognize a less apparent aspect of the problem of enclosure: the pressure on those who in the end were responsible for internment, for they were bound by the code of honor to keep their promise of protection.

Devoting oneself to pious deeds was onerous but also rich in positive possibilities—for instance, in increasing personal prestige through the enlargement of client networks and in reinforcing valuable interpersonal relationships by means of collaborating on the same charitable activities. Thus, Don Giacomo Negri agreed to hold the office of president, for some time vacant, on the condition that he was allowed both to introduce whomever he wanted into the Casa and to submit as a *fait accompli* the ratification of his decisions to the rest of the Congregation.[51] And the gentlewomen who were "visitors" (*visitatrici,* in practice the real agents of control over the girls and often relatives of members of the Congregation themselves) often clashed with members to claim greater authority in the management of the Casa.[52]

I turn at this point to some case histories of women enclosed in the Casa del Soccorso di S. Paolo to understand what in practice this fall into sin meant which ideologically justified the institution. Angela Silvestri, Cecilia Cavazzi, and Ippolita Cortesi were actual prostitutes (a regulation issued at a later time lumped together all women "fallen through misfortune" under the label of public prostitute).[53] Their names appeared in the registers of the Ufficio delle Bollette, a council set up to control public prostitution, between 1601 and 1606.[54] The dates and sums paid certify the periods when these women had obtained a "license" to practice their trade.

In the case of Angela Silvestri we note that the name of the person who made the payment to the Bollette, probably a lover or more likely a pimp, was the same as that of the benefactor who assured the Casa del Soccorso of her maintenance. The regulations of San Paolo acknowledged that "carnal friends" could pay alms "for the salvation of the penitent life" of their ex-lovers.[55] Cecilia Cavazzoni had a very brief stay in San Paolo: within a month she was sent back to the Casa della Probazione, from which she came.[56] Ippolita Cortesi entered San Paolo under the protection of Panina Fasanini, who promised her 100 lire.[57] In the years that followed, Ippolita decided to devote herself to the religious life, but that sum was certainly not sufficient to pay her monastical dowry as well as the cost of the candles and the ceremony of investiture. The aid of another benefactor was necessary, and Ippolita was able to obtain it only after three years of internment when, in 1608, Count Giovan Battista Bentivoglio agreed to help her. In the same period, the members of the Congregation named Signor Banzi and Bentivoglio himself as aides (*assonti*) for the survey of all members of the Congregation in order to obtain the necessary sum to allow Ippolita to enter a convent or the Convertite.[58]

Maria Gandolfi, the eighteen-year-old daughter of Paolo and Gentile, made buttons and enjoyed a good reputation among their neighbors.[59] In her own testimony recounted to the judge of the Foro Ecclesiastico, a court responsible for sexual offenses, she claimed that she had never "spoken" with a man until she met Pietro Padoano, son of a tailor whose shop was near the one where her brother Matteo, also a tailor, worked. Their love began one September evening when Maria, her mother, and Matteo were standing at the entrance of their house to enjoy the fresh air. Pietro had passed by chance, recognized Matteo, stopped, joked with his mother, and had seen Maria. After several other casual encounters, finally Matteo arrived at her house one evening "with a bunch of fragrant hyacinths which I accepted and in this manner Pietro made known his love for me." But later Pietro left Bologna rather than be faithful to the promises of love and marriage he had made. In Maria's house, tragedy literally exploded; Angelo, her older brother who was already married and lived elsewhere even threatened to kill her. But their mother, Gentile, intervened, and the two women, alone, went to the archbishop to ask for justice and protection. Gentile knew that all the neighbors would testify to Maria's honesty and report the tender talks with Pietro at the entrance of their house. In fact, it was probably for this reason that it was resolved to take legal action by turning to the authorities. Quickly it was decided to rescue Maria from her brother's wrath by sending her to San Paolo. This account, given by Maria herself, was confirmed by two neighbors. It is possible, however, that her brother's anger was merely a pretext to make the authorities intervene in a more decisive manner than if a simple rape, always difficult to prove, had been denounced.

For some women, their lives themselves were in danger. For Livia Tederisi, living with her "evilly bewitched" husband meant "the danger of offending God and endangering her own life." San Paolo was, then, a safe place, a refuge.[60] But when her benefactor, Cesare Bianchetti, suggested to her that she should return to her husband, she had to obey. Although she worked for the Casa, she clearly was not in a position to pay the entire cost of her maintenance. Yet everyone knew that her situation was difficult, and thus it was decided to "reserve a place in the Casa for her each time she has just cause to leave the said husband." This decision was further justified because Livia "was a very good woman meriting every assistance."[61] Six months later she made use of this guarantee, staying for awhile in San Paolo before returning again to her spouse. We do not know much about the story of this couple, but it does reveal that in moments of particularly acute conjugal crisis, San Paolo could become a safe refuge for a wife, and, given the almost monastical characteristics of life there, it guaranteed, perhaps better than any family, the safeguarding of female honor indispensable to reconciliation. All this was done without any suspicion about the behavior of the woman before internment.[62]

Some women ran away from San Paolo. One such case involved Messina Vignola, confined in 1626, wife of Signor Flaminio Segnelli, a doctor and one of the few higher-status people about whom we have concrete information. It appears that in this case we are dealing with a private punishment carried out with the help and protection of a series of influential people.[63] There is no trace of any action taken either by judicial authorities or by religious ones: instead, we find a large gift donated by her husband, a promise to pay her living expenses, and a security promise provided by individuals both noble and rich. The procedure of internment was, moreover, quite irregular: while various statutory norms, such as the woman's consent, the medical visit, the requirement not to accept married women, and the visit of the aides were ignored, economic conditions were carefully negotiated in the context of an extreme discretion toward her family.

In this, as in other cases, when the president refused to reveal the name of the woman until the Congregation had agreed to admit her, apparently without obtaining the usual background information, it appears likely that there was a desire not to spread news of a private scandal. Class and group cohesion seemed to have imposed a certain discretion in aid. Messina fled her prison after about sixteen months, with violence that involved breaking down the door and scuffling with the porter.

Isabetta Dini's case history was different. This time, things moved from love to homicide to capital punishment. The events took place in Oliveto, a hill town in the Bolognese countryside, a short distance from the Modenese border. Isabetta, about eighteen, the only child of a very poor family, loved Tommaso Gardiani, the standard-bearer of the Bazzano militia, who was well-to-do, married, and described as having a "mind given to dreams."[64] At a certain moment, she decided to flee with him, saying that she was tired of poverty and mistreatment by her father. Her father, Biagio, reacted immediately: he went to Bologna, lodged a denunciation, and had the notary from the Foro Criminale come to Oliveto. The result of the trial was to make Tommaso pay the cost of maintaining his deserted wife and to incite his ferocious anger. On the last night of October 1616, Biagio was killed on the doorstep of his house by a shot from a harquebus. After a trial that lasted several months, the authorities decided to condemn

Tommaso to death in absentia for abduction and homicide. At the beginning of February 1617, Tommaso and Isabetta were found by the Modenese police and extradited. Isabetta was immediately interned in the Casa della Probazione, where she remained until the beginning of September, when she was transferred to the Casa del Soccorso. In March of the following year, she entered the Convent of Saints Giacomo e Filippo on "probation."[65]

Internment in the Casa della Probazione may be explained by the fact that the girl, besides having to pay in some way for her indiscretion, was not able to return to her village where by now she was more than dishonored, having been the indirect cause of her father's death. Her moving from San Paolo and later to the Convertite instead seems linked to other factors: besides the obvious psychological problems that must have tormented her, Isabetta was the heir to 100 scudi. That sum did not come from her father, a poor man, but from Tommaso, who, before being executed on 25 February 1617, made a will and left various bequests to many charitable institutions and that money to her.

These cases reveal that the women enclosed in the Casa del Soccorso had very different personal histories. Some even seem to have been innocent of the sin that was supposed to be the reason for confinement. This multiplicity of individual situations points out an ambiguous aspect of the institution, at least with respect to its declared ideological intention: to offer the possibility of redemption to sinners. Perhaps this ambiguity can be understood by referring to another moral code, different from the religious one but equally important in the society of early modern Italy: the lay code of honor.[66] The disjuncture perceived between the institution's declared intentions and its actions is perhaps a consequence of a reading based only upon the parameters of a Christian ethic. It is a gap that may, in fact, reflect the interaction of two systems with different values in the activity of the Opera. The problem is recognizing each and understanding it. While notions of sin and grace have sufficiently precise theological definitions, those of honor and dishonor are more elusive, because many factors are involved in their evaluation.

Economic, social, and familial conditions were significant for determining levels of honor in accordance with rules that we barely understand.[67] Moreover, while the state of grace was an individual matter, since it was the realization of a personal and internal relationship with God, honorability in Mediterranean society, at least from an anthropological perspective, was an eminently social fact.[68] Honor could not exist outside relationships with others: The value of an individual was determined by the estimation of others. This value, which was comparable to a material good, could be socially damaged, destroyed, or reconstructed.[69] Female honor, although it was, above all, sexual, did not escape these realities.[70] To thoroughly understand the criteria used to enclose women it would be necessary, for example, to understand the social evaluation of the simple suspicion of sin in terms of the loss of honor. Did a similar suspicion have the same relevance for the unmarried woman as for the married one? For the daughter or the wife of a wage earner as for the wife of a shopowner? For the orphan as for the girl with parents? The most likely hypothesis is that in different cases the suspicion weighed in a different way upon the reputation of the woman and her relatives, kindling responses contingent upon the gravity of the damage feared.[71] What is certain is that the women who entered San Paolo found themselves in a situation where honor had been lost. A counterexample demonstrates this: the refusal to admit Lucia Cavazzi's young daughter was defended with the claim that her sojourn in San Paolo under any conditions would be "prejudicial" for her, a young girl still a virgin.[72]

The request of Gentile Machiavelli, who had already lived once in San Paolo and wanted to return there in order to get married with "her reputation at its greatest," provides only an apparent contradiction.[73] For Gentile, another period of time spent in the institution meant arriving at the ceremony that sanctioned her reinsertion in society with the greatest possible honor, given her condition as a woman who had already fallen.

A stay in the institution could cut either way, removing or adding honorability according to the quality and quantity of the honor possessed at entry. The importance of honor in that society and the care placed in safeguarding it are testified by the existence of "conservatories," institutes conceived expressly to guard what was considered a young girl's most precious good.[74] Within this cultural context it is possible to understand the reconstruction, carried out at San Paolo, of a certain type of honorability for women who had in some way lost it. This delicate operation was based upon melding together the principles of the Christian ethic (the rites of penance and forgiveness) and those of the lay ethics of honor. Obviously one must not overlook the cases where practical motives led to internments in which regaining a good reputation was only a secondary goal.

**Table 2.** *Women by Formally Declared Reason for Leaving*

| | |
|---|---|
| Married | 110 |
| Entrusted to family | 107 |
| Entrusted to a fiduciary[a] | 89 |
| Without indications[b] | 81 |
| Became domestic servants | 33 |
| Became nuns | 25 |
| Total | 445 |

a. Included in the category "Entrusted to a fiduciary" were all women for whom a nonfamilial guardian was named.

b. Grouped within this category were those women whose exit was listed without motive and those who were sent away. Many things suggest that the motives of these cases were similar.

❧ To confirm these hypotheses about the reconstruction of honor through internment in San Paolo, I shall examine some social factors related to the way in which women left the institution and the duration of their confinement.

The 445 women who left the institution with a formal certification were analyzed in terms of categories suggested by the sources.

Marriage, for the most part with artisans, and becoming a nun involved an acquisition of status that clearly seems to attest that honor had been restored. Interpreting other reasons for leaving which did not necessarily represent a failure (an exception being made for the "exits" without any motive, which in large measure were probably due to being sent away for bad conduct) was more problematic. For example, among the women re-entrusted to family were included those who returned to their husbands. Some were real or suspected adulterers, while others seem instead to have been mistreated (abandoned, battered by their husbands).[75] After 1618 it was decided to exclude married women from San Paolo, but in fact they continued to enter. In the entire period studied, 56 married women entered; of these, 22 were reconciled with their spouses when they left the Casa del Soccorso di San Paolo.[76]

Given the Congregation's care in picking the guardians of the women when they were allowed to leave, the information on this transferral of custody should be significant. Receiving a young woman in trust seemed to be a sign of particular involvement in her affairs. From this perspective, the large number of close relatives involved (uncles and aunts were rare) would appear to indicate that the problems connected with female sexual conduct were managed within the more intimate familial circle. A decisive role seems to have been played by the maternal figure: the number of mothers actively involved with the institution was equal to that of fathers, brothers, and sisters combined.[77] In numerous cases, mothers managed the situation—securing confinement, saving the dowries, taking back their daughters themselves. Even in cases of married women, we glimpse the presence of maternal tutelage which was prolonged beyond the abandonment of the natal family and intervened in moments of acute conjugal crisis.[78]

The precariousness of the life of domestic servants is well known: we find that when a woman left the Casa for such service, the possibility of returning was not typically conceded. This was probably in order to strengthen an image of San Paolo as a place of definitive redemption.[79] Lucrezia Ruggieri was told that after "she will have done domestic service for two continuous years without having committed any indecent act, it would be possible for her to return to our Casa." In other cases as well, it was specified that if a position was lost through no fault of one's own and one had "behaved honorably," reentering the institution would be permitted.[80]

In fact, some ten or so women spent several periods of their lives within the walls of the Casa del Soccorso. This was a sign that above and beyond the reform and good conduct that were the goals of the stay in the institution (assuming that those confined were truly culpable—and they were not always), many women found themselves living in unstable affective, familial, or social situations. For such women, the institution of San Paolo was in practice an auxiliary structure. Barbara Manza entered at least five times in the span of twenty years: already there in the spring of 1636, paying a reduced maintenance fee, she entered a second time in September of the following year owing to the "many dangers which she faced . . . because of her husband." About a year later she left to be a domestic servant in the house of the Biondi family, but "because she did not wish to remain there," she was sent to her mother's house. In April 1639 we find her again returned to the institution by Signora Lucrezia Malvasia. This time she was pregnant but was accepted nonetheless. At the beginning of August, she was turned over to Signora Malvasia "to give birth, then to return." In the register of entrances and exits for the date 11 November 1639 we read, "Barbara Manza returned in order to continue to be a good young woman." In May 1640, she was re-entrusted to her protectress, who promised to "accommodate her in an honored place." Fifteen years later, in 1665, "Barbara Manza was again reaccepted having stayed other times in the Casa, paying the usual maintenance fee and giving therefore the usual pledge."[81] She was an exception, and her by now mature age did not constitute an obstacle.

Recurrent marital crises clearly seem the cause of multiple internments: Caterina Lanzini asked if she could enter for a month in May 1612 because "being in conflict with her husband" she thought that the stay in San Paolo would be useful "to better repacify herself with the said husband." Nevertheless, things did not develop according to her desires, and a year later she was readmitted for three months, "being beautiful and in great danger because she had displeased and was in the bad graces of her husband and other members of his family." There still seemed to be the hope that reconciliation could occur in a brief time, but it did not work out that way. Catarina remained confined in San Paolo not three months but three years—until 1621, when finally, after she had long asked to be freed, she was entrusted to her mother.[82] Obedience and a willingness to reform, demonstrated during confinement, were the principal bases for subsequent admissions; thus, Camilla Galiari was able to reenter after childbirth "as another time she had given much satisfaction."[83]

Marriage or becoming a nun were ways of leaving that more realistically represented an assured reacquisition of honor. If, as it seems, this was a function of several factors, then verifying evidence must be sought in several areas. But because the identification of these areas is anything but clear and the information in my possession is relatively scarce, for the moment I shall consider only one aspect of the problem: the economic dimension. The most evident characteristic shared by women who were to be married or enter the convent was the possession of a dowry. Without it, there were few prospects of marrying or becoming a nun.[84] Was the dowry to be considered, then, a constitutive element of honor? Might not one posit that a good reputation could be bought with a good dowry?

How were marriage dowries for the women in the Casa del Soccorso gathered? From examining marriage contracts, it appears that the potential donors were three: family, patrons, and the Congregation, combined in various ways (each type of donor appeared in about two-thirds of the cases in a sample of about thirty cases altogether).[85] The dowry was generally composed of two parts, one in cash (from a minimum of 100 to a maximum of 650 lire) and one in "movable property and accouterments" (about 200 lire).[86] While minor sums were always paid immediately, larger ones at times were paid in several installments at an expected annual interest rate of 6 percent. At times a clause appeared in the agreements that a portion of the money was to be spent for the acquisition of *ornamentata* (necklaces, rings, bracelets) and new clothes for the woman.[87]

The norms that regulated the marriage contracts of the women in San Paolo were similar to those that underlay every other transaction of the same type in the period in Bologna, from the obligation to conserve and eventually to restore the dowry "salva parte lucranda per maritum illi uxore premoriente sine communis liberis" to the obligation to invest the larger sums "in aliqua re stabili in civitate vel guardia vel comitatu Bononiae ideoneo fideiussore." And there were various guarantees, both to assure the spouse that the promised portions of the dowry would in fact be paid and to promise the donors that the spouse would always be in a position to return the sum received. The Congregation seemed particularly attentive to this condition each time it paid a portion of the dowry, at times imposing its own control on the use of the dowry even after the marriage.[88]

Given that families did not always contribute or that they did not contribute enough to constitute the dowry, it would be extremely interesting to know how a woman succeeded in obtaining one for herself. The case of Violante Guicciardini seems significant. Violante was "introduced at the request of the most Illustrious Ippolita Boncampagni" on 3 July 1602 and entrusted to the same Lady Ippolita in order to marry Benedetto, a textile worker, on 1 April 1603.[89] In March of that year, the marriage contract was drawn up by the notary Achille Canonici; it included a dowry that promised some furniture that was not appraised and 650 lire, part to be paid immediately and part to be paid later.[90] That sum was raised as follows: Father Ortensio Giovanelli, an Augustinian, gave 200 lire "from the money which he had as alms given for love of God" and promised to give another 200 in payments over the next two years, with Signor Cesare Gessi, goldsmith, as guarantor. The president of the Congregation pledged to pay, in its name, another 200 lire on the day of the "marriage ceremony before the church." Domenica, Violante's sister, "gave, provided and paid out" 50 lire in sound money of gold and silver. Finally Lord Gerolamo Boncampagni, Ippolita's husband, promised two wedding chests and some furniture "to be decided upon." Violante was without a father, and we do not know if she had many other relatives besides her sister, but it is possible to identify Domenica as a key figure. In fact, Domenica, at the time of the stipulation of the marriage contract, was "living as a wet nurse in the house of the most illustrious Lord Gerolamo Boncampagni." This same Boncampagni was one of the more active members of the Congregation del Soccorso, and it was in his house that the notary Canonici wrote the marriage contract. The interplay of wet nurse/wife of Congregation member/Congregation member/Congregation could provide an explanation for the generosity of the Opera toward Violante. It is likely that submissive conduct during the period of internment was an important element in obtaining some help, but it is probably not the entire explanation.[91]

As we know, not all the girls who got married received their dowry from the institution. Yet this did not ever prevent the Opera from overseeing the marriage contract. In many cases, even when the entire sum was given by others, we find members of the Congregation as "agents and authorities." Even when the marriage was contracted by the father, they were "witnesses and supporters."[92] Marriages negotiated by the Opera, in turn, even when the father was living, could occur without his consent.[93] We know, moreover, that one of the tasks of the members of the Congregation was to obtain husbands for their "daughters" and that when a suitor appeared an inquiry was set up to verify if they should approve "the forming of a family."[94] The institution seems, then, to have assumed the characteristics of *pater potestas* to the degree of even turning away young males from families who were judged unworthy and of protecting their ward's hereditary rights from her own relatives.[95] The Opera thus created a new, prestigious family consisting of nobles, ecclesiastics, lawyers, and bankers, which took women under its tutelage.[96]

The institution's role as a family created a web of artificial relationships that encircled the woman. Given the hypothesis that honorability did not exist for the isolated individual, but only for one who was part of a group that evaluated honor, what did this set of relationships mean? In such a situation, evaluation was based upon the process of redemption; the group that measured it was composed of noble, rich, and esteemed citizens who, during the period of confinement, watched over the process of moral regeneration of the confined woman. The members of the Congregation, "witnesses and supporters" at the highly formalized moment of the marriage contract, explicitly expressed this recognition by guaranteeing to the spouse the good conduct of the woman during her stay in the institution. Good conduct itself did not regain honor; rather, it did so only if recognized by someone worthy of faith, by an honorable person. It seems as if the guarantee brought about a sort of transferral of honor from the patron to the protected/enclosed.[97] It was a transaction not without reciprocity, if we remember that a true redemption attested to the efficacy of the institution and proved the credibility of those who managed it.

In this context, the importance of the economic factor in honor is not denied, but rather made more complex by adding a series of other conditioning elements. One did not buy a good reputation with the dowry; rather, a certain way of obtaining that money could help to regain it. To prove this hypothesis it would be necessary to know whether women who had "fallen into sin" and who had dowries got married, and, if so, how many of them. And supposing that there were some, how many enjoyed the protection of a patron. It would be necessary, in short, to understand if repentance and redemption developed outside the institution and sustained by a personal relationship with a rich and honorable citizen obtained the same result as the restoration of honor found in San Paolo. Not being able to determine this, we can at least say that the stay in the institution seemed to represent a sort of ritual of purification that was certainly not devoid of efficacy. I speak of a ritual of purification and not of punishment because the punitive sense of the "penitent's life," which undoubtedly existed, was limited by the relatively brief duration of the internment: on the average less than a year, often a few months.[98]

The period of time spent within the walls of the Casa del Soccorso seemed to have a symbolic value almost independent of its duration, a value residing in a concept of an honor that could be regained through physical contact with the place of purification.[99] This hypothesis of the symbolic value of confinement seems plausible in a society that was characterized by "a heightened sense of symbolism," at least regarding transactions of honor.[100]

After attempting to analyze the objectives and methods of the Casa di San Paolo, it is necessary to query the importance of an institution that housed a small number in a city that had more than sixty thousand inhabitants. Beyond suggesting the analogy with the relatively small homes for converts from Judaism, which certainly did not anticipate receiving all the Jews, but only the "best," I would suggest that the institution served a symbolically integrating function that affected the entire citizenry. In fact, on the political level, San Paolo represented a place of encounter and mediation among different social groups (I am not thinking only of relationships between women and Congregation members but also of relationships among the members of the Congregation themselves, all honorable, but not socially homogeneous). On the cultural and ethical level, it also provided a place of mediation between the moral/religious code and the lay code of honor, holding together norms and criteria of both, such as the reconfirmation of the principle of female modesty. The Congregation, responsible for and guaranteeing these mediating activities for the city, managed a patrimony that was essentially symbolic. The complex and delicate operations necessary for the at least partial reacquisition of honor by women who had gained the right to aspire to a dignified reentrance in society,[101] seem to suggest a sort of redistributive mechanism embodied in the Casa di S. Paolo which manipulated an important resource, civic honor, analogous in certain ways to the distribution of subsistence goods to the poor.

## Notes

1. The existence of institutions for sinners between the sixteenth and seventeenth centuries in Turin, Venice, Genoa, Florence, and Rome is discussed in S. Cavallo, "Assistenza femminile e tutela dell'onore nella Torino del XVIII secolo," *Annali della fondazione Luigi Einaudi* 14 (1980): 142; B. Pullan, *Rich and Poor in Renaissance Venice: The Social Institutions of a Catholic State to 1620* (Oxford, 1971), pp. 391–94; A. Barzaghi, *Donne o cortigiane? La prostituzione a Venezia: Documenti di costume dal XVI al XVIII secolo* (Verona, 1980), pp. 145–52; E. Grendi, "Pauperismo e Albergo dei Poveri nella Genova del Seicento," *Rivista storica italiana* 87, no. 4 (1975): 645–46; S. Cohen, "Convertite e Malmaritate: Donne 'irregolari' e ordini religiosi nella Firenze rinascimentale," *Memoria: Rivista di storia delle donne*, no. 5 (1982): 46–63; B. Pullan, "The Old Catholicism, the New Catholicism, and the Poor," in *Timore e carità: I poveri nell'Italia moderna, Papers from the conference Pauperismo e assistenza negli antichi stati italiani* [Cremona, 28–30 Mar. 1980] (Cremona, 1982), pp. 13–25. In this last essay, Pullan develops the theory of a cultural atmosphere characterized by "aggressive religion" (p. 25), typical of the Counter-Reformation, in which institutes for sinners were conceived (p. 16) as analogous with others for the poor and for converts to Christianity.

2. Archivio di Stato di Bologna (hereafter cited as ASB), Opera Mendicanti, Notizie Storiche, cart. 2, Statuti (1560).

3. Ibid. (1574), reprinted in 1603.

4. ASB, Demaniale, SS. Giacomo e Filippo, 99/6918, Libro dove si scrivono le donne quali entrano in S. Paolo del Soccorso, 1589, cols. 6v, 23v.

5. G. Calori, *Una iniziativa sociale nella Bologna del '500: L'Opera Mendicanti* (Bologna, 1972), pp. 45–57.

6. Begun in 1589 by Bishop Gabriele Paleotti, Bonifacio Dalle Balle, and Pazienza Barbieri, widow of Bolognetti, the Casa, first called the "Malmaritate" and later the Soccorso di S. Paolo, after moving to S. Petronio Vecchio and to the Seliciata di Strada Maggiore, remained in Broccaindosso for twelve years until it found its permanent

residence in Via Galleria, where it moved in 1602 (G. Guidicini, *Cose notabili della città di Bologna,* 4 vols. [Bologna, 1868–73], 2: 191). Pope Benedict XIII did away with the Casa del Soccorso in 1729; he gave its property to the monastery of SS. Giacomo e Filippo, which was called the Convento delle Convertite "because similar women—those of S. Paolo—accustomed to sin, although apparently converted when dismissed from the aforementioned Casa, more often then not they returned to the[ir] first standard of an indecent and scandalous life" (*Costituzione di nostro Signore Benedetto Decimo quarto sopra la confermazione, rinnovazione et ampliazione de' privilegi e ragioni del monastero e monache de' SS. Giacomo e Filippo di Bologna, Bologna, 1745*). This essay examines the period from its foundation to 1662, because some of the sources on which it is based, that is, the minutes of the congregation and the registers of those who entered and exited, are limited to these years.

7. Biblioteca Comunale dell'Archiginnasio di Bologna (hereafter cited as BCAB), Raccolta Gozzadini, 244, n.d. [c. 1640]. Although this document appeared well after the institution's founding, its contents seem to be confirmed by the documents that will be analyzed later in this essay for the preceding period.

8. Only beginning in 1644, that is, from the moment when the Casa received the inheritance of the Marchesa Virginia Malvezzi Ruini, was a woman's maintenance provided completely free of charge in accordance with the stipulations of the marchesa (ASB, Ufficio del Registro, registro 404, col. 176v).

9. BCAB, Raccolta Gozzadini, 244.

10. The Casa della Probazione was situated in the Via S. Mamolo and was founded in 1600 (ASB, notary Achille Canonici, Atti 1631, 5 Sept., "Emptio Congregationis Domus Probationis a Garberio"; ASB, Demaniale, SS. Giacomo e Filippo, 99/6918, Sessioni della Congregazione della Casa del Soccorso di S. Paolo, Libro primo, col. 120).

11. ASB, Libro dove si scrivono, cols. 3, 6, 24, 62, 78, 118.

12. G. Guidicini, *Cose notabili,* p. 315; G. Zarri, "I monasteri femminili a Bologna tra il XIII e il XVII secolo," in *Atti e Memorie della Deputazione di Storia Patria per le Provincie di Romagna* (Bologna, 1973), pp. 141, 180.

13. The dowry that a woman who wanted to enter the Convertite had to pay was much higher than that usually required for women from the Soccorso to marry. As we shall see, their cost of marriage seldom exceeded 600–650 lire; in contrast, the sum of 1,400 lire donated by a woman who wanted to enter the convent of SS. Giacomo e Filippo in 1663 was defined as a "usual dowry" (Archivio Archivescovile di Bologna, hereafter cited as AAB, Miscellanee vecchie, 266, fasc. 14c).

14. ASB, Demaniale, SS. Giacomo e Filippo, 3/6822, Libretti delle provisioni che si pagavano le malmaritate e mondane che habitavano nelle Convertite.

15. During the entire period, we find women who moved from S. Paolo to the Convertite. In 1630, the Archbishop of Bologna explicitly asked the Casa del Soccorso di S. Paolo to assume the function of "probation" for the Convertite (Sessioni, col. 112).

16. Libro dove si scrivono, cols. 60v–61r.

17. Ibid, col. 6.

18. Determining the number of women effectively present in the Casa del Soccorso is a problem, because they seem to be absent from the parish registers of S. Benedetto, of which the Casa was a part, and the registers of the institution contain only partial information (Sessioni, col. 96). In 1627 they refer to twelve *ordinarie,* but in response to the changing economic situation the numbers shifted dramatically.

19. A. Guenzi, *Pane e fornai a Bologna in età moderna* (Venice, 1982), pp. 20, 55.

20. Sessioni, cols. 120, 127.

21. The subdivision into *ordinarie* and *straordinarie* continued, but it is not possible to ascertain if a fixed relationship existed between the numbers of one and the other.

22. The Opera tended to confirm the perception that the young women confined would have been provided with everything. (See the various printed sheets distributed which requested charity; particularly explicit is the one that begins, "Most Reverend Father Preacher in the Casa del Soccorso di San Paolo there are received young women fallen into sin . . ." BCAB, Raccolta Gozzadini, 244 [1640]). But we know that it was not so: the women paid a maintenance fee limited to three lire for *ordinarie*, but that reached fifteen and sixteen lire for *straordinarie* and married women (Sessioni, col. 96, judgment of 4 Feb. 1627; ibid., col. 153, judgment of 7 Dec. 1648). These figures do not vary for the years around the middle of the seventeenth century. For a point of reference on the value of the lira we note that a *tiera* of bread which cost two soldi weighed fourteen ounces in 1654 and in 1660. This means that the price of bread per kilogram was in these years equal to L. 0.23 and to L. 0.15, respectively (Guenzi, *Pane e fornai*, p. 63). On the other hand, work was expected to be a necessary educative corollary of a penitent's life (BCAB, Raccolta Gozzadini, 244, "Condizioni che devono havere le donne per essere ammesse e potere stare nella pia Casa del Soccorso di S. Paolo"). Catarina Ferrari in 1615 risked being expelled because she was not or "did not want to be inclined to earn what she had to for herself and for the Casa . . . in compliance with her obligations." This was all the more true because she was heavily in debt to the Opera (Sessioni, col. 30).

23. Sessioni, col. 52.

24. Ibid., col. 24. Caterina Rossi "paying L. 16 a month, given that she has made a petition, and that her qualities and relations are good and her poverty . . . is given the privilege of not paying more than L. 10 a month" (Ibid., col. 162).

25. Ibid., col. 121.

26. I use the term *total institution* in the sense defined by E. Goffman, in *Asylums, le istituzioni totali: I meccanismi dell'esclusione e della violenza* (Turin, 1968), p. 34ff. (*Asylums: Essays on the Social Situation of Mental Patients and Other Inmates* [Garden City, N.Y., 1961]). Using the five categories that Goffman used to subdivide total institutions, the Casa del Soccorso would fall in an intermediate position between the third (prison) and the fifth (monastery).

27. Laura Bordoni entered S. Paolo in order to escape the death threats of her husband, Giovanni Zagni. Some time later, the same Giovanni, having renounced his threats, implored the Congregazione to concede a reduction of her maintenance fees (Sessioni, col. 143; Libro dove si scrivono, col. 134v).

28. Anna Maria Spighi, who in 1654 paid L. 16 a month, was allowed to pay only 14, but continued to pay 2 lire "for the room that was conceded to her" (Sessioni, col. 163). In the same period, Vittoria Guaraldi was allowed to pay one and a half lire "for the room that she enjoyed as it was small" (ibid., col. 167), and it was decided to petition "signor count N. N. [unnamed] who supported Domenica Manfredini's stay in the institution in order that he pay what she owes for food and the comforts of a separate room" (ASB, Demaniale, SS. Giacomo e Filippo, 99/6918, Libro di memorie, unnumbered sheet, 14 Jan. 1660).

29. At the moment when their petitions for admission to the Casa del Soccorso were presented, several women were found in the houses of Congregation members or in the Casa di Probazione, whose function was described in 1635 by signor Alessandro Massarenti: "Once the Casa del Soccorso understood the progress made in the said Casa di Probazione (it too for penitent women) it seemed good to ask those of the latter Casa if they wanted to be admitted to the said [Casa] del Soccorso . . . because in the said [Casa] del Soccorso they did not accept [the young women] except after a

length of time and in the [Casa] di Probazione they accept [them] immediately and they tested them to see if they had the good desire to do well, then if they were suited for the Soccorso they accepted them, if they were not they proceeded otherwise" (Sessioni, col. 120).

30. Ibid., col. 130v.

31. Ibid., col. 21.

32. Ibid., col. 130.

33. On the night between 26 and 27 July 1615, Angela Vaccari, Isabetta di Messer Antonio, and Antonia dalla Mano escaped (Sessioni, col. 38); in 1626, Messina Seghelli imitated them; in 1630, Susanna Rizzi "escaped from the Casa on the roof-tiles" (Libro dove si scrivono, unnumbered sheet, 5 Aug.). Women who were expelled for bad behavior numbered about twenty altogether. An allusion to bribes for the guards appears in a case in 1662, where it was decided to increase their salary in order to assure greater fidelity to the Congregazione (Sessioni, col. 130). Lucia Magnani "was expelled for being possessed" in 1592 (Libro dove si scrivono, col. 5), and Lucrezia Fani was forced to leave in 1616 "because of the suspicion that she was taken by a melancholic humor" (ibid., col. 38). Among the sixty-three women for whom a petition for admission was presented, but who did not enter, many let the examiners know that they did not have any intention of entering S. Paolo.

34. The years 1636–40 witnessed the addition of seven women to the staff and the strong preoccupation of the Congregazione with custody (Sessioni, cols. 126, 136; Libro dove si scrivono, cols. 90v–91r, 102v–107r, 109v–111r, 114v–115r).

35. On 21 Mar. 1624, "il signor Canonico Ringhieri and signor Vitale Bonfioli were made aides to go to the Casa and to repress the disagreements and brawls among the women" (Sessioni, col. 82); see also n. 33.

36. Sessioni, cols. 28 (15 Jan. 1613), 41 (27 Oct. 1615), 69 (25 June 1621).

37. Libro dove si scrivono, cols. 102v, 122, 103, 110.

38. Sessioni, col. 121.

39. Ibid., cols. 21, 35–36; Libro dove si scrivono, cols. 12v, 13, 23, 28v, 29, 35.

40. Libro dove si scrivono, cols. 7v–8r; notary Achille Canonici, Atti 1615, 22 Jan., "Absolutio Domini Sinibaldi de Claris a Congregatione Succursus Sancti Pauli." From 1595 to 1611 she had received the assistance of a benefactor, who had then formally stated that he wanted to suspend payments.

41. Libro dove si scrivono, cols. 9v–10r; Sessioni, cols. 27, 43.

42. See the forms for requesting charity (BCAB, Raccolta Gozzadini, 244) and the minutes of the Congregation (Sessioni, cols. 75, 109, 120, 121, 131, 158).

43. In 1602, the Congregation of the Soccorso bought from the brothers Annibale and Giovanni Pellicani a house set in Via Galliera for 6,500 lire paid in successive installments and with the primary contribution made by Lorenzo Banzi, future canon of the metropolitan church of S. Pietro (Guidicini, *Cose notabili,* 2: 191; notary Achille Canonici, Atti 1603, 26 June, "Absolutio Congregationis Succursus Sancti Pauli a Girandinis pro Pellicanis"; idem, Atti 1606, 13 Mar., "Absolutio Congregationis Succursus a Pellicanis, Ruccola et Giraldinis"). This house would be enlarged in 1616 with the acquisition of part of a contiguous building paid for in part with the money from the inheritance of Signor Giovan Domenico Locatelli, a banker, already a congregation member (L. 400) and Mario Orsi, also a member of the Congregation (L. 500). In 1606, the Opera di S. Paolo received an inheritance from Signora Lucrezia Zancheri, widow of Savenzani, consisting of a house also in Via Galliera and L. 1,000, but burdened by numerous debts and mortgages on the property (idem, Atti 1606, 24 May, "Inventarium hereditatis quondam Dominae Lucretiae Zancariae Saventiae").

44. While emphasizing that the sources studied cannot be considered exhaustive for the economic situation of the Soccorso, I would argue that the type and frequency

of the testamentary bequests encountered can be considered indicative of the patrimonial state of the Opera, which, at least for the period examined, certainly could not live on the revenue of its capital. Moreover, while on one hand the testamentary bequests seem neither rich nor numerous, on the other there were many disputes over the bequests (Sessioni, cols. 14, 25, 28, 88, 100, 156; notary Achille Canonici, Atti 1611, 15 Dec., "Procura Dominorum Officialium Congregationis Succurus Sancti Pauli"; idem, Atti 1613, 18 June, "Absolutio Dominorum Marii et Pompilii de Ursis a Congregatione Succurus Sancti Pauli"; idem, Atti 1628, 12 Oct., "Absolutio Heredum quondam Domini Sfortiae Gandulphi a legato Sancti Pauli"; idem, Atti 1628, 10 May, "Procura Dominorum Congregationis Sancti Pauli pro legato Luminasii"; idem, Atti 1629, 12 Dec., "Procura ominorum Congregationis Sancti Pauli pro legato Luminasii").

45. In her will, Marchesa Malvezzi Ruini established that the young girl maintained with the revenue of her bequest could enjoy this benefit until she married and could remain in S. Paolo if she wanted to enter the religious life. Entry into the Convertite or in any other convent would have brought about the immediate loss of any subsidy (ASB, Ufficio del Registro, registro 404, col. 176v; Sessioni, cols. 137, 152; Libro delle memorie, unnumbered sheets, 14 Mar. 1659, 20 Apr. 1660; Costituzione di nostro Signore Papa Benedetto Decimo quarto, p. 20).

46. Libro dove si scrivono, col. 70v; Sessioni, col. 118; notary Achille Canonici, Atti 1630, 21 Jan., "Procura Dominorum Congregationis Sancti Pauli pro Domina Elisabeth de Serantoniis"; idem, 8 June, "Cessio Congregationis Sancti Pauli a Domina Elisabeth de Serantoniis."

47. Libro dove si scrivono, col. 6v; notary Achille Canonici, Atti 1595, 16 Feb., "Obbligatio Domus Succurus Sancti Pauli a Lucia Piazza."

48. Libro di memorie, unnumbered sheet, 14 Jan. 1660.

49. BCAB, Inquisizione, Processi, MS. 1883. I would like to thank Milena Brugnoli, author of a thesis on the Bolognese Inquisition in the seventeenth century under the direction of Professor Carlo Poni at the Facoltà di Scienze Politiche of the Università di Bologna presented in the academic year 1982–83, who kindly pointed out this source.

50. Ibid., col. 473.

51. Sessioni, col. 108.

52. Ibid., cols. 34, 130, 133. Noblewomen were seen as serving a mediating function between their own social class and those below. See P. Burke, *Cultura popolare nell'Europa moderna* (Milan, 1980), p. 30 (*Popular Culture in Early Modern Europe* [New York, 1978]).

53. "Condizioni che devono avere." This document, issued later than the period when the prostitutes cited entered S. Paolo, seems to reflect a stiffening of admission criteria not found in the other sources.

54. The Ufficio delle Bollette was an older body set up to control foreigners, bars, prostitutes, and in the beginning Jews (L. Simoni, "L'ufficio dei forestieri a Bologna dal secolo XIV al XVI," in *Atti e Memorie della Regia Deputazione di Storia Patria per le Province di Romagna,* ser. 4, vol. 25 [1935], pp. 71–91).

55. ASB, Governo misto, Ufficio delle Bollette, Campione 1606, unnumbered sheets in which the names are listed in alphabetical order; ASB, Demaniale, SS. Giacomo e Filippo, 99/6918, Libro dove si scrivono, unnumbered sheet, 22 Sept. 1607; "Condizioni che devono avere."

56. Campione 1605; Libro dove si scrivono, col. 16v.

57. Campioni 1601, 1604, 1605; Libro dove si scrivono, c. 15v.

58. Sessioni, col. 7.

59. AAB, Foro Arcivescovile, Processi criminali (1691), col. 7ff. Maria's version

of the events was confirmed, at least regarding her honesty and her association with Pietro in general, by two neighbors, Maria Brunetti, a widow, and Maria Ferrari.

60. Libro dove si scrivono, col. 14v.

61. Ibid., col. 15.

62. Barbara Miola was forced to enter in 1635 on the order of the monsignor vicar, "not for an error committed but for the peace of her house" (Libro dove si scrivono, col. 100v), while a certain Anna was admitted "because she was forcibly taken from her husband by a gentleman" (ibid., col. 128v). In both cases, an unstable family situation was the cause rather than the woman's guilt.

63. Libro dove si scrivono, cols. 64v, 65; Sessioni, col. 86. The secrecy surrounding the internment and the fault committed, which involved safeguarding the honor of an entire familial group, must have been an enormous problem, even if, in practice, it was one that was unlikely to be solved. In eighteenth-century France, dishonor caused by requesting confinement for a member of one's family in such institutions was exorcized by direct recourse to the authority of the sovereign (*Le desordre des familles: Lettres de chachet des Archives de la Bastille,* ed. Arlette Farge and Michel Foucault (Paris, 1982), pp. 350–56.

64. ASB, Tribunale Criminale del Torrone, lib. 4793, col. 299ff. In the course of this trial, although numerous witnesses were heard, including Tommaso Gardiani, no deposition from Isabetta Dini appears.

65. Sessioni, cols. 51, 55.

66. The importance of realizing that there were systems with different values, based not only on a religious ethic but on a lay ethic as well, is argued by E. Grendi, "Ideologia della carità e società indisciplinata: La costruzione del sistema assistenziale genovese (1470–1670)," in *Timore e carità: I poveri nell'Italia moderna,* papers from the conference *Pauperismo e assistenza negli antichi stati italiani* [Cremona, 28–30 Mar. 1980] (Cremona, 1982), p. 62: "Since the real object of analysis is social behavior, this implies a complementary analysis of common values, that is, values not reducible to strictly religious inspiration. Traditionally these are viewed in the context of references to the theme of honor as another category of analysis which, in effect, functions within society's vision of orders and different 'conditions.' "

67. Although I accept the notion of differentiated honor, taken from anthropology, I am nonetheless well aware of E. P. Thompson's criticisms of the indiscriminate use of concepts deriving from anthropology for history (E. P. Thompson, "L'antropologia e la disciplina del contesto storico," in *Società patrizia, cultura plebea* [Turin, 1981], pp. 251–73). I nevertheless think that the use of certain concepts in this work indicates their utility without exceeding the limits imposed by the particularity of the historical sources.

68. The characteristic of honor as a uniquely social fact is extensively discussed by J. Pitt-Rivers, *The Fate of Shechem, or the Politics of Sex: Essays in the Anthropology of the Mediterranean* (Cambridge, 1977), pp. 2–3 and passim. A convincing application of this concept for history appears in Chapter 4 of this volume. Another confirmation comes from the field of literary criticism: H. Weinrich, "Mitologia dell'onore," in *Metafora e menzogna: La serenità dell'arte* (Bologna, 1976), pp. 227–49.

69. Pitt-Rivers, *Fate of Shechem,* p. 5; Chapter 4, this volume, p. 75.

70. Grendi, "Ideologia della carità," p. 64.

71. Weinrich, "Mitologia dell'onore," p. 230.

72. See n. 41.

73. Libro dove si scrivono, col. 124v. To have stayed in the Casa di S. Paolo was considered an indication of having been a prostitute, as an official of the Ufficio delle Bollette explicitly explained. Among the causes that had driven him to investigate the

case of Vittoria Balzani, he said, was that Vittoria "had been in the Casa di S. Paolo where women who have done evil go in order to withdraw themselves from doing evil" (ASB, Governo misto, Ufficio delle Bollette, Filza 1605, 3 Feb.).

74. On the relevance of female conservatories, see L. Ciammitti, "Fanciulle, monache, madri: Povertà femminile e previdenza a Bologna nei secoli XVI-XVIII," in *Arte e pietà: I patrimoni culturali delle opere pie* (Bologna, 1980), pp. 461–547.

75. It seems clear that Isabetta Machelli was an adulteress, married and confined in the archbishop's prisons at the moment of her request for admission. In fact, adultery was an offense usually handled by the Foro Ecclesiastico. In this case, the connection between imprisonment for an offense of a sexual nature is suggested by the order of the Monsignor Suffraganeo, who allowed her release from prison only on the condition that she be admitted to S. Paolo (Sessioni, col. 91). Flaminia Duci, on the other hand, a "very modest woman," had returned a second time to S. Paolo after her husband "sold almost all of her things" and threatened to take her away from Bologna to a destination that was not well defined, but was certainly unhappy (Libro dove si scrivono, cols. 127, 131v).

76. Sessioni, cols. 53, 59.

77. Of the 107 women who returned to their families, excluding the 22 who returned to their husbands, 30 were entrusted to their mothers, 10 to both parents, 10 to the father, 10 to a brother, 10 to a sister, 10 to aunts or uncles, and 5 to cousins. I interpret these data as signs of a particular involvement by women in these matters, at least at the moment of internment and in relationships with the institution.

78. We already know about Lucia Piazza (see n. 47). Isabetta Ughi and Caterina Ortolani, who entered in 1633 and 1640, respectively, and who were both married, lived their institutional life under strict maternal control (Libro dove si scrivono, cols. 86v–87r, 121v–122r; Sessioni, col. 115).

79. "Condizioni che devono avere." In 1611, Fiordimonte Nicolini was readmitted to the Casa after her husband, to whom she was given in marriage several years earlier, abandoned her. But the uniqueness of her case, which was not to be an example for the future, was emphasized (Sessioni, cols. 19–20).

80. Sessioni, cols. 83, 21.

81. Libro dove si scrivono, cols. 106v–107r; Sessioni, cols. 123, 165. It was noted that pregnant women normally were not accepted.

82. Libro dove si scrivono, col. 42v; Sessioni, cols. 49, 55, 56v, 68.

83. Libro dove si scrivono, cols. 41v–42r; Sessioni, cols. 50, 52, 54v, 56, 64v, 79.

84. Yet, the dowry does not seem to have been enough to contract a marriage, at least through the mediation of the institution. Francesca Agostini and Gentile Gioannelli, both coming from the Casa della Probazione, were made to return, although they possessed substantial sums of money (Libro dove si scrivono, cols. 47v–49r; Sessioni, cols. 66, 69). These events suggest that when confronting behavior that they judged negatively, the Congregation did not permit matrimonial negotiations, even though positive economic conditions existed.

85. In addition to the dowries that we know about from the register of entrances and exits and the minutes of the Congregation, about ten others were found in the deeds of Achille Canonici, notary of the Congregation and himself a member for more than half a century. The fact that these contracts were concentrated in great part in the first twenty years of the existence of the institution and in the third decade of the seventeenth century leads me to hypothesize that in other periods a second notary worked instead of Canonici. The examination of the deeds of Vittorio Barbadori, also a notary and a Congregation member, did not bear any fruit. A detailed analysis of the economic and juridical mechanisms that governed the distribution of the dowry, with particular reference to a Bolognese female conservatory, appears in L. Ciammitti,

"Quanto costa essere normali: La dote nel conservatorio femminile di S. Maria del Braccano di Bologna (1630–1680)," *Quaderni Storici,* no. 53 (1983): 471–99.

86. Two relevant exceptions are Angelica Ghedini, who, besides 700 lire, brought movable property valued at 1,156 lire; and Anna dall'Oro, who gave her husband 1,540 lire, to which was added movable property valued at 219 lire (notary Achille Canonici, Atti 1604, 9 Sept., "Dos Angelicae Ghidinae et Leonardi Gardiani"; idem, Atti 1628, 14 July, "Dos Annae de Auro et Joannis Baptistae de Mezzettis"). Leonardo Gardiani and Giovann Battista Mezzetti were a fishmonger and a hemp worker, respectively.

87. Lorenzo Leli, for example, spent 38 lire on "a gold link necklace" and 18 lire on two gold rings, "one with a white stone and the other with a red stone"; the money came from the 200 lire that Lucrezia Alberghetti had brought to him as dowry. The dowry came in part from her brother and in part from the Congregation (notary Achille Canonici, Atti 1606, 18 Jan., "Dos Lucretiae de Alberghetti Leliae").

88. When Silvestro Rizzoli, a hemp worker, went to receive the 400-lire dowry of Angela Turlaia, he promised the Congregation (which had not given him even one soldi) to invest that sum in acquiring the hemp necessary for his profession and, in case he changed professions, in something else that was stable. In no case, however, could he use the money for anything else, even in the presence of a suitable guarantor, "absque consensu . . . Dominorum dictae Congregationis" (notary Achille Canonici, Atti 1600, 21 Jan., "Dos Laurae Turlaiae et Silvestri Rizzoli").

89. Libro dove si scrivono, cols. 20v–21r.

90. Notary Achille Canonici, Atti 1603, 18 Mar., "Dos Violantis Guicciardinae Montanariae."

91. In 1618 a collection was made for Francesca Parmesani, "a well-deserving young girl" (Sessioni, unnumbered sheet, 1 Feb.).

92. This was the case for Angela Turlaia and Angelica Ghedini (see nn. 88 and 86).

93. Notary Achille Canonici, Atti 1610, 3 July, "Dos Iustinae Venturae et Bartolomei Sabatini."

94. Sessioni, cols. 28, 23. In 1624, two aides were delegated "to gain marriages for the women who are in our Casa" (ibid., col. 84).

95. Count Francesco Caprara was officially charged by the Congregation to "be concerned with the negotiations" of Persia Giacomazzi, who was reclaiming her portion of an inheritance (ibid., col. 84). Again, the Congregation, which had donated Lucia Magnani's entire dowry, imposed on her new husband the obligation to claim from her brothers and mother the same sum that they had given as dowry to Lucia's sister, Tommasa, and which they had denied her (notary Achille Canonici, Atti 1596, 12 Aug., "Dos Luciae de Magnanis uxoris Dominici Consolini"). Angela Maccari was supposed to declare that she had repented "her grave error" and promise to never see her mother again in order to be readmitted to the Casa (Sessioni, col. 55); when Angela asked that she be allowed to leave to go take care of her sick mother, the members of the Congregation, suspecting that the woman had invented a pretext in order to lead her daughter again into evil, decided to obtain some verification and eventually find a solution that permitted the daughter to stay far away from her mother (ibid., col. 43).

96. Concerning the confraternities that assisted those condemned to death and that over time restricted their social base to people of high prestige, Adriano Prosperi pointed out: "To become involved with the executioner and with the gallows would mean meddling with things which are of themselves ignominious, certain to reverberate dishonor on anyone who is no longer protected except by one's own qualities (A. Prosperi, "Il sangue e l'anima," *Quaderni Storici* 17, no. 51 (1982): 968). Having made the proper distinctions between those condemned to death and female sinners, we can

glimpse a certain analogy in the management of both. In both cases, the intervention of more honorable citizens occurred, because "just as capital assures the credit, so the possession of honour guarantees against dishonour" (Pitt-Rivers, *Fate of Shechem,* p. 15).

97. The hypothesis that honor could be transferred from members of the Congregation to those confined seems plausible, because male honor and female honor "are aspects of honour manifested by either sex rather than opposed concepts of honour, for they are united in the family honour of which they are the external and internal facets" (Pitt-Rivers, *Fate of Shechem,* p. 78).

98. The length of confinement has been calculated for 351 of 445 women. The remaining 86, although we know the conditions of their leaving the institution, were not included in this calculation because either the conditions or the date of entrance or exit were not known with absolute certainty. Concerning the symbolic value of the punishment in relation to the "condition" of the punished, see Grendi, "Ideologia della carità," p. 64.

99. Pitt-Rivers, *Fate of Shechem* p. 5.

100. The notion of a society with "a heightened sense of symbolism" is argued by J. M. Lotman, who defines it as arising from a situation "where a certain social activity . . . became significant only by changing itself into ritual" (J. M. Lotman, "L'opposizione 'onore-gloria' nei testi profani del periodo di Kiev del medioevo russo," in J. M. Lotman and B. A. Uspenskij, *Tipologia della cultura* [Milan, 1975], p. 225). Lotman's analysis, although referring to medieval Russia, offers an interpretive schema because his work pertains specifically to the semantic analysis of the code of honor.

101. As to knowing "who marries whom," the data do not allow one to identify clearly the social strata into which the women of S. Paolo married before and after their sojourn in the institution. I have sporadic information about artisans and merchants, but I do not know if it pertains to shop owners or dependents, and the difference is significant. Nevertheless, I believe I can say that neither wretched nor truly rich were involved—nor, certainly, were nobles. The best characterization seems to be simply "poor" people who lived by their own labor.

# 4 ❧ Female Honor and the Social Control of Reproduction in Piedmont between 1600 and 1800

*by Sandra Cavallo and Simona Cerutti*

In this study we consider the topic of heterosexual relationships, their characteristics and modifications in a society of early modern Europe. More precisely, we propose to analyze the nature of female honor, which was at that time viewed as an object of exchange in the sexual relationships between men and women. The interest that different groups and individuals showed in the fate of such honor has led us to analyze the connections that existed between the social control of honor and the control of sexuality and female reproductive power. Our primary sources are the matrimonial lawsuits heard before ecclesiastical judges in the period from the beginning of the seventeenth through the second half of the eighteenth century, in particular the great number of cases regarding broken promises of marriage.[1] This type of documentation, which deals primarily with situations before or outside of matrimony, has permitted us to examine the social and institutional attitudes toward extramarital sexual relationships and maternity.

First, we examine the nature of the transaction[2] that occurred between a man and a woman at the beginning of an amorous relationship and sexual activity. Then we add context and complexity to this model, analyzing individual relationships in terms of the social networks in which they developed. This permits us, in the final section, to advance a hypothesis about the nature of significant changes that,

---

"Onore femminile e controllo sociale della riproduzione in Piemonte tra Sei e Settecento," *Quaderni Storici,* no. 44 (1980): 346–83. Translated by Mary M. Gallucci. Research and writing was done in collaboration: Simona Cerutti drafted the materials for sections 1 and 2, and Sandra Cavallo did the same for sections 3 and 4.

from the second half of the sixteenth century, marked heterosexual relationships and gained particular force in the context of a different attitude toward illegitimate maternity and natural children.

Couples involved in matrimonial lawsuits appeared at the Curia's initiative or following a denunciation by the local ecclesiastical authority either before the judge of the Curia or before a delegated vicar. The motives given usually regarded marital disagreements profound enough to involve separation, which legally required ecclesiastical ratification, or else, more frequently, default on a promise of matrimony. In our analysis we have concentrated on the second type of dispute, which, by focusing on a crucial phase in the relationship between a man and a woman—its beginning—lends itself better than any other, in our opinion, to a reconstruction of the workings of heterosexual transactions.

The institution of the marriage promise, which before the Council of Trent was unanimously recognized and practiced as the decisive moment in the formation of the couple and of the new family,[3] was relegated by the new norms of Trent[4] to a secondary ceremony. It might precede the marriage rite *in facie S. M. Ecclesiae* (before the Holy Mother Church) officiated by the parish priest, but it was subordinated to the latter in terms of importance; for the Church reserved the power of legitimating sexual practices and cohabitation only for the marriage ceremony. The importance attributed to marriage promises, nevertheless, still remained, and, throughout the 1600s, depositions reveal that "carnal coupling"—sometimes even cohabitation—almost always followed such a promise, often resulting in pregnancy. Even when the necessity of formalizing the union in the eyes of the Church was acknowledged, the promise of marriage still maintained its social impact of legitimating the couple before the community.[5]

The 1700s, however, were profoundly marked by the Counter-Reformation, and sexual relations were only rarely associated with a promise of matrimony. Such promises did, however, preserve the character of a binding and socially recognized obligation toward a person and his or her group.[6] The promise of marriage, then, remained as a form of community control over heterosexual activities and matrimonial choices. In light of these considerations, the Church's declared intent to discipline the great variety of situations beyond its control appears to have been an attempt to oppose itself to and substitute itself for the old order. In turn, resistance to the introduction of these new norms was not an effect of inertia, but a defense of a traditional system of organization and social control that belonged to the community.[7]

The very events that protagonists and witnesses described during a matrimonial case, recalling various moments of meeting and courtship, of conflicts and break-ups that led to judicial action, illuminate how individuals, in their daily decisions, made reference to a code of rules and values by which they evaluated each other and through which the community regulated the conduct of its members. Their testimonies contribute to delimiting the contours of a system of social control bent on regulating the distribution of matrimonial resources and, more generally, heterosexual relationships.

According to the depositions, the attribution of honor and dishonor was one of the principal ways a judgment was publicly expressed about the degree to which conduct adhered to common expectations. Reference to honor was, in fact, constant: witnesses referred to it frequently, defining themselves through it, in order to furnish a guarantee for the honesty of their intentions and, at the same time, using it to describe the character of the relationship under question. They measured their own and others' conduct in terms of honorability. Honor was presented, then, as a personal virtue of variable measure, susceptible to change: an action worthy of rebuke or appreciation in the eyes of the community modified the opinion one had of a person, since it implied a diminution or an increase in that person's honor. But public reputation was also defined by hereditary factors, not individual but belonging to the family group. These were determined by its social position, by the esteem and respect it enjoyed in the community, and even by the power that its social relationships might give it. In part, this consisted in the sum of personal honors, and in this sense the individual's conduct could influence the image of the entire group; but on the other hand, it represented a solid protection and cover for individual actions.[8] The measure of honor, then, constituted a significant indication of the consensus that common opinion conferred on behavior. On the basis of this material, however, it is not possible to construct a classification of accepted or disapproved behavior, because this community judgment does not appear to conform rigidly to a binary scheme of adherence to or deviation from the norm. Rather, as we shall see, it was able to differentiate individual situations in terms of the specifics that characterized them.

But, aside from these more general considerations, the narratives that constitute our sources bring to light a particular aspect of personal honor: the honor involved in making love. Within heterosexual relationships, the concept of honor was different for men and women; the extreme frequency of references to honor in the woman's testimony and its direct link to sexual relationships are immediately evident. Women themselves referred to it for the first time when faced with a man's insistence on sexual intercourse, which in their terms seemed to assume the character of aggression against their honor: "Don't take away my honor." Hesitation at the moment of the proposal of "carnal commerce," which often occurred after a period of "familiarity," was expressed as the fear of suffering a loss, whose consequences created anxiety or uncertainty: "What will become of me if you take away my honor?" At this stage, female honor was already described as a quasi-material good that the man could take away, but that he also had the power to restore. The expressions with which he countered the woman's defenses had, in fact, a reassuring character, inasmuch as they prefigured a restitution of honor:

> After having greeted her and there having passed loving words between them, he began to grab her in order to put her, the complainant, on the bed, and she, resisting, said to him that she did not want him to take her honor; the said Thomaso responded that, after taking her honor, he would restore it to her by promising her, swearing to God, that later he would marry her and he would never marry another besides her. Because of that promise she pleased him and he knew her carnally one time, in which practice of copulation they continued for a bit.[9]

The same terminology was used by women who were forced to go to an ecclesiastical judge in order to obtain satisfaction for their honor: "Insisting, therefore, that the said Francesco be sentenced to marry me in conformity with the promise made, to *restore to me* the honor *taken from me.*"[10] The obligation to marry, then, had the value of a restitution, and a promise was enough to overcome female resistance to sexual intercourse, even more so if accompanied by a claim of male honor. "I am a man of honor"; "I have but one word only." This progression of events repeated itself in a great number of the cases examined: even when the reference to honor was not explained, the understood dynamic was the same. The man's word permitted the initiation of sexual activity, as is obvious in the story, similar to many others, of Caterina Richiardo di Collegno:

> The said Blasio began to be familiar with her, the complainant, as is typical between young men and women about to marry. Then, a little later he asked her to please him sexually, saying not to doubt anything and that he would marry her and take her as wife and that he did not want any other woman but her, the complainant, and moreover that he wanted to be a man and maintain his word. *And thus with such a promise she, the complainant, acquiesced and was willing to please him sexually* as pleased him.[11]

The language we have seen used to describe the dynamic of the relationship—losing, taking, restoring—reveals the *material* aspect of female honor and underscores the possibility of its transference. Accepting a request for sexual intercourse, a woman entrusted her own honor to her partner; awaiting its restitution, she found herself in a liminal position,[12] where her honor was in a state of suspension. The man at that moment possessed the power to reintegrate her into an honored condition, and thus he enjoyed the power of decision over that reintegration. The fulfillment of the obligation he assumed was nevertheless conditioned by pressures that, as we shall see, the social environment could exercise on his honor and by the consequences that his unkept word carried for his reputation. What could elicit sentiments of faithfulness to his word, then, derived from the larger social context: the woman—by herself—was unable to create the conditions for her reinsertion into a socially defined and accepted situation. A relationship of dependence was already inherent in the disparity of the terminology used for the transaction carried out at the moment of sexual intercourse: the honor/material good of the woman was exchanged for the honor/word of the man. From this perspective, *la strenna* (the gift),[13] which according to custom accompanied the promises, might be understood as an element of compensation for the inequality of the exchange. Most often this was nonreciprocal, an act of homage to the man, yet its character as a material good underlined the male word, and, as it was a public affirmation of the relationship, its credibility was increased.

Nonetheless, the honor entrusted to a man did not undergo a simple transferral. From the woman's perspective, it was restored, increased in quality, and validated: in a relationship, a woman pledged her sexuality, obtaining from the man, through his promise of marriage, the guarantee of a new condition that assured her a permanent state of honor. The marital relationship, by legitimating female sexuality, represented the situation of greatest security and was recognized as fully honorable. Outside of this form of stable bond with a man, the female figure was, in fact, regarded with suspicion and distrust, because she carried continually in herself the peril of an aggression against her honor and, as a consequence, a possible loss of reputation. The deception to which only the woman was exposed was so frequent and endemic in this system of heterosexual relationships that it was designated by precise linguistic forms: *dare la burla* (to give the trick); *gettare la burla* (to throw the trick); *burlare* (to trick or deceive in the sense of making a fool of). These expressions indicate in general the man's ability[14] to negate the value of the word he had given, turning a promise of marriage into a trick or joke. The "trick," then, had the capacity to stand on its head an emotional moment that a male did not wish to continue by ridiculing the woman and those who with her had believed in the sincerity of the obligation undertaken.[15]

This situation is encountered most frequently when a real problem existed in the relationship; for example, in those cases in which disparate social conditions or enmity between families made doubtful the possibilities of an enduring and stable bond. Lucia Gariglia of Volvera, "daughter of a poor carpenter of low status and no holdings," could not press any expectations about the sexual intercourse she had had with Giuseppe Baudino, "of honored status, being the son of a notary." He could admit without qualms that he had "contracted friendship with the same [Lucia] yet not at all with a mind to marrying her, but rather to trick her [*burlarla*], as she very well should have known, not being of equal status."[16] Frequently, the fact that the trick's perpetrator had an elevated status seemed to guarantee particular license to behave as he pleased, as a compensation of the prestige and power proper to a privileged situation. For this reason, it became more difficult to press public sanctions against this type of individual.[17] Beyond such considerations, the discredit that ill-considered male sexual behavior earned the man was sometimes tempered by the range of situations in which male honor was involved. Unlike women, the sexual conduct of men, if it contributed to their public image, did not entirely define it. Instead, the consequences of the trick fell upon the woman, who, paradoxically, assumed the bulk of responsibility for the deception that had compromised her honor. The public derision to which she was often subjected and the "insults and banter" that were turned against her for her credulousness seemed to contain elements of recrimination toward behavior that did not conform to the conventional model of matrimonial options.

The instance of the trick is an extreme example of the precariousness and peril involved for the unwed woman, whose honor was the target of continuous attacks and insinuations; this position was one of great ambiguity upon which the man could play. And actually, in some instances, the woman was pressed into sexual intercourse against her wishes with threats of being defamed and dishonored no matter what.

It is evident what the woman's position was in relation to the promise of matrimony and how, assured only by the man's word, with apparent surrender she agreed to sexual intercourse. It was the desire to escape a condition of ambiguity and danger that justified the anxiety with which she entrusted her own honor to a man in order to obtain protection: only male control could eliminate all suspicions about her honor, which, as a result, was defined by a bond with a man. With the transfer realized at the moment of sexual intercourse, a man took upon himself a woman's honor; with the promise of marriage, a man undertook to become a woman's protector, assuming all responsibility for her. The transaction implicit in heterosexual relationships thus brought different investments of resources, expectations, and behaviors for men and women; the shared moment broke down into an experience of value and meaning different for each member of the couple. The particularity of behavior can no longer be explained as the fruit of imprecise, contrasting feelings—masculine and feminine—but rather as the consequence of the different content found by each person in the relationship.

Following the transfer of honor, any attacks on the woman's honor became a direct offense against the man's. The married woman's condition was thus defined by the plenitude of her honor assured by the presence of a man at her side.[18] As we have seen, her opponent was the unmarried woman, especially the widow, who, detached from her own kin group by marriage and from her husband's by his death, was unable to claim clear-cut membership in either her family of origin or that of orientation: control of her honor, if not nonexistent, was undefined. She was the archetypal ambiguous woman, to whom, not without reason, characteristics of wildness and sexual rapacity were traditionally attributed.[19] As a result, she was forced to present herself before the ecclesiastical court with a stereotypical formula, which had the sense of preventive defense: "chaste and honest widow."

The woman's honor, because of its significance in the evolution of heterosexual relationships as described in the depositions, appeared, then, in the context of the degree of control established over her sexuality. Married, single, widowed—the women whose portrayals we have described were situated precisely in a hierarchy defined by the measure of honor, or more exactly, by the control exercised over it. The complex code of honor was one of the channels through which a relationship of power and dependence between the sexes was guaranteed and reproduced, and because of this the protection assured by a man was the condition of an honorable sexuality. In this sense marriage was, for the woman, an almost obligatory choice.

The most significant implication of this situation, which matrimonial documents throw into particular relief, was the domination that the man, by assuming responsibility for honor, established over female reproductive power and used to assure himself a guaranteed paternity. Several factors reveal that the preoccupation with certain paternity was one of the principal motives behind the attribution of honor and dishonor. In this context, the emphasis in the depositions on fidelity to one man rather than on the importance of virginity gains meaning: indeed, some women who had already had an unfortunate emotional and sexual relationship were not necessarily perceived as dishonored, nor were they viewed as excluded from other marriage possibilities. Fidelity to the new partner might render her desirable as a bride,[20] even more so in the frequent cases where the previous partner provided a dowry, which publicly recognized his responsibility and the woman's good faith.

The threshold of honor, then, was not virginity. Certainly this constituted a value, but primarily because it represented the maximum guarantee of control over female reproductive power. The real importance of a woman as the agent of reproduction was at times made explicit, and presumed sterility was an adequate motive to renege on all promises:

> Since you were pledged to another and I see that you have still not conceived, it is not right that I marry you, having need of a woman who can give me sons; for this reason we each ought to remain free, and I acknowledge the pleasures received from you, for which I will give you something.[21]

Moreover, the man, following sexual intercourse, often manifested a sense of ownership over the woman with expressions such as "I am with my own," "I am boss," "I am working with my own." Finally, the seventeenth-century custom that gave the father, not the mother, full responsibility for a natural child was an element of great significance, representing a kind of social recognition of the male control of reproduction. The man, in fact, did not hesitate to give his name, to maintain, or even frequently to accept into his home the fruit of a momentary or temporary union. This phenomenon—which we will discuss in more detail later—clearly demonstrated how the father was perceived as having the principal responsibility for offspring, and represented an institutionalized expression of the male right over the reproductive power of women.

❧ The possibilities for license that this same sexual code of honor offered the male—the trick being the most typical example—were opposed by different interests characteristic of the groups and individuals who, in various measure, were involved with the fate of female honor. Also, the community in all its complexity exercised different forms of control over conduct, which tended to guarantee an equilibrium within the system of relations whose expression was measured by degrees of honor. This activity of control, which was translated into the defense of individual honor, had particularly important ramifications for the woman, whose honor, weaker and more exposed, constituted a threat to the status of her entire community should it be lost. For this reason, the family was, first of all, involved in the protection of female honor; one member's fall into dishonor threw into doubt the authority and power of the family, proving its weakness and incapacity to defend the reputation of its members. In this sense, an attack against the honor of a woman was an offense against her kin group as well: through an emotional relationship, the promise of marriage touched the lives of the men of the family—the father, the brothers, the closest relatives—who, by protecting female honor, were defending their own name.

Thus, the discourse that mattered for the man was with these males, for it was their presence that could create concern for the reputation of his word that was capable of conditioning his attitude toward the relationship. His behavior toward the woman, then, implied a message to her group, even if indirectly: for this reason, the man who played a trick, as a "destroyer of family reputations,"[22] provoked contradictory sentiments. On the one hand, he was the object of sanctions. On the other, he was the victorious protagonist of a challenge to the honor of the men of the family: his aggression fell not only on the woman's personal honor, but on family honor as well. The result of all this was that the strength of the support network, understood as the capacity to assist and protect, upon which the woman could rely influenced the attitudes of potential partners and even conditioned others' perception of the woman herself.

The family's protection was not limited to the premarital phases of a relationship, but at times continued after the wedding. Ties were often maintained with the new couple—even when the new home was distant. The desire for information about the condition of the bride at her in-laws' home, for example, could be interpreted as the kin group's continuing concern about her treatment, which reflected on family honor.[23] We see examples of this type of concern especially among the upper classes, where prestige and name seem to have played a considerable role. In the case of the gentlewoman Maria Mariani, married to Signor Bartolomeo Rovati, the family several times lamented the treatment she received, sending letters of remonstrance to Maria's brother-in-law, the head of the family, who had imposed on her a life deemed inappropriate to her rank. Her mother's protests referred not only to affronts of a personal nature, but also to those perceived as harmful to the family's reputation:

> He holds her in servitude, forbidding her now from going to make certain visits, now from wearing certain clothes, ordering her to attend to the cooking and similar things; for this reason I wrote to said Signor Giuseppe that I had not put in his house a servant and that I wanted him to treat my daughter differently.

Even when suspicions of infidelity fell upon Maria, the mother still intervened, asking for an explanation not from Maria but from her son-in-law, holder of the daughter's virtue and thus responsible for the reputation that the Mariani family name enjoyed.[24]

This case represents a recurring example among groups of a certain rank and condition where the pressure of family decisions upon personal decisions was justified by preoccupations with prestige. But turning to the more general customs of the romantic relationships covered by our documents, the picture changes dramatically, and, at least in the preliminary stages of a relationship, the intervention of the kin group was less direct and less pressing. What is more striking in the reconstruction of the first stages is, in fact, the absence or at least the marginal role given parents, relatives, and persons of a similar age and authority. At this stage, the family did not actively exercise a protective function toward the couple's honor, but seemed to delegate to other individuals the responsibility for following the relationship's evolution. In essence, peers provided the milieu in which the relationship began; youths, in other words, of the same generation. The control of heterosexual relationships seems, then, to have been characterized by a specialization of the forms that conditioned it and of the people to whom it was entrusted depending upon the stage of the relationship.

The meeting, choice of partner, and development of the relationship occurred amidst the regular forms of youth socialization. In a society marked by profound divisions, of which the separation into a social hierarchy was but one aspect, the young on their own constituted a defined and recognizable group.[25] As such, they had autonomous forms of association that had specific powers and provided internal mechanisms of control. But these characteristics were revealed in the context of groups of the same sex, which so often divided youthful society.

The different levels of organization of these groups seem to constitute a primary, distinctive element. The male group was characterized by intense internal relationships and a strong sense of belonging, which developed through codified social activities. The female group was more dispersed and, in contrast to the male, had little geographic mobility, being limited primarily to the home and thus having the neighborhood as its principal focus. Dances, visits, evening gatherings—places favored for courtship and love—were the accepted occasions for contact between the two groups. There sociability and, especially, relations between the sexes assumed concrete and formalized forms and expressions. The formalized character of the gestures or words exchanged was certainly not a sign that rigidity was imposed on relationships. Rather, it revealed a ritual significance that had precise functions, contributing to the definition of individual sexual roles and, at the same time, to the description of the nature of the relationship that might be established.[26] This type of intermixing, because of the characteristics of such groups, had as its recurring locus the home of the young woman, where potential suitors, usually accompanied by friends of the same age, went to pay their calls:

> He began coming to a stable . . . near my house where I usually spent all evening, sitting up with other girls and with the youths who would come to court [*far servitù d'amore*] other girls and there the said Pirra . . . used to discuss amorous things with me.[27]

On such occasions, parents were often absent, or their presence did not cause concern about parental control.[28] Rather, at this point, control of the development of the relationship and individual behavior appears to have been delegated to groups of peers. They accompanied the couple at every stage of the development of their relationship: they were witnesses to each meeting between the couple; to the expressions of love exchanged; to the gestures of affection given; and they were often responsible for bringing gifts or messages to the betrothed. It was not unusual, then, in cases that treat of broken promises, where testimony was gathered to support the opposing position, that most testimony came from peers: that is, those who saw themselves also as "children of family" still to be married, as youths tied by friendship to the parties involved in the dispute.[29]

In turn, the family assumed an active role in the later stages of the relationship. The parents had to give or withhold their consent when confronted by an official request to marry, which usually capped a period of lovemaking between the two betrothed. In more critical situations, when the honor of the group was directly threatened by an offense perpetrated against a woman, it was still the family who, even with violence,[30] intervened to obtain reparation for honor by securing marriage, payment of a dowry, or an official promise in the presence of witnesses.

The peer group, however, was recognized as significant for a long time: its members, grouped by age and being unmarried, were further united by the different roles they played contemporaneously as work partners, neighbors, relatives, and friends.[31] Because of these ties they could exercise a great deal of control just by virtue of their continuous participation in different phases of a relationship. This control was especially effective over individual conduct and over the man's word in particular, restricting the freedom that verbal promises seemed to offer him. As potential rivals for one of the parties and possible partners of the other, the group was immediately concerned with an equitable distribution of matrimonial resources, which seems to have been inspired by egalitarian principles governing the possession of goods.[32] The youth groups' competence in controlling such resources was recognized by the community itself and assumed institutionalized forms such as the *chiabra*, barriers, tolls, and compensation.[33] By means of such controls, the youths expressed dissent with an unsatisfactory alliance, and they called for an indemnity—if only symbolic—in order to reestablish the ideal equilibrium. While in our sources these initiatives appeared to be mostly the male group's prerogatives, possibilities also existed for women openly to express forms of sanction possessing the same potential for control. Gossip and chatter, in particular, constituted an autonomous mode of evaluating what men did to women; in more than one case a woman broke a promise of marriage, claiming as her principal motive the unworthy behavior of the male in a previous relationship where he had compromised and abandoned a future bride. Thus, Martina Mutta withdrew from an engagement contracted with Alfonso Rizzioni, having been informed that he "had had carnal commerce with a certain Maria who had borne him a son."[34]

The community, then, through the peer group, succeeded in extending control to even the more private moments of the relationship; moreover, the tensions and conflicts that a more direct control by elders might have generated were eased by peers equal in age and authority. This role of mediation was evident in the initial stages of the relationship when ritual aspects of avoidance between the potential son-in-law and male relatives of the woman were made explicit by the absence of the family.[35] The presence of the group postponed a direct relationship between a false suitor and the family and still warned him fully of the implications of an offense to the family's honor. The tensions implicit in this relationship explain the regular custom of engaging an outsider, often a peer not directly involved in the contract, to act as mediator by requesting the marriage and conducting the negotiations.

Giò Andrea Giardino, friend of Giò Battista Siminino, played the role of mediator for the Gillio family from the earliest phases of the relationship:

> In the company of Gian Battista Siminino I went to the place of residence of Giò Antonio, father of the engaged girl. . . . There the said Siminino stayed for about one hour with Lucia Gillio, talking

> about love to her in her [family's] stable, where even Anna Gillio her mother was; and I at that time went into a room, the kitchen I think, and I remained there talking with Giò Antonio Gillio until we left.

It was Giardino, then, who controlled the contacts between Lucia and Giò Battista, and, together with other youths, Giardino accompanied him on visits and assumed the onus of conducting marriage negotiations.

> On the night of the above-named day, a Sunday, along with Felice Berardo and Giò Vaudagnotto, we all went on horseback . . . to the house of the above-named girl of the Gillio family who, however . . . had already left with her mother for Carignano in order to be blessed . . . and we all went to Carignano by road, and in the vicinity of that city we overtook those women and we talked there for awhile . . . but at that time her mother said that perhaps the youths of Carignano would "talk,"[36] seeing all of us in the company of her daughter. It was agreed that the said mother and daughter would let themselves be seen alone entering Carignano and the Duomo, and that we should go along after them . . . and no one complained about that. . . . Then we all went to the house of the said girl of the Gillio family where the said Siminino and said Gillio girl showed themselves to be very happy and they made the promises of marriage . . . first though . . . in order to speak to him, I went into the room where the above-named Giò Antonio, the father, was found tucked into bed because he had a migraine, saying . . . that I wanted to know if he would be content to give his daughter in marriage to him [Siminino]. And finally, I later told the mother that on Thursday . . . I would come to plan the expenses that would have to be paid . . . and the day when in the presence of the closest relatives they would exchange the marriage gifts.[37]

We have reported this testimony more fully because it seems to summarize the active role played by the peer group in courtship and marriage. We would like, at this point, to dwell a little on the characteristics of the control that not only such groups, but the whole community, exercised over heterosexual relationships. First, it should be noted that there was little in the way of a rigid code of behavior; what code there was did not present strictly established boundaries that, if transgressed, would call down sanctions. Rather, public judgment had an elasticity that was capable of adapting to individual circumstances.

In the trials it is, in fact, very difficult to discover the limits of the community's tolerance toward its members' conduct—the threshold of dishonor, in short. We find irregular relationships that were prolonged for many years and seem to have been accepted without dispute; other cases, instead, barely different in their essential dynamics, met with sanctions from the community, publicly expressed through irony and ridicule or in more marked forms, such as the refusal of a greeting or the exclusion from some social events[38] or directly through ostracism. The dynamic between the community and the protagonists in a relationship influenced its development and outcome and determined the judgment expressed about it. Control was continuous, not sporadic, since it was constantly exercised at the level of information: the relationship was observed throughout its evolution, and this permitted timely and decisive intervention. The community performed, in fact, both a preventive and a protective function, assessing conduct and transmitting messages of rebuke when faced with the peril of deviance.

Angela Alberico, a "poor daughter" of Balangero, while carrying on a relationship with a young, well-to-do lawyer and counting on his promise to marry her, received numerous warnings about the impossibility of a marriage marked by such a pronounced social disparity. At first she was warned by her parish priest, then she was made the object of public "tricks and rough songs," and finally, although she assured an innkeeper in a nearby district that she was by then married, that woman denied her and her "husband" a common bed.[39] Disapproval was expressed more symbolically about the behavior of Mathea Paglieta, suspected of being "easy to get to know carnally": surprised during a break at harvest time in a too-familiar position with a youth who was not her betrothed, she met with the sanction of a fellow worker who, without speaking, threw a sheaf of hay on her. Mathea insisted, however, on having relations with different men, thus earning for herself the disfavor of neighbors who, at last, requested that the owner of the field dismiss her along with her family.[40]

The relationship between a private relationship and the community, then, was dialectical in the sense that opinions expressed by the latter were delivered in order to correct conduct before punishment became necessary. Moreover, punishment and judgment were at times able to adjust to individuals' responses to the pressures exerted on them. Community control was distinguished from institutional control: while the former was continuous and developed along with the relationship, thus contributing to its evolution, the latter was irregular and acted upon an already static and defined reality. The difficulty that the Church encountered in introducing new matrimonial customs, whereby the promise of marriage would be subordinate to an institutionalized marriage ceremony and sexual intercourse would be legal only after matrimony, provides a telling index of a different concept of control. To demand an official ceremony required the ability to concentrate intervention in a definite moment, thus making it possible to define deviance clearly. In contrast, following the entire development of a relationship permitted the community greater flexibility of judgment, which went well beyond a precise distinction between licit and illicit behaviors.[41]

This description of how a community controlled sexuality might make it appear extremely rigid, with each member of the community equally committed to preserving the social order. We would like to examine, however, certain underlying codes of conduct that did not obstruct the efficiency of the system of control but that made its dynamic more flexible.[42] What we will say below, for example, about the different quality of control exercised by the allies of the family and the peer group introduces the concept of client-patron relationships, which cut across other social bonds and created a new variable capable of strengthening or weakening judgments on personal conduct. But in addition there were other groups that hoped to adapt the rigid behavior codes to their own ends, without necessarily trying to overthrow those codes.

Women's networks, for example, often served as a defense against controls that, even if they were used to protect a woman's honor, were before all else a way of forcing a woman into a role of dependence. Gossip, the form of communication traditionally viewed as dominated by women, was used in matrimonial cases as an effective weapon against an aggressive husband: through confiding in female neighbors, the wife made her husband's misbehavior part of the public domain, exerting in this manner more incisive pressure on him. This was one reason husbands feared female gossip, because when reported within other family circles it eventually had an impact on their relations with other men. In moments of conflict, worry about bad-mouthing drove the male to warn his wife to avoid contact with female neighbors.[43] Only rarely did women's networks demonstrate external, disruptive behavior: one of the few examples that we have encountered involved a close alliance between a wife and a woman servant being sexually harassed by her husband. Both agreed to surprise the man and unmask his betrayal, but this action did not obtain the desired effect, provoking only a violent reaction from the husband.[44]

In the vast majority of cases, the alliances among women were less explicit; they were expressed in secret but effective forms of solidarity. They can be found, for example, in family relationships, particularly those between mother and daughter, in which the former was often disposed to force situations favoring the latter and work on her behalf virtually to the limits of conventionally accepted behavior. In the case of Antonia Bertina, who had received two different offers of marriage, it was her own mother who suggested the possibility of disregarding the rule of precedence that would have had her marry the suitor that she found unattractive, so that she could marry the man whom she preferred.[45]

Infractions of this type, which revealed hidden networks and thus were difficult to discover, even in such a descriptive source, demonstrated that such networks had a decisive impact on individual experiences. The picture that emerges, then, from even a summary analysis of underlying codes, and in particular from examples of female solidarity, reveals that the measure of their presence and efficacy actually was to be found in subtle and barely perceptible forms. These forms, nonetheless, are to be read as attempts to rebalance the power relationship between the sexes, modifying, to one's own advantage, a rigid and constricting code of conduct.[46]

❧ We have seen how, in the last analysis, in one model of heterosexual relationships, when the woman was threatened with a loss of honor, the control exercised by the environment provided some protection, restricting male license. The presence of people and groups who, in different measure, shared in the fate of the woman's reputation not only could guarantee decisive interventions in her favor, but by increasing the respect given females, could actually protect a woman from incidents harmful to her honor. This protection grew out of the necessity felt by males to defend the integrity of their own name; and, more generally, from a preoccupation with the control of female sexual behavior. For a woman, the result was double-edged: while this state of affairs protected her from being marginalized, it did impose an oppressive situation in which her choices were restricted and were continually exposed to outside judgment. To define female honor by the degree of control exercised over a woman's sexuality meant defining, in turn, the existing relationship between control and honor: to the degree that a woman's relationships were perceived as capable of exerting pressure on her and creating support for her, her state of honor would be defended and augmented even more effectively. This was perceived as a quality not fixed but variable, which was measured not only by the social context but also in terms of its own characteristics.

In the cases where there was a network of strong and cohesive relationships, one notices in the woman's conduct a sense of the protection she enjoyed. Such a woman, in fact, could easily accept a request for sexual intercourse advanced by a man whom everyone recognized as her official partner. And concern about her honor, typically heightened in other cases, in such an instance was tempered by the strength of the network of relationships she could count on. For her, the man's word was, in fact, guaranteed by pressures exerted by a network that, in extreme moments, could even use violence in defense of her honor. For example, in the case of Domenico Lampiano, who was suspected of bad faith for not having yet acted upon his promise of matrimony, even though Margarita Vinazza was "pregnant with his seed," coercive action was planned:

> It was necessary that I [Domenico], having terminated my service at the above-named Rigoletto's [at whose home both Margarita and he had been servants], return to Marentino on the feast of last Christmas, where a certain Giacomo Antonio of the said Moncucco, inhabitant of the place called Marentino, told me that Matteo the brother of Margarita Vinazza wanted to speak to me and I answered that I would go the next day to Moncucco and I asked him to accompany me. And in fact, we did go together to Margarita Vinazza's house, where we actually found Matteo, who only after various discussions left the house, having told us to wait, as he would soon return. And in fact, he did return in the company of the parish priest of Moncucco. Then after them the Lord Giorgio Campagnola, Signor Nodaro Medino, Giò servant of the said Signor Medino, and Matteo Vinazza, cousin of the said Margarita also joined us. Signor Medino had a sickle in his hand, the Lord Giorgio and the servant of said Signor Medino and the cousin of said Margarita each had big clubs in their hands; and having entered the said room, the parish priest said to me that it was necessary to marry Margarita Vinazzi, who was present there, and whom I had made pregnant. And having answered them that I absolutely did not want to marry her, they—

> all of the above-named—said that I must actually resolve to marry her, otherwise my end was near; at that Signor Medino raised the sickle and the others the big clubs that they were holding in their hands. And I persisting that I did not want to marry her, the said Matteo left and brought in Margarita and locked the door anew. The said parish priest began again to question me, asking if I wanted to take the said Margarita Vinazza as my wife to which I said no, that rather than marry her I would give something to her for the commerce I had had with her. But the said Matteo with all the others, having then protested to me that if I did not marry her I would never get out of that room for they would have put an end to me; I, fearing to be killed, said to her that I would marry her. Having heard this the parish priest asked me if I wanted to take for my wife the said Margarita Vinazza. I responded yes to him, then the said Margarita being asked if she wanted me for her husband said indeed yes. That done, the parish priest said to us that we were married; that we could go to bed together.[47]

The possibility for interventions of this type was well known to the woman, who could use it as a warning when she accepted a request for sexual intercourse:

> He said that he wanted her for his wife and that he wanted to marry her and she warned him that he had better for if he would not marry her for love, there were people who make him marry her by force. He replied to her that he would marry her, and he knew her carnally one time in the said room.[48]

The weight of such interference was so great in some cases that nothing remained for the man to do except to leave the community to escape an imposed marriage. Giovanni Ferrere, Giacomo Belli, and Giorgio Molliassa declared under oath that they knew Ludovico, a factor for Battista Petito,

> who, although he was supposed to work for [Battista] until the feast of the Purification of the Madonna, nevertheless, it having been discovered that he had impregnated Anna, daughter of the deceased Francesco Iarbione, and that, for this reason, they wanted to make him marry her he, Ludovico, therefore fled from there without leave from his patron and went to Settimo Torinese.[49]

But aside from these extreme cases, cancellation of marriage plans was the more normal outcome when faced with the intransigence of one of the parties, with disagreement about the provisions of a dowry, or even with hindrances such as being related or having been previously engaged.[50] In such situations, protection of female honor was expressed in other forms: through the custom, already mentioned, that required a reluctant man to provide a dowry[51] and, more generally, in the duty acknowledged by the woman and attested to with regularity throughout the seventeenth century, of giving the father's name to the natural child. The control of relationships was so effective that a declaration of paternity by the mother alone before the parish priest and preselected godfathers was sufficient for the baby to be baptized and even registered in the father's name. Fathers, as we have already seen, usually accepted responsibility for a child, provided that the woman's reputation was not clouded by suspicions of infidelity and looseness. Providing a dowry and, more importantly, recognizing the child were, then, significant because they confirmed male responsibility and restored an honored status to the woman.

Such important effects resulted from the protective nature of the control exercised by the community, whose power resided before all else in the control of information. But disseminating the news, judging it, and intervening in behavior were possible only if the social network was characterized by high density or internal cohesiveness, understood as the strength of relationships among members.[52] The strength of the network did not depend so much on its size as on its cohesion; that is, on the presence of strong bonds that linked its components. In fact, in situations of mobility, where interpersonal contacts could be numerous yet sporadic and unstable, the pressures exerted on behavior to make it conform to common norms were minimal and of a different nature. In the woman's case, such conditions had great potential for attacks against her honor, while the man, less worried by the requirements of loyalty, was offered greater license.

Certainly, situations of this type were frequently encountered in cities of early modern Europe characterized by movements of unstable masses and marked by strong conflict and insecurity in social relationships contrasted with small islands of organized groups.[53] Nevertheless, an analysis of social networks allows one to avoid oversimplifications and to distinguish the responses given by different social groups in analogous circumstances. Transferring customs from the environment of origin to the new social environment was not, in fact, rare even in cities. The promises, for example, exchanged by Matheo

Opperti and Bernardina Vigna, both originally from Bra and at the time residents of Turin, illustrate the strength of the social network among immigrants from the same village, both in the way in which the incident unfolded and especially in the active participation of the relatives and fellow citizens.[54]

More often, the characteristic that seemed to dominate relationships in the urban environment was fragmentation, which resulted in modifying not only the forms through which control was expressed but its very functions. The attributes that we have revealed as peculiar to control in situations of greater social cohesion, that is, its active and protective character and the capacity to intervene promptly in behavior, did, in fact, disappear. The witnesses called to testify about events in the city did not seem to have been participants in the entire history of the relationship; rather, they recalled isolated episodes about which they offered hypotheses and insinuations. Their control was not continuous but fragmentary, and it concentrated on certain moments that were assumed to be representative of the whole history. Domenica Azano of Turin, known as "Pellizzara" (the furrier's woman) because of the occupation practiced by her husband, was investigated by the fiscal solicitor, following "murmuring" about her in the courtyard where she lived. She was accused of excessive "familiarity" with Bernardino Bussi, to whom she had given assistance, keeping him as a boarder and appearing in his company in public. No witness was able to testify to actual scandalous doings; rather, she was charged on the basis of a series of interpretations of acts in and of themselves so very insignificant that they were easily redefined by the investigation and by the court, so that in the end, she was absolved.[55]

Those who testified about the behavior of the "Pellizzara" did not constitute a controlling group organized around the defense and reconfirmation of common norms and interests that had been established by peers. Instead, they were presented as a collection of people of different ages and circumstances—similar, if at all, because they frequented the same inn, not because of that plurality of bonds which was the guarantee of efficient control. Their contributions to unraveling the incident were as observers (passive ones at that) and were expressed essentially in terms of surveillance. With respect to the community that we described earlier, these social groups appear more difficult to define, characterized as they were by extreme heterogeneity—especially in the absence of peer groups—and by a marked instability that was caused by the mobility of members. Such elements reveal that these groups were scarcely cohesive nuclei, and that the functions of control they exercised were modified. In fact, the preoccupations which motivated the "Pellizzara"'s neighbors were not dictated by problems in maintaining the equilibrium of resources but by the need to maintain order in the residential area and courtyard. The attempts at control revealed characteristics of policing;[56] they did not form a part of the people's business; rather they spied on others' movements.

Francesca Clario, a young woman of Savoy who came to Turin, having as her only reference a woman from the same village, was lured by a procuress, who, keeping Francesca secretly hidden in her home for a week, forced her to prostitute herself against her will. As was evident by the richness of detail that they later furnished during the interrogation, neither the other village-woman, nor the neighbors who had "observed" the entire incident, intervened in any way to save Francesca from the violence that was used against her. It is no wonder that many of these trials involved young women who came to the city without having a defined group to whom they might turn—"like a young person who does not have anyone to assist them"—thus, they remained victims of people who profited by their isolation.[57] Maria Sacchetta, for example, under the cover of a "small collar-maker's shop," was a procuress, who with ease led astray some young "wanderers and homeless women," luring them with the pretext of learning a career into becoming prostitutes for the servants of the ambassador of Venice.[58]

The indifference or the limited support of the urban environment, as well as the climate of insecurity and precariousness so often testified to in these documents, seemed to weaken the woman's vigilance when faced with male offers of protection. The dynamic of the relationship was, in the initial phases, identical to that already described: sexual intercourse immediately followed the promise of marriage. Yet, in these cases, because the relationship was not subject to a definite control but only to the woman's pressure, it often developed into a form of temporary concubinage rather than a stable bond. Sometimes the man broke off the relationship; then, at his pleasure, took it up again. He could be arrogant and treat the woman badly, while she seemed unable to escape the state of dependence in which she found herself waiting for the restitution of her own honor.[59] In a system of unstable social relationships, she appeared fragile and incapable of defending her honor on her own; the incidents encountered often expressed, in dramatic tones, the difficulties and pain that the absence of stable contacts entailed for women.

This reality is in stark contrast with the image of a woman emancipated and freed from restrictions, which has often been assumed for a female far from her family and her original community.[60] At the same time, it is difficult to maintain that such a detachment implied in itself the abandonment of community values and an adherence to new models of behavior; overall, if one looks at emigration before matrimony, such hypotheses appear even more unfounded, as the element that characterized such women was the goal of "return."[61] Emigration was, in fact, temporary. It often was seasonal; and thus it implied an adherence to the customs and traditions of the original community. This type of emigration involved a great part of the female population, for whom servitude represented a phase of life. The fact that female servants so often found themselves as protagonists in suits about broken promises was not so much a result of claims to "sexual liberty" practiced in a new environment, but rather of the absence of control and protection the community had assured them. This absence left them more vulnerable to a loss of honor and made them the most likely victims of seduction. In fact, while they counted on the customary practice of relations between the sexes, in their new environment pressure on the male was virtually nonexistent. As a result, the relationship ended most often with deceit and abandonment. Nevertheless, the mechanisms of control typical of the local community could be partially re-created, and sometimes we find new individuals, especially companions from work, who assumed the role of guarantor of female honor. The case of Gianna Marzonet, a servant in Turin from Aix in the duchy of Savoy, re-created to an extent the violent intervention that characterized the story of Margarita Vinazza:

> In the act of having sexual intercourse, they were caught by one of the shepherds of said Signor Boggia [for whom they all worked], who, having seen that, became very angry against the defendant, threatening him with beating. And he, the defendant, answered him in the formal words or similar ones that he would work out his problem and that he wanted to marry her.[62]

Still, the constant reference to the original community sometimes manifested itself in the desire to link the relationship to the community by making it known directly to the family or to a relative or fellow villager now living in the place emigrated to; these became the original community's representatives, thus involving family honor in the incident and guaranteeing it a certain protection, even if indirect and ideal.

This preoccupation found its source in the very nature of the group's honor, which assured steadfast support for the individual. As we have already seen, the behavior of a single person influenced family honor, even if that honor, by spanning generations, was not as easily corruptible as personal honor. This honor, however, was not only the sum of moral qualities but varied with social status, power, and the reputation that the family enjoyed. What seems clear is that the level of the protection that the family was able to furnish was all the more potent the more able it was to mobilize power when its reputation was threatened.[63]

The nature of this power is seen clearly in the context of the suit that Mathea Paglieta of the city of Racconigi brought against Giò Paulo Accastello, accused of having broken a promise of marriage after having had sexual intercourse with her.[64] The witnesses called to confirm or deny the accusation of dishonest behavior that Giò Paulo used as a counterattack against Paglieta (who attempted to defend herself) can be neatly divided into two groups: on one side were certain notables from Racconigi, who seem to have had "something to do with" Mathea's father on several occasions, renting a house to him, bringing him "the silk to work on," "having him carry things from place to place," and so on; these connections were then reinforced by "those who were familiar with the family" and, at least in one case, by relations of patronage. This group of testimonies had the function of affirming the good name of the Paglieta family. Mathea's conduct was mentioned only as a consequence of the reputation that the family enjoyed. For example, the noble Agostino Pistone replied to questioning that he had known "the couple, Giovanni and Beatrice from Paglieta, for many years. He knew them as good people, with a good name, condition, and reputation and publicly known and recognized as such in Racconigi; their daughter he knew named Mathea, who has the same quality as her said father and mother."[65]

On the other hand, a group of Mathea's peers seemed to serve the function of supplying information on her behavior with Giò Paulo and other suitors, as evidence for a judgment of her personal morality. Their numerous depositions made reference to precise episodes in which, "as young people all from one place," they had been participants along with her. There seems to be, in sum, a sort of division in competence and lived realities: the first group did not refer to Mathea's conduct, nor to her own honor, but, motivated by strong ties with her family, affirmed her reputation; the second group, essentially her peers, expressed, on the contrary, a type of direct reportage on her personal honor.

Mathea Paglieta worked seasonally as a servant in the fields of the castellan of Racconigi. She and her family were of modest means, yet they could count on the support of people who were very influential and superior to them in social and economic status. A family's power, then, was not necessarily and solely dependent on social position, but also upon the force of a series of client relationships of asymmetrical reciprocity that cut across the social hierarchy.[66]

The family's protection consisted, then, in mediating the community's judgment of the individual's conduct. Concerning the behavior of "Pellizzara," her Turinese neighbors freely advanced suspicions and insinuations; in the testimonies one finds no reference to her family, and the judgment ends with an evaluation of individual behavior, isolating the person from the complex of events that constituted her past. For her there was not a trace of that group, even urban-based, which had furnished a guarantee for Mathea Paglieta, recognizing the latter as belonging to an honored family. Explicit in these examples is the power that social relationships could ensure: while a stable network of relations could sustain a woman in the defense of her own honor, so that responsibility for it was shared, at the same time the recognized membership in a family group meant that consideration of personal qualities was strictly tied to qualities of the group.

As a result, an examination of networks makes it possible to understand more clearly the variety of behaviors, observed even within the limited circle of local contacts, which are difficult to explain in the context of rigid categories such as, for example, rural society versus urban society. From this perspective, in fact, behavior would appear to be distributed along a continuum, and only the extreme poles of that behavior would correspond to well-defined social categories with definite characteristics. Accordingly, situations that did not fit such a classification would be overlooked as "moments of transition," unimportant because unrepresentative. To examine the network of relationships and its characteristics has meant, instead, to consider the different social realities, not as anticipations or inheritances of predefined models, but in terms of an internal logic that presents the specific nature of the situation.

❧ The analysis of the exchange between sexual partners has provided us with a basis for reading their love stories, which from time to time need to be corrected in the context of individual events. It is possible to explain a relationship's specific progression and the choices that distinguished it—to determine, that is, the nature of the variations characterizing each relationship—by examining the influences exercised on the development of a relationship by the people and groups to whom a couple was in some way tied. What we would like to propose, and are here advancing as a working hypothesis, is that we can analyze the network of relations in order to interpret even slow processes of change, changes for which our sources offer many clues. There are, in fact, many indications of a gradual mutation in the relations between men and women, which became clearer from the middle of the eighteenth century.

In the first place, the moment of the marriage promise assumed new meanings. Earlier it had consisted essentially in an exchange of consent between peers, which needed at most casual witnesses but did not require formal sanction to legitimate it. In the early decades of the 1700s, an official ceremony became necessary to assure its reality. The public aspect of the promise, then, assumed great weight, and in this sense the observance of a strict ritual—requiring the exchange of gifts, a toast, the presence of witnesses, and the consent of the parents—became the only affirmation recognized for the future contract. Through the new importance accorded to the official moment, the family took on a more central role in controlling the couple's relationship, which had previously been dominated by the community.

This tendency seems to be a measure of a loss of faith in the social network's ability to act, and can be understood as an effect of the penetration of ecclesiastical rule on matrimonial custom.[67] By assuming an official character, the marriage promise gained ceremonial significance as a prelude to marriage, while less frequently it initiated sexual intercourse and cohabitation. Our sources reveal a great repression of premarital sexual relationships over the span of two centuries, which became particularly intense in the second half of the eighteenth century. The incidence of sexual intercourse in cases of broken promises was greatly reduced, and what had been the common practice of the masses in the seventeenth century became an exception in the eighteenth, presented as anomalous by even its practitioners.[68]

The most significant aspect of these cases was the change in the tone used by a woman to present her experience to the judge: intercourse was described as a form of violence from which she had been unable to escape or as the consequence of a long negotiation with the man. Her attitude seems to reveal an awareness of having committed a disapproved and blameworthy act. While in the depositions especially at the beginning of the 1600s the woman had admitted without reserve her consent to sexual intercourse, protected as she was by the male word, now, in an attempt to exculpate herself, she strongly underscored her resistance to the man's pressure. The violent moment of sexual intercourse often contrasted with other phases of the incident, characterized by tones of reciprocal affection, as is evident in the account of Caterina Ghiga, servant in Turin:

> The said Nicolao Bianco having entered said kitchen, greeted me, saying to me "Good evening, my bride" and having seated himself beside me near the fire, he began to make illicit touches, that is, to my bosom, and kissing me and hugging me, he called me "my dear joy and bride." Refusing him, I defended myself with my arms, but he, having taken me by the arms, put me on the bed which served for me to sleep alone in, in a room adjoining the above-named kitchen, and there he tore my blouse and had sexual intercourse with me and though I had used all my strength in order to defend myself so that that man could not have sexual relations with me, nonetheless the greatest force was used by that same man, and illicit touches from the same having been made to me, on the modest parts, and also on the breasts, I, left half-alive, could not escape allowing him to vent his passions. . . . Afterwards both of us having gone into the pantry and I, having immediately taken out the wine for my mistress's supper, we drank that same wine, he first and I after, and he was toasting me "to my wife," and I toasted him "to my husband."[69]

And in other cases, not only the first, but every sexual encounter between the couple, was presented by the woman as involving force:

> He took me with violence. He laid me down and without saying anything to me as he usually did, he lifted my clothes and had sexual intercourse with me; it was then that I began to be pregnant. . . . Various other times the same thing happened, he having sexual intercourse with me and when I was all alone he took me and laying me on the ground he did with me whatever he liked.[70]

The woman's insistence on male aggression seems to express an admission of her own weakness and isolation in defending her honor;

it no longer sufficed to state that sexual intercourse followed a promise of marriage in order to demand that the man fulfill that promise. Now it was necessary to present sexual intercourse as a crime of violence in order to implicate him and make him share the consequences. The woman's fear of being held solely responsible for safeguarding her own honor appears evident.

With respect to the details of violence, the promise assumed a secondary position in the economy of the narrative: the man's word appears to have lost all value as a proof, which had formerly been assured by the active presence of groups implicated in the defense of female honor. These had once permitted a rebalancing of the relationship of unequal power between a man and a woman. In consequence, sexual intercourse had lost its character as a prelude to marriage and had to be presented as an act of force in order not to appear sinful and thus dishonorable. It is significant that exactly in these years, for the first time, sexual practice came to be explicitly associated with an idea of guilt consciously evaluated. This can be seen in the very words with which Maria Gavatta of Piobesi refused the proposal of Bartolomeo Cerruti:

> He, Cerruti, having come to my house and I being all alone in the room in which I usually slept, after having given me various kisses and touching my breasts, he asked me to permit him to have sexual intercourse with me, assuring me that he would marry me, *but I, pointing out to him that it was a sin* and that after having enjoyed me he would then have abandoned me, he assured me always that he would marry me.[71]

All these elements unite, in our opinion, in supporting the hypothesis that the responsibility which once had been broadly shared was now concentrated on the woman. This dynamic appears reducible to a larger process of isolating the individual from the protective context of broader relationships; this was one of the principal effects of the penetration of ecclesiastical institutions into the social fabric.[72] The means and the language with which this process was affirmed were many. In the area of relationships between the sexes, the continuous warnings contained either in manuals of instruction or in the Piedmontese synods[73] had a definite role in discouraging the most organized forms of socialization among youths, which used to exert a collective control on such relationships.

The weakening of these forms of solidarity, and therefore the smaller amount of pressure exerted on the man to keep his word, left open to men wide margins of license. The most important fact that reveals this is the disappearance of that phenomenon, described earlier, which held the father above all responsible for the natural child. It is already suggestive that in eighteenth-century cases, following the news of the child's birth, its fate was rarely mentioned; moreover, this always happened more frequently in the city, where greater guarantees of anonymity and the possibility of temporarily or more permanently leaving the child existed. But generally there was no trace of the father's involvement. He left the scene at the notice of pregnancy, or, in rare cases, followed the case until the moment of birth, sometimes providing the woman with necessary money. But the mother had to assume entirely the onus of the illegitimate child; and this responsibility and the thought of her own good name at times prompted her to abandon the infant.

This phenomenon, entirely absent from our sources for seventeenth-century premarital relationships, appeared at the beginning of the next century with ever-greater frequency. It developed as the most striking effect of a changed attitude toward birth outside marriage. Control over heterosexual relationships had diminished sufficiently that the vision of the illegitimate child of unknown parentage, deprived of any identity, tended to prevail over that of the natural child whose origin was known to all. Even if the original community could have taken on the burden of the consequences of noninstitutionalized relationships, it showed now an ever-greater propensity to delegate to central institutions a problem that had assumed new features. The increase in hospitals for abandoned infants and for expectant mothers can be interpreted as a consequence of two parallel tendencies, the changes in custom and the assumption by centralized institutions of new functions. They constituted, in part, a response to the phenomenon of rapidly increasing abandonment of infants, which, in a broader context, may also be seen as indicating a new vision of and a new policy toward the population.[74]

Even a rapid glance at the measures adopted by the state of Savoy on illegitimate children permits one to see once again the evolution of the process we have described. The custom often reported in local customary regulations,[75] that presumed fathers were required to provide for natural children, was attested to by an edict for the city of Nice, promulgated in 1591 by the Infanta Caterina of Savoy. She established

> that the mothers, having declared with their solemn oath in court, which will be stronger yet if accompanied by some supporting testimony, could constrain those who will be respectively declared fathers to promptly give food to their children until they will have proved the contrary, under pain of law, and of paying 100 scudi to our fiscal authority.[76]

The illegitimate child was, then, the father's responsibility, but in the cases in which the parents were unknown and the child was brought to the urban hospital, this obligation fell to the community of origin, which itself assumed the onus of its maintenance. In 1609, the statute of the Hospital of Casale, "erected for the infirm, the exposed and pilgrims under the title of the Santo Spirito," declared:

> that natural sons and daughters having been brought to the said hospital, the managing rector at that time must use every diligence in order to know the father and mother of the offspring in case they come from the same city [but] if it be that they have been brought by others from outside the city, the rector must equally use diligence as above in order to know from whence they have been brought and immediately send them back to the community of that place which will have the responsibility of nourishing them.[77]

This custom, which carried the assumption that the onus of illegitimate children would fall to the community, was confirmed in an edict of 1675. It still required that abandoned babies who were not from Turin should be sent back to the communities of their origin; and, as was the case earlier, grave penalties were levied against those who, not from the city, had recourse to abandonment there, as well as against midwives who did not notify the authorities about them.[78] By 1728, however, the great number of "infants and women giving birth" in Turin made it necessary to erect an obstetric institute adjoining the hospital of San Giovanni Battista, "in order to save the hospital from the burden of the abandoned infants," who had to be sustained by subsidies from the state.[79] In 1745 an ordinance of the Most General Congregation of Carità (Charity) allowed "the Hospital of Racconigi to assume the obligation for the maintenance of abandoned babies in order to unburden the Commune." Thus began an important transition: the community's gradual escape from this obligation. Significantly, this provision seemed to be an intermediate stage in this development; the Commune of Racconigi was still compelled to donate 864 lire yearly to the Congregation as a contribution for the foodstuffs used.[80]

With the deliberations of 1770 in Turin, which prescribed "the formation of a court for dealing with the infants who would have been abandoned at night and the appointment of a guard to receive them,"[81] those who abandoned children were *de facto* freed from responsibility and cloaked in anonymity. The problem became ever more pressing. Abandoned babies apparently overwhelmed the hospitals of the city, so much so as to force the Congregation of the Hospital of San Giovanni to present a request, in 1774, to the king for help with this burden. It lamented the presence of women who were delivering and the cost of "the maintenance and care . . . begun there only forty years ago, without as yet the actual establishment of funds to sustain the burden of it." But, overall, there was the heavy presence of abandoned infants who "were secretly left"; their numbers were enormous, exceeding those of the sick by more than a third.[82] The hospital requested the creation of appropriate new institutions, or at least some kind of support. Finally, at the end of the eighteenth century, the process described here seems to have reached its conclusion: communities were no longer burdened with any obligation for abandoned babies; urban hospitals that took them in would provide for their custody and maintenance, no longer distinguishing between "natives of the city and its territory, and others from the province."[83]

The example of illegitimate children considered here suggests that an analysis of interpersonal relationships and the social networks that condition them is capable also of drawing upon an analysis of an institutional dynamic and providing some context for understanding the impact of the latter on individuals. This in turn permits one to escape a misleadingly formulated problem: the attempt to decide which comes first, the developmental change of a custom or institutional intervention.

The evolution of the attitude toward illegitimate infancy certainly has other, more complex aspects not discussed here; nevertheless, it reveals an implication central to the broader process that we have tried to describe, an evolutionary process whereby the bonds that guaranteed solidarity and protection to the woman were weakened, creating in turn a progressive focusing on her of all responsibility for sexual relations.

## Notes

1. Our primary source is the Cause matrimoniali, preserved at the Archivio della Curia Archivescovile of Turin. Among the documents collected between 1570 to 1772 by the Diocese of Turin, we considered a group of more than 600 trials. In addition, at the Archivio di Stato of Turin (sec. 1) we examined the sources contained in Materie criminali, with particular attention to trials concerned with family issues. We would like to thank Marisa Bona and Monica Pratelli, who have allowed us to consult documents from their theses.

2. On the transactional nature of heterosexual relationships, the fundamental work is that of F. Barth; see in particular *Models of Social Organization,* Royal Anthropological Institute (Glasgow), Occasional Papers, no. 23 (1966). We have also gained important ideas from the psychoanalytic school of Palo Alto. See P. Watzlawick, J. H. Beavin, and D. D. Jackson, *Pragmatics of Human Communication* (New York, 1967).

3. See A. Esmein, *Le mariage en droit canonique,* vol. 1 (Paris, 1891), and G. Le Bras, "La doctrine du mariage chez les théologiens et les canonistes depuis l'an mille," in *Dictionnaire de théologie catholique* (Paris, 1927). Some interesting material can be found in J. Gaudemet, "Législation canonique et attitudes seculières à l'égard du lien matrimonial au XVIe siècle," *Dix-septième siècle,* nos. 102–3 (1974): 15–30. For Italy in particular, see A. C. Jemolo, *Il matrimonio nel diritto canonico* (Milan, 1941); P. Rasi, *Consensus facit nuptias* (Milan, 1946); A. Marongiu, "La conclusione non formale del matrimonio nella novellistica e nella dottrina canonistica pre-tridentina," in *Studi Giuridici in onore di F. Vassalli,* vol. 2 (Turin, 1960). On this theme there is also a rich folkloric literature: see, for example, A. Van Gennep, *Manuel du folklore française contemporain,* vol. 1, pt. 1 (Paris, 1938–58); A. De Gubernatis, *Storia comparata degli usi nuziali in Italia e presso gli altri popoli indo-europei* (Milan, 1869); and E. Milani, *Usi nuziali piemontesi: Il contratto di matrimonio nelle Langhe, Archivio per lo studio delle tradizioni popolari,* vol. 23 (1907).

4. Sacro Concilio Tridentino, session 24, "Doctrina de Sacramento Matrimonii," esp. "Decretum de Reformatione Matrimonii," chap. 1.

5. By the term *community* we mean a generic entity defined by unified territory, the center of strong bonds of society and kin, characterized by feelings of identification and belonging (see esp. R. Redfield, *The Little Community and Peasant Society and Culture* [Chicago, 1963]), and R. Frankenberg, *Communities in Britain* [London, 1966]). This abstract concept, necessary for the earliest phases of our work, will, in the following pages, be partly revised to accommodate greater individual detail. A debate on the definition of community can be found in A. Macfarlane, "History, Anthropology, and the Study of Communities," *Social History* (May 1977).

6. On the evolution of matrimonial customs in relation to ecclesiastical norms, see S. Cavallo, "Fidanzamenti e divorzi in *ancien régime:* La Diocesi di Torino," *Miscellanea Storica Ligure* 9 (1978).

7. On the intervention of the Counter-Reformation Church on community social organization, see J. Bossy, "Controriforma e popolo nell'Europa cattolica," in *Le origini dell'Europa moderna,* ed. M. Rosa (Bari, 1977).

8. In the course of our research, the most useful studies on the theme of honor in society came from anthropological literature concerning the Mediterranean regions, especially the works of J. Pitt-Rivers. See the entry for "Honor" in the *International Encyclopedia of the Social Sciences* (New York, 1968); *Il popolo della Sierra* (Turin, 1976) (*The People of the Sierra* (London, 1954); *The Fate of Shechem; or, the Politics of Sex* (Cambridge, 1977). See also J.-B. Michaud, *Cohesive Force: Feud in the Medi-*

*terranean and in the Middle-East* (Oxford, 1975); J. K. Campbell, *Honour, Family, and Patronage* (Oxford, 1964); J. Davis, *People of the Mediterranean* (London, 1977); J. G. Peristiany, *Honor and Shame: The Values of Mediterranean Society* (Chicago, 1966); J. Schneider, "Of Vigilance and Virgins: Honor, Shame, and Access to Resources in Mediterranean Societies," *Ethnology* 10 (1971); P. Schneider, "Honor and Conflict in a Sicilian Town," *Anthropological Quarterly* 42 (1969).

9. Archivio Arcivescovile di Torino (hereafter cited as AAT), 9/1 3 (1618), Sargato-Boganone case.

10. AAT, 9/1 2 (1616), Ollivero-Cravero case. Emphasis added.

11. AAT, 9/1 2 (1616), Richiardo-Bosca case. Emphasis added.

12. For a definition of this state, see in particular V. Turner, *Simboli e momenti della comunità* (Brescia, 1975), p. 14ff. (*Dramas, Fields, and Metaphors: Symbolic Action in Human Society* [Ithaca, 1974]).

13. The object exchanged generally had a pronounced symbolic significance: one is dealing with *stringhe, bindelli,* rings that called to mind the bond being formed. On the nonreciprocal character of the gift, see A. Burguire, "Le rituel du mariage en France: Pratiques ecclésiastiques et pratiques populaires (XVI–XVIII siècles)," *Annales E.S.C.* 3 (May-June 1978).

14. Rarely are cases encountered where women trick men; and it is significant, given what we say below about this, that widows were almost always the ones who might get away with tricking a man.

15. Often the woman's family, attracted by a good relationship, aided the couple and thus later became involved in the sanctions.

16. AAT, 9/1 37 (1737), Gariglia-Baudino case.

17. On the protection that "honor-rank," that is, the social position of the family, could furnish to "honor-virtue," and thus to personal conduct, see Pitt-Rivers, *Fate of Shechem,* and J. Davis, *People of the Mediterranean.*

18. Because of the number of couples who did not fit institutional modes of definition, this discussion refers not only to matrimonial relationships but also to all stable relationships.

19. On the characteristics attributed to widows, see Pitt-Rivers, *Fate of Shechem,* p. 44ff.

20. G. Borgiato, for example, insisted that he wished to marry M. Tortona only on the condition that she "abandon the evil company with whom, more often before than now [after their acquaintance], she had had sexual intercourse." AAT, 9/1 36 (1731), Borgiato-Tortona case.

21. AAT, 9/1 43 (1750), Grosso-Tortona case.

22. See Pitt-Rivers, *Fate of Shechem,* p. 25.

23. See Michaud, *Cohesive Force,* p. 221.

24. Archivio di Stato of Turin, sec. 1, Materie criminali, mazzo 36, fasc. 2 (1738).

25. On youth groups and their organizations in early modern Europe, see, especially, N. Z. Davis, "The Reasons of Misrule," in *Society and Culture in Early Modern France* (Stanford, 1975), and, by the same author, "Some Tasks and Themes in the Study of Popular Religion," in *The Pursuit of Holiness in Late Medieval and Renaissance Religion,* ed. H. A. Oberman (Leiden, 1974). See also S. T. Freeman, *Neighbors: The Social Contract in a Castilian Hamlet* (Chicago, 1970), esp. chaps. 2 and 4, and E. L. Peters, "Aspects of the Control of Moral Ambiguities: A Comparative Analysis of Two Culturally Disparate Modes of Social Control," in *The Allocation of Responsibility,* ed. M. Gluckman (Manchester, 1972.)

26. On the function of ritual, see M. Gluckman, ed., *Essays on the Ritual of Social Relations* (Manchester, 1966).

27. AAT, 9/1 37 (1737), Rossi-Pirra case.

28. On the freedoms accorded by parents during courtship, see P. Caspard, "Conceptions prénuptiales et développement du capitalism dans la Principauté de Neuchâtel (1678–1820)," *Annales E.S.C.* (July-Aug. 1974).

29. The high number of male testimonies, beyond confirming the role of control attributed to that group, suggested the tendency to accord less space in the courtroom to depositions by the female group. This characteristic of the documents accentuated the difficulty in reconstructing the functions of this group, difficulties that were already created by its structure.

30. See the example of forced marriage on pp. 90–91.

31. On the effect on social control implied by the superimposition of more roles, see M. Gluckman, "Coesione e conflitto sociale in Africa," in *La politica della parentela,* ed. G. Arrighi and L. Passerini (Milan, 1976).

32. On the egalitarian motives present in peasant society, see G. M. Foster, "Peasant Society and the Image of Limited Good," *American Anthropologist* 67, no. 2 (1965), esp. pp. 296–97, and Pitt-Rivers, *Fate of Shechem,* pp. 32–34.

33. On the diffusion of these practices in Piedmont, see C. Corrain and P. Zampini, *Documenti etnografici e folkloristici nei sinodi italiani* (Bologna, 1970), pp. 207–8, 223–25. More general sources are A. van Gennep, *Les rites de passage* (Paris, 1909), and N. Z. Davis, "Reasons of Misrule."

34. AAT, 9/1 39 (1742), Rizzioni-Mutta case.

35. See, for example, Pitt-Rivers, *Il popolo della Sierra,* pp. 102, 107.

36. Both Felice Berardo and Giò Vaudagnotto were 21 years old, outsiders to the community, from the outskirts of Turin, and sons of good families. Their interest in Lucia Gillio could be interpreted by their coevals of Carignano as aggression, a threat to an owned resource in their territory.

37. AAT, 9/1 37 (1752), Siminino-Gillio case, deposition of Giò Andrea Giardino.

38. For example, the youths of Varisella stopped visiting the house of Domenica Bertina, who had broadcast the fact of her pregnancy far and wide. AAT, 9/1 37 (1736), Bertina-Audiero case.

39. This severity was not aimed at preventing the relationship. The promised marriage would later be staged as a farce in order to make fun of her. AAT, 9/6 36 (1769), Alberico-Franceschetti case.

40. AAT, 9/6 9 (1608), Paglieta-Acastello case.

41. Some useful observations on the characteristics of community judgment of sexual conduct may be found in E. P. Thompson, "Rough Music: Le charivari anglais," *Annales E.S.C.* 27 (1972).

42. On the capacity of this type of group to define and diffuse norms for behavior, see A. L. Epstein, "Gossip, Norms, and Social Network," in *Social Networks in Urban Situations,* ed. J. C. Mitchell (Manchester, 1969).

43. On the functions of female gossip and the sanctions to which it was subjected, see J. Naish, "Desirade: A Negative Case," in *Women United, Women Divided,* ed. P. Caplan and J. M. Bujra (London, 1978), and M. Wolf, "Chinese Women: Old Skills in a New Context," in *Woman, Culture, and Society,* ed. M. Z. Rosaldo and L. Lamphere (Stanford, 1974).

44. Archivio Comunale di Chieri, vol. 44, art. 114, par. 1 (1567), Caterina-De Vittoni case. We would like to thank Luciano Allegra for pointing out this case to us. It seems important, even if it is from an earlier period than the one we are examining.

45. AAT 9/1 41 (1744), Enrietto-Bertina case.

46. On female solidarity, see V. Maher, "Kin, Clients, and Accomplices: Relationships among Women in Morocco," in *Sexual Division and Society,* ed. D. L. Barker and S. Allen (London, 1974); Caplan and Bujra, *Women United, Women Divided,*

the entire anthology; L. Lamphere, "Strategies, Cooperation, and Conflict among Women in Domestic Groups," and C. B. Stack, "Sex Roles and Survival Strategies in an Urban Black Community," both in Rosaldo and Lamphere, *Woman, Culture, and Society.*

47. AAT 9/1 39 (1742), Vinazza-Lampiano case.

48. AAT 9/1 4 (1632), Ollivero-Grosso case.

49. AAT, Registrum Sententiarum, 9/2 3 (1607). This page was erroneously inserted into the register of sentences.

50. On the *Impedimenti Dirimenti* of the promise, see *Degli sponsali e del matrimonio secondo il gius canonico e civile* (Turin, 1939), p. 10.

51. The determination of the correct amount of the dowry was based upon the status of the woman's family. On the controversies caused by this custom, see F. Arro, *Del diritto dotale secondo i principi del gius romano e della giurisprudenza dei magistrati* (Asti, 1834).

52. In our research, we made use of the methodology of network analysis, which has been widely discussed in the anthropological literature: in this essay, we wish to suggest its importance and applicability for historical research, even with all the limits that historical documents present for this type of reconstruction. For an essential bibliography, see J. Boissevain, *Friends of Friends, Networks, Manipulators, and Coalitions* (New York, 1974); E. Bott, *Family and Social Network* (London, 1957); A. Mayer, "The Significance of Quasi-Groups," in *The Social Anthropology of Complex Societies,* ed. M. Banton (London, 1966); J. C. Mitchell, "Networks, Norms, and Institutions," in ibid.; J. C. Mitchell, "Social Networks," *Annual Review of Anthropology* 3 (1974); Mitchell, *Social Networks in Urban Situations,* entire anthology. We use the term *cohesiveness* in the sense indicated by Bott, in *Family and Social Networks,* p. 59, and in A. L. Epstein, "The Network and Urban Social Organizations," in *Social Networks in Urban Situations.*

53. On these characteristics of early modern cities, see, for example, C. H. Chevalier, *Classi lavoratrici e classi pericolose* (Bari, 1976); R. Cobb, *The Police and the People* (Oxford, 1970); Y. Kaplow, *I lavoratori poveri nella Parigi pre-rivoluzionaria* (Bologna, 1976); and R. Muchembled, *Culture populaire et culture des élites* (Paris, 1978), esp. p. 147ff.

54. AAT, 9/1 4 (1632), Opperti-Vigna case.

55. AAT, 9/6 11 (1649), case heard by the fiscal solicitor against Bernardino Bussi and the married couple, Domenico and Domenica Azano.

56. Such permutations in the urban situation are also revealed by N. Z. Davis, regarding the function of control by youth groups. See "Reasons of Misrule," p. 109ff.

57. AAT, 9/6 20 (1709), Acta criminalia fisci contra Mariam Movinam.

58. AAT, 9/6 9 (1623), Acta inquisitionalia fisci contra Margheritam Sachettam.

59. Economic independence could sometimes reequilibrate the picture; some women, mostly widows who had inherited property (land or shops), seemed to have been able to behave more freely outside of the schemas of conduct required for their sex, taking for themselves roles traditionally reserved for men, whether in choosing marriage or in refusing it in favor of pursuing their own activities. In a large majority of the cases, however, because work was personal, it apparently did not free the woman from the necessity for male protection; the society we are describing anticipated that women would work, even outside of the domestic sphere, but not as an alternative to matrimony. Small-scale sales, particularly of greens and herbs, was the occupation we have found most frequently among married women. If these activities could furnish them with greater security and respect, especially in the family circle, and could create a resource, for example, in moments of matrimonial crisis, they nevertheless did not substantially alter the decisions about life and the quality of relation-

ships with men. Cultural pressures were such that an attitude of greater independence in relation to a man—often accompanied by manifestations of nonprejudice and irony vis-à-vis men—were found more easily in females filling roles such as widowhood that in themselves were already ambiguous and characterized by undefined honor, rather than in young, unmarried women. On the theme of female labor in traditional societies, see the important article by L. A. Tilly and J. W. Scott, "Women's Work and the Family in Nineteenth-Century Europe," in *The Family in History,* ed. C. Rosenberg (Philadelphia, 1975).

60. E. Shorter has often advanced the hypothesis of a "revolution of erotic customs," tied to the diffusion of extradomestic labor. See especially "Illegitimacy, Sexual Revolution, and Social Change in Modern Europe," *Journal of Interdisciplinary History* 2, no. 2 (1971): 237ff. Among the numerous criticisms of this interpretation, see J. W. Scott, L. A. Tilly, and M. Cohen, "Women's Work and European Fertility Patterns," *Journal of Interdisciplinary History* 6 (1976).

61. On the characteristics of this emigration, see G. Levi, "Mobilità della popolazione e immigrazione a Torino nella prima metà del Settecento," *Quaderni Storici,* no. 17 (May–Aug. 1971): 553.

62. AAT, 9/1 38 (1740), Marzonet-Garbolino case.

63. See especially Michaud, *Cohesive Force,* p. 226.

64. AAT, 9/6 9 (1608), Paglieta-Accastello case.

65. Deposition of nob. ms. Agostino Pistone di Racconigi.

66. For analyses of this type of relationship, see, for example, Boissevain, *Friends of Friends,* chaps. 6–8; Campbell, *Honour, Family, and Patronage,* pp. 213–66; E. Wolf, *Peasants* (Englewood Cliffs, N.J., 1966), esp. pp. 60–95; Wolf, "Kinship, Friendship, and Patron-Client Relations in Complex Society," in *Social Anthropology of Complex Societies.*

67. A measure of this change in custom seems to be those same ecclesiastical norms, which became even sterner than those of the Council of Trent, defining more restrictively the rules for the validity of marriage promises. Depositions by Benedetto XIV, Instit. Eccl. 46, no. 15.

68. The results of three twenty-year surveys of matrimonial disputes between the beginning of the seventeenth century and the second half of the eighteenth make it clear that the percentage of marriage promises accompanied by sexual intercourse suffered a notable decline: present in 89 percent of the cases between 1600 and 1630, they appeared in 34 percent between 1730 and 1750 and shrank to 16 percent between 1752 and 1772.

69. AAT, 9/1 38 (1739), Ghiga-Bianco case.

70. AAT, 9/1 36 (1731), Peirato-Chiaberta case.

71. AAT, 9/1 42 (1746), Gavatta-Cerruti case. Emphasis added.

72. See Bossy, "Controriforma e popolo."

73. See esp. *Constitutioni della Prima Sinodo Diocesana di Torino celebrata dall'Ill.mo e Rev.mo Monsig. Carlo Broglia Arcivescovo . . .* for Pizzamiglio Stampatore Archiepiscopale (Turin, 1596), pp. 66–77; the 1666 Synod of Vercelli, cited by Corrain-Zampini, *Documenti,* p. 221; *Sinodus Diocesana Taurinensis habita in Ecclesia Metropolitana ab Illustrissimo et Reverendissimo Domino Micaele Beyamo Archiepise Taurinensi,* (Turin, 28 May 1570), p. 36. Among the manuals, we note, in particular, *Raccolta di vari esercizi di Pietà e Istruzioni* (Turin, 1792).

74. See, in this regard, W. Kula, "Histoire, démocratie, statistique," in *Mélanges en l'honneur de F. Braudel* (Toulouse, 1973), pp. 279–88.

75. For example, the local law of Valsesia (Curia Maratella, cap. 144, *De spuriis alendis*) established that "quod si quis rem habuerit cum aliqua muliere, et quae postea infantem aliquem seu infantes aliquos provocaverit, et negaverit ipsum talem infantem

seu tales infantes esse suum vel suos, quod statur juramento illius talis matris; et quod postquam illa juraverit illum vel illos esse suos, qui negabat ille talis compellatur per Jusdicentem curia Maratellae omnibus juris remedis ad suscipiendum et alendum, et suscipiant et alent illum talem infantem seu infantes pro suis et tamquam suos"; cited in F. A. Duboin, *Raccolta per ordine di materie delle Leggi* (Turin, 1846), vol. 12, p. 46.

76. "Lettere Patenti di S.A.S. la Duchessa di Savoja . . . ," 13 Dec. 1591, in Duboin, *Raccolta,* vol. 12, pp. 46–47.

77. "Ordini dell'ospedale riformati nel 1609," in Duboin, *Raccolta,* vol. 12, pp. 478–79.

78. "Ordine per la città di Torino," 14 Sept. 1675, cited in G. B. Borelli, *Editti Antichi e Nuovi dei Sovrani Principi della Real Casa di Savoja,* (Turin, 1681), bk. 1, tit. 13, p. 263.

79. See Duboin, *Raccolta,* vol. 12, p. 633.

80. Ibid., pp. 573–74.

81. Ibid., p. 634.

82. Ibid., p. 631.

83. Ibid., p. 489.

# 5 ❧ The Spirit of Fornication: Virtue of the Soul and Virtue of the Body in Friuli, 1600–1800

*by Luisa Accati*

By the seventeenth century the phenomenon of European witchcraft was, according to historians, in decline. In a few villages in mid-seventeenth-century Friuli, however, the documentation suggests the importance of trials, even in this period. In fact, the intensity of sixteenth-century battles having cooled, these trials enable us to see how the Church intended to reassert its system of control. Also, female and male witches were interrogated as witnesses of a substantially tamed phenomenon, whose meanings could now be determined more precisely. And crucially, the diminished tension between the inquisitors and the faithful allows an analysis of how the prevalence of women in witchcraft was linked to the female body.

"We collect the products of the body's labor, we collect its written and oral texts; but the very numerous and varied possibilities of this instrument, universal and understood by all, that is the human body we ignore."[1] Marcel Mauss realized very clearly the social relevance of the use of the body and how behavior was affected by education and by the duties that society assigned to individuals: "The physical education of all ages and of both sexes constitutes an enormous quantity of unobserved particulars which need to be observed."[2] Moreover, in "Les éléments de la magie," he affirmed that women "are considered everywhere more suited to magic than men, due more to social perceptions of them than to their physical characteristics."[3]

Although Mauss intuited the importance of the body's diverse

---

"Lo Spirito della fornicazione: Virtù dell'anima e virtù del' corpo in Friuli, fra '600 e '700," *Quaderni Storici,* no. 41 (1979): 644–72. Translated by Margaret A. Gallucci. Marina Sorzano transcribed many of the documents used in this article. The documents are preserved in the Archivio Archivescovile of Udine (hereafter cited as ACAU).

meanings and uses as well as the way the Inquisition had exploited and sustained prejudices against women,[4] he did not link these elements. Perhaps he was led astray, more than he knew, "by an intellectual and moral formation as prudish as was that of the neo-Kantianism" reigning in universities at the end of the nineteenth century.[5] The documentation that we find at the Archepiscopal Archives in Udine demonstrates, in fact, that the particularities of the female body seemed to be the source of many of the "social perceptions" regarding women in general and witches in particular.

Polidoro della Frattina, priest of Brazzano, was a scrupulous and precise man. On 18 May 1645 he wrote to the Inquisitor of the diocese of Aquilea and Concordia, assuring him that "I am not far from taking action, and each day I receive greater enlightenment . . . so much so that even daughters denounce the superstitions of their mothers. I take minute notes, which I keep near me, in the presence of witnesses to validate to a greater degree what has been attested."[6] In effect, he collected all sorts of *preenti,* that is, spells and invocations, in abundant detail, sending for anyone reputed to know about such things. In the course of the depositions, whoever was named he summoned and interrogated, making note of those who did not come forward. He moved from city to city to ease the process of collecting testimony and the investigation.

From 10 May to 24 May 1645 no fewer than thirty people, twenty-seven women and three men, came before him. They were successively denounced in a chain reaction, one after another and by each other. In Brazzano and Giassico, a great fear of being caught and unmasked as a person who knew and performed spells spread. But the chain of denunciations also involved Percoto, Farra, Visinale, Cormons, Chiopis, and Rutars. The tension was at a fever pitch among women; men were less involved. It could not have been otherwise, given that spells were divided into two types, both relating to women. Some had a feminine sexual component; others were popular medical practices, spells against illnesses. Women were the ones who treated the sick; moreover, the illnesses were mostly those affecting children or connected with childbirth and lactation.

On 10 May 1645, in Brazzano, Margherita and Antonia del Conte, aunt and niece, denounced Madalina del Conte, wife of Bastiano, and Zannuta Morguto.[7] On 19 May, Madalina presented herself and confirmed Margherita and Antonia's accusations: "About ten years ago I made the said Zannuta . . . ride naked on a yoke [Editor's note: this appears to have been the curved piece of wood used by women to carry heavy loads in the fields] and go around through the fields imploring often at dawn, 'Flee, flee, furry caterpillars or my cunt will eat you.' " ("Fui, fui ruie et il mio con[8] ti mangiuie.") She had not done it to offend God, but to drive away the caterpillars from the fields. Her mother had taught it to her "when she was young": she also taught her the "spell of crossing herself on her breasts, in the name of the Father and of the Son and of the Holy Spirit. She further adds that her aforesaid mother is a woman given to superstitions. It is remembered about her that once, threatened by a storm, she lifted her skirts from behind and cried against the wind this formula: 'Nothing, nothing may do more harm than this ass' ['Nul, nul fa tant mal, cu' po fa chist cul'] and the said mother knows the spell for caterpillars, for adoring the nettle and another to drive away fever."[9]

Madalina, before coming to testify, had already been to her mother Svalda's house in Rutars to persuade her also to tell the priest about "these matters concerning the Holy Office." But her mother had refused because the chaplain of Rutars, Don Zorzi Salomon, had given her absolution and had told her that confession was sufficient for her sins. Svalda, however, was worried and went to confide in a neighbor, Pasca, daughter of Nadal: she admitted having used spells and unwisely recounted some of them to her. Svalda also confessed to Pasca that her husband, Gioseffo, would not let her go to the priest, as her daughter requested; and even that Gioseffo wanted to beat the daughter if she continued to insist. Pasca went immediately to report this conversation to the priest;[10] poor Svalda, caught between two fears, decided to present herself, unbeknownst to her husband, on 22 May at the parish in Brazzano.

Svalda knew many spells, and she explained each in detail:

> She has gone about with her clothes raised showing her shameful parts in order to chase away the caterpillars which were causing damage there, always saying while she was moving, "Flee, flee, furry caterpillars or my cunt will eat you." . . . When there was danger of a storm and also after getting married she raised up her skirts, and exposing her genitals, she said these words towards her rear: "Nothing, nothing may do more harm than this ass" and in doing this action she said the words only once. She had cast the spell on a woman's breasts more than twenty times and while saying the spell, she took a comb and with it she made a circle around the breasts three

> times, saying each time, in the name of the Father and of the Son and of the Holy Spirit. . . . When her daughter Madalina was sick with fever she took a live frog and, attaching it to a string, put it around her neck and wore it for the space of three days and then she threw it away. After becoming a mother she did the same to her little son for a fever, making him wear it around his neck three days in the aforesaid manner.[11]

But Madalina del Conte was still not satisfied; she returned again to the priest. On the way she met her son Bastiano, who "admonished her, saying that she should be ashamed . . . and that they were astonished at her and he did his best so that she would turn back."[12] Madalina was not dissuaded; she went on to Don Polidoro's. This time she denounced her sister-in-law: even she had invoked the spell against swollen breasts (*madrazza*).[13] Then she went to Farra, searched for Zannuta, and brought her to the priest. Zannuta confirmed having used the spell for caterpillars: "when she did this she was a little girl."[14]

Meanwhile, the priest summoned Menia, wife of Mattia of Rutars, the sister-in-law accused by Madalina, as well as the daughter-in-law of Svalda. On 25 May Menia came forward and confirmed Madalina's accusations, naming many other women. Even her mother had taught her some spells: when Menia was a child she made her go naked astride a yoke, and "she taught her to cast a spell on male witches, a spell she had recited often before she knew that it was a sin." Two other women taught her some ways to foretell who her husband would be and how many years she would live; a third woman taught her and others when they were young the spell against storms, raising their skirts. She also accused a man, Simone of Nadal, who knew a spell against animal illnesses.[15]

Orsula Miano was present at Madalina's first deposition. She denounced in turn a sister-in-law, Zannuta Bon, widow of Zuan, as "a woman truly given to superstition." Zannuta allegedly had had a woman come to her house and had chatted familiarly with her for three days about spells; she knew some spells for deafness and possessed an unguent that could make one grow, by applying it behind the knees, under the arms, and below the ribs. On 22 May Zannuta Bon arrived at the priest's, infuriated, and "with improper words" protested her innocence and declared that "she had not done any acts of witchcraft."[16]

Meanwhile, other women presented themselves to the priest: on 20 May Catarina Visintino, denounced by Madalina Giacopito, admitted having learned many spells from Giusta Monchias of San Andrat,[17] including a spell for foot problems. Don Polidoro reported that "she did it believing that it wasn't a sin and she believed this to a greater degree because once my predecessor Reverend Father Gasparo admonished her in confession, having heard that this Maria of Biasio from said Villa of San Andrat was doing this spell for serious foot problems. A short time afterwards it happened that this above-named priest sprained his foot. And he sent for her to come and because the words cured him he even gave her permission to continue to do this spell. And because of this she, judging that she was doing good, continued to do so for many years. He added that people even went to her with as much devotion as if they had gone to a priest's house to get Jesus's blessing for a fever." Catarina also knew *preenti* for fever, caterpillars, and catarrh. Her daughter, Apollonia Miano, accused by Antonia Fabro, admitted to her brother, in the presence of her mother, having used the spell against caterpillars and said that she had learned it from her grandmother: "she had done it at other times to many people, believing that it wasn't a sin and in the future she will not do it."[18]

On 21 May, Madalina Piano confirmed the denunciation made against her by two of Visinale's sisters-in-law: she had climbed nude on the yoke in order to drive away caterpillars.[19] On 23 May, a new series of denunciations followed: Antonia Vidir, a married woman from Giassico, denounced Madalina del Conte, wife of Antonio, who was also from Giassico. Madalina denied having cast spells against storms: "she said it was not true that . . . she had shown her rear parts in broad daylight, but that it was quite true that she had taken her baby son once and lifted his shirt off the said parts, marking the weather and saying, 'Nothing, nothing, may do more harm than this ass.'" Madalina Piano reported that when she was a child her mother had sent her out "nude on a yoke to ride around the garden with the typical incantation, 'Flee, flee, furry caterpillars or my cunt will eat you.'" She had also said the spell for swollen breasts and, like all the others, asserted that she had performed these actions not knowing that she was offending the Good Lord.[20]

On 24 May, Marcolina Bresciotto came before Don Polidoro and admitted what she had already learned from her sister-in-law Maurizia. Marcolina had said to Maurizia that, in order to drive away the caterpillars from a turnip field, "she should find a virgin and have her sit naked astride a yoke and go around the turnip field saying,'Flee, flee, furry caterpillars or my cunt will eat you.' " Marcolina "only did this because she had learned it when she was a child and she had actually done it once as a child in order to obey her sister-in-law. . . . but she had not done it to offend the Good Lord."[21] Maria Del Bon taught Pasca Silvestro how, in order to cure the headache of one of her children, "she should find two young girls who were menstruating. The girls should carry the child to a vineyard of cividin grapes [*vite di cividino*], holding the creature by the hand so that they made him pass between the vines three times, passing him from one to the other back and forth and saying certain words"; she denied, however, "the part about menstruation."[22] Appolonia Favietto was sent to Don Polidoro by her confessor: she had used the spell against caterpillars and, like Pasca and Maria Del Bon, knew spells against fever.[23]

❧ Don Polidoro also searched out the "superstitions" of men, which divided into two basic categories: spells for animals and magic for seducing women. On 10 May 1645, "blind Zuan of Giassico" said that "it's been about twelve years since he started to do this spell, which will be explained below. It was taught to him by his grandfather, and to do it he used this ritual of speaking into the ears of sick animals nine times, and he did this really believing that it cured them."[24] He was so convinced of the effectiveness of his spells that he recounted how he had gone from stall to stall doing this, and people had paid him: so salutary were his spells that when Hortensio of Mariano did not keep his promise to pay him for a spell used on his animals, Zuan spoke to "the justice of Cormons and in the end—the report concluded—it was decided that Hortensio would have to pay him the whole sum." "Besides this, he said spells in the aforementioned manner for other people's animals . . . and in particular, for an animal of Nardino of Vitinal he received as payment four portions of soup. He also treated nine animals of Zonte Visintino of Giassico and one of Giacomo del Conte of Brazzano; these animals were the only ones to survive and if Zuan had not healed these animals with his spell, he firmly believed that they all would have died."

Zuan was unwilling to renounce his profession of popular veterinarian, as was Gasparo Gasparutto, also of Giassico. Gasparo knew how to keep wolves away: "he had demonstrated this with experiments many times."[25]

Don Giacobbi, priest of Auronzo, "knew how to make it rain and how to swell the river waters." But his techniques were quite different from those used by the women of Brazzano: "he did this because he has inherited certain books, as was commonly believed."[26]

This agrarian and therapeutic male magic was dominated by tools or by knowledge. It made no use of the body, because no part of the male body had magical powers. Only one male body participated in the spells of women—the newborn infant of Madalina del Conte of Giassico. She raised the clothes from his bottom in order to perform a spell against bad weather, but it did not work: "a storm struck in these parts the baby, who, crying, she brought back into the house."[27] The presumed magical power of the son derived from his still being a part of his mother, or more specifically, a part of her womb. In this sense, the magical virtues of the Benandanti (examined by Carlo Ginzburg in *The Night Battles*) were also of a feminine nature: the sign of their magical predestination was in fact the *camisiutta* (the afterbirth, or caul). Having been born enveloped in the placenta, they brought into the world with them a piece of the maternal womb.

The magical power of the female womb was central; its capacity to give life also had the strength, by analogy, to confront and destroy that which was opposed to life and fertility—just as, by analogy, one who knew how to give life also knew how to give death. Women, then, had a direct relationship with the afterlife. Thus, women were the most dangerous adversaries of priests: they literally made problematic the priest's hegemony over the sacred.

During the seventeenth century, the Church set out to absorb into the ecclesiastical-religious category of the sacred any and every magical phenomenon.[28] The capacity to intervene in life and death had been a part of both the world of magic and the world of the sacred. The magical sphere in mid-seventeenth century Friuli was feminine and was enclosed in the womb; the sacred sphere was masculine and resided in knowledge of the divinely revealed order. The Church was guaranteed the interpretation of the revealed order: each man traversing the ranks of the ecclesiastical hierarchy could have access to it. At the same time, understanding had various levels; the Church reserved for itself the highest ones but recognized an area of "professional" knowledge suitable for combating sickness and death with earthly remedies linked to empirical practices. The efficacy of these practices did not interfere with the power of the priest; they were placed on another level where they could then coexist with the clergy's power. Don Polidoro's approach toward blind Zuan or Gasparo Gasparutto fell within a more general concern to define the still-uncertain boundaries that would authorize and contain lay knowledge. Masculine therapeutic magic in seventeenth-century Friuli was without boundaries in lay consciousness; popular doctors or veterinarians and learned professionals could coexist. On 24 April 1648, Giulio Superchio testified before the Inquisitor, "I was more than begged by Signor Cristoforo Federli of Gemona who, in love with one of his servants, could not fulfill his designs with her, that I should help him by means of some superstitious aid, since he felt that *as a doctor* I would have some secrets."[29]

The magical power of these men was manifested not only beyond their bodies but also in an area that was no longer linked to the supernatural. Reaffirming the effectiveness of their spells, Zuan and Gasparo limited their responsibility to the sphere of a type of popular medicine and veterinary science based on "knowledge" that was handed down and of assured success. The doctor Giulio Superchio, for his part, wanted to eliminate every suspicion of magic from his "science."

Women, on the contrary, were not able to discuss their powers with priests. It was impossible to distinguish levels between their power and that of priests: such powers were, in fact, not homogeneous but irreconcilably opposed. In the end, how could women defend the efficacy of their spells without affirming more or less indirectly that life and death were rooted in the body, not the soul?

Even men, in the magic used for seducing women, in contrast to their other spells, took a stand as direct enemies of the priest. But, without a magical autonomy of the body like that of women, magicians and priests had to compete for the same sacred quality. The magic for seducing women consisted in putting some herbs under the altar and letting nine masses be said over them: thus rendered magical, the herbs allowed the seduction of as many and as diverse women as one wanted. Don Polidoro warned that there was, in this practice, a clear opposition to the Church which could not be negotiated and which had to be confronted, rejected, and suppressed as sacrilege: men were trying to obtain the same powers over the sacred as the priest. Thus, when one of these rituals came to his attention in December of 1647 in Rutars, he notified the Holy Office and straight away called together the parochial priest of Rutars, Don Zorzi Salomon (whom he could not have had much faith in after the quick absolution conceded to Svalda), and three men.

> Father Inquisitor, I received a letter from Your Most Reverend Father around one o'clock yesterday to come to you as soon as possible for matters of the Holy Office. In the letter . . . you asked me to bring together Domenico of Perin, Giovanni, son of the said Domenico Perino, and Blasio, son of Giorgio Cantiano, all of Rutars. In order to obey the Holy Tribunal, I immediately had the three citizens present themselves yesterday, and early this morning I left my house again and I have brought with me the said three citizens.[30]

Don Zorzi recounted that while celebrating mass, after drinking from the chalice, he noticed under the altar cloth some clover, rolled up in a leaf and secured with an herb. At the end of mass, he showed the herb to the faithful and reminded everyone, with severe words, what a reproachable sin such an action was. Leaving the church, he met the three men and told them about the incident; the three imprudently revealed that they had already heard about this magic, and this was enough to make them suspects.

Giovanni Perino repeated to the Inquisitor what he had already told Don Zorzi: "Someone wanted to teach me also that a four-leaf clover, if I would put it under the altar cloth and would have nine masses said over it, with that herb, I could have had any girl come to me, and any woman whom I might want."[31]

Magic *ad amorem* of this type was extensive and known to all; Giorgio, Giovanni's brother, a child of eight or nine, joking on the street with some girls who were talking about what happened in church, "said that that herb had been put under the altar cloth so that he could go to bed with the *polzetis* [young chicks] and he said it laughing," and the girls laughed, too, in their turn.[32]

This magic is most significant for understanding the changes wrought by the conflict between the Church and the faithful. The sacred and the powers over the sacred had been sources of great ideological battles: from the fourteenth to the sixteenth century, the Church aggressively repressed whoever contested its definition. Heretics, mostly men, thought they could interpret the sacred and have a direct, unmediated relationship with it. Persecutions first, religious wars later, suppressed and rejected this hypothesis. The complexity and variety of issues contested during the Reformation and the

Counter-Reformation were reordered in the seventeenth century; the points reached were very different, but, in substance, full individual liberty in relations with the sacred was not observed in Protestant countries and was wholly denied in Catholic ones.

In Friuli in 1645, ideological power over the sacred was solidly in the hands of the Church, and no one dared to oppose its monopoly anymore. To those who wanted to use the sacred for their particular and unmentionable ends, there remained nothing but to steal a little of it from the priest, with ingenious strategies. The persecution of heretics eliminated the mostly ideological male magic; the persecution of witches completed the task, destroying the mostly corporal female magic.

The grotesque medieval body of which Mikhail Bakhtin spoke was a body in motion. It was never finished or defined: it was always in the process of construction, of creation and, in turn, on the verge of constructing another body. Such a body absorbed the world and was absorbed in it. For this, the essential role of the grotesque body was entrusted to the womb and the phallus, its own parts, the places where it went beyond itself, broke its own limits, began to build another (second) body. All excretions and orifices were characterized by the fact that they were the frontiers where the boundaries between two bodies and between the body and the world were overcome.[33] Such a body, in mid-seventeenth century Friuli, was still the body of Madalina, Svalda, and Zannuta; it maintained its functions of continuity with the world. The vagina freed the earth from caterpillars; the anus kept tempests at bay, humbled the heavens, and turned the world upside down. Of the Dionysian splendors of the phallus, there remained only a weak trace: the comb used to make the sign of the cross on the breasts in the spell against swollen breasts.[34]

The grotesque period had been in essence a juxtaposition, two phases of development at once coexistent: beginning and end, winter and spring, death and birth. The relationship between mother and daughter, between daughter-in-law and sister-in-law, between the old woman Svalda, the young woman Madalina, and the little girl Zannuta was tied to a conception "of the cyclic time of natural and biological life,"[35] for which each moment of life, as each season, produced and consumed its own fruits.

Virginity for these Friulian women peasants was the moment of maximum potentiality of the female body, when fertility was at its fullest and when no measure of it had yet been utilized, analogous in this to flowering plants. This virginity ended with menarche, when blood issued from the flesh, "because the life of all flesh is blood." A woman who had menstruated, then, had to realize her fertility with procreation, otherwise the generative force would flow away from her with her blood. Madalina had children; her vital force was already focused, applied, and used in part, while that of Zannuta, a virgin, retained a complete and generalized "symbolic efficacy."[36] In the spells based on the use of the body, the quantity of fertility necessary varied according to the amount of danger to be confronted. Virginity was the female status that could combat death, death of the harvest and death of children, while one could use spells against a storm "even after marriage," as Svalda said.

The virginity of the Madonna, in its ecclesiastical-religious conception, seems to have some aspects in common with the physical virginity of Zannuta: the Madonna was the woman who, although a mother, had not lost anything of her fertility. In reality, the Church based its concept of virginity on the model of biblical sanctity.

Regarding the body, in Leviticus "the idea of holiness was given an external, physical expression in the wholeness of the body seen as a perfect container."[37] It was an impervious membrane that had no continuity with the world, with the Earth, with corporal baseness;[38] rather, it was of God as an image and likeness, and of heaven with its spiritual and ascetic heights. It was a body based on domination of itself, on completeness and on separation from anything that was not of its nature.[39] The saint of Leviticus is a male saint, whose body eschews its own contaminated secretions. The Church transferred these norms of sanctity to the female body, rendering fertility a good that, in order to be realized, had to be contaminated and degraded: virginity and fecundity became contradictory. The Church set out to transmute the virginity of Zannuta, an active, fertile, and inalienable virtue of the body, into a passive virtue of the soul. Physical integrity was the objectification of this, an objectification rendering it expropriable and threatening.[40]

In Friuli, the second half of the sixteenth century was marked both by an ever more rigid distinction between the culture of the dominant classes and that of artisans and peasants and by the imposition of a single vision on the masses.[41] If we see the grotesque medieval body as the image and root of peasant culture, preaching and indoctrination seem to have struck first and most easily at the grotesque phallic body rather than the grotesque uterine body.

The masses' indoctrination was a process that could not be reversed, but the images and means of this indoctrination were obtained, suggested, and reinforced by the results of the Inquisition. During the entire fifteenth century, resistance by the faithful was strong; many beliefs were difficult to stifle; and many were the Church's uncertainties about which cults to support, which customs to absorb into Christian practice, and which to destroy.

❧ Between 1640 and 1650, the confessions of "diabolical witches" closely adhered to the model of the diabolical sabbat spread by the Church. The testimonies regularly included all the nefarious deeds attributed to witches: the journey to the sabbat, the sabbat, sexual intercourse with the devil, offenses to sacred images and to Christian worship, theft of consecrated objects. Their aims were to kill babies, to dry up women's and cow's milk, and so on. These were narrations, then, whose principal purpose was to please the Inquisitor by confirming the ecclesiastical demonological model. "Diabolical witches" were all in ambiguous situations: they were widows, orphans, unmarried women.

Bartolomea Golizza, wife of Simone di Lenarduz, had been born sixty years earlier in Colloredo but lived in Farra. She remained there even after the death of her husband, barely supporting herself as a spinner. Bartolomea's companions in witchcraft, Lena Zampara and Sabbata Lorenzona, were also widows. But Bartolomea and Sabbata were not natives of Farra; therefore, after becoming widows, they escaped all control, lacking even the kind of control that living near one's natal family normally entailed. Domenica di Camillo from Faedis had lost her mother and been thrown out by her father—psychologically fragile, she was jealous, unhappy, and extremely miserable. Maria Danellis from Forni di Sotto in Carnia, though thirty years old, was still single.[42] Their power was negative, but similar in nature to the positive power of agrarian and therapeutic witches: only women, in fact, could bring death, because they could create life; only women could make breast milk disappear, because only they could lactate; only women could become liminal as widows, orphans, or spinsters, because they lacked an independent status—their social identity was based on a relationship with a father or a husband.[43]

The continuity and the homogeneity between positive and negative witches was, therefore, provided by the body. The spontaneity of the therapeutic witches, shown in raising their skirts, riding nude through the fields, and making the sign of the cross on their breasts, denoted in a manner of speaking a naturalistic relationship with the body, a knowledge of its virtues and of the positive presence of all its parts. In the case of "diabolical witches," as we shall see, this type of spontaneity became an explicit affirmation of the body's sensual propensities.

When we compare the depositions of "diabolical witches" with those of therapeutic ones, we see a single female body emerging: it was one that expressed with great intensity the positive nature of the flesh. In the accounts of Zannuta, Svalda, and Madalina, the generative fertility of the body was affirmed; in those of Bartolomea, Domenica, and Maria, it was pleasure as a prerogative that emanated spontaneously from the body. Both these visions had deep roots in peasant culture and a precise point of reference in the festival. By the mid-seventeenth century, the Church had long been trying to reduce and to Christianize the peasant festivals, which were spread out through the year; gradually, it gathered them within the brief period of carnival. Carnival, then, united and concentrated the meanings of festivals; it became the theater in which agrarian rituals were played out. Bit by bit, non-Christian ones were expunged from the calendar. Carnival celebrated the death of the old season, the birth of the new one, fertility, and fecundity; at the same time, it satirized the absurd pretensions of the dominant hierarchy and its members to eternity and immortality.[44] Both witch and jester drew inspiration from each other, as we can see when comparing the deposition of Domenica di Camillo of Faedis with the description of a carnival. The witch and the masqueraders parodied the sacrament of penance, the instrument with which the Church, particularly in those years, tried to penetrate into and impose itself upon the countryside. Domenica set out the ecclesiastical framework of the devil, but if looked at closely, we find in her account details of *diablerie* brought to the girl's mind from the streets of her village.[45]

Domenica declared that in Faedis the devil once presented himself

> in the form of a red-colored horse, with the hair on his red head cut short, with a saddle . . . with a black tail, and I was exhorted by Sabbata to go and confess to the Devil in the form of a horse. Never in my life would I have made a similar confession. And the three of us, having entered the aforesaid kitchen, and again finding the devil in the form of a horse, Giacoma began to speak to him, saying,

> "Lord Father, listen to the confession of this girl," and then the devil was transformed from the figure of a horse to the figure of a handsome young man dressed in a blue-aster color like *priests* wear, and he had on his head a black beret like a priest's, and in his hands a red book, and as to his feet they looked like an *ox's hooves* and he told me that he did not want me to ever confess.[46]

Many aspects of this account are to be found in the festivities of carnival. On Saturday, 4 March 1652, the priest of San Clemente in Povoletto came before the Inquisitor with three peasants: Giovan Domenico Tomadino, twenty-two years old, Antonio Decano, twenty-two, and Guiseppe, the son of Giovanni, fifteen. He began:

> On Saturday evening of the last carnival before the Sunday of the sixtieth day these three young men were masked to enjoy carnival, and while they were going around the village clowning around, they met Gregorio Cocolo, called Guverlo, Battista Cainero, Gregorio Schitulo, Battista, Giuseppe and Francesco, sons of Daniele Bastianutto, Antonio Bastianutto, Menia and Maria, sisters of said Gregorio Schitulo, and Biasio, brother of said Giovanni Domenico Tomadino, all masked, and all from the said village of Povoletto. Among them, Gregorio Cocolo was masquerading as a priest, and Battista Cainero was dressed in a dried, untanned bull's hide, worn in such a way that the horns came out over the hide yet adjusted so that they couldn't be seen. Still, he was pretending to be a demon. The said three willingly accompanied the other masked troop: it was nighttime, and they were going to parties at people's homes. The masquerade consisted in this, that the said Gregorio Cocolo in the priest's habit acted as confessor; he invited the masked and unmasked people to confess to him, such as the aforesaid Antonio Decano, a simple person who has suffered mental problems. In three places he pretended to be confessed by the false priest, that is, at the house of Vincenzo di Bastianutto, at Giovanni del Decano's, son of the deceased Domenico, and at the said Gregorio Schitulo's. These other two, that is, the said Giovanni Domenico Tomaldino and Giuseppe del Decano, willingly accompanying them, saw and heard that the said Gregorio Schitulo was pretending to be a priest and even a confessor, and hearing how at the parties and at people's homes he called to this one and that, saying "Come here, I want you to confess and for penance I want to give you a *corona* [a series of prayers said in sequence as with the rosary]." Everyone was laughing, and he was saying to those who did not want to confess that he wanted

> them to be carried off by the Devil. For that he called Battista Cainero, who was dressed in an ox hide as the Devil, and he said, "Come here, Devil, and carry away those who do not want to confess." And he would do a rapid turn about the house, striking terror in the people and then leave.[47]

Biasio Tomadin confirmed, "The said Devil came in and ran around all the rooms and everyone laughed."

This carnivalesque devil was ambivalent; he represented the power of the base, both material and corporal, which gives death and regenerates life. But the regenerative laugh, one that let everyone feel the continuity of life in the public square, mixed with the folly of carnival, was disturbed by a young man who, invited to mask himself as a devil, refused. Giustina, mother of Antonio Decano, had warned him that "one should not mask oneself as the devil with a hide because another young man masked as the devil for a little while suffered great pains and tribulations and if one wanted to free himself from this one had to go to the Madonna of Grace in Udine. Having heard this, Battista Cainero made the sign of the cross and said: 'this is not done out of contempt, nor to do ill, but to be merry at Carnival time' and thus he put on the hide."[48]

The element of fear and intimidation generated by the ecclesiastical devil broke the unofficial atmosphere of the festival; the carnivalesque element in Domenica's confession shed a mocking light upon her. The intense sensuality of her account to the Inquisitor had the flavor of a great mockery, a self-satisfying burlesque, full of maliciousness and pleasure:

> when one came to those words "Blessed are you" they taught me, and ordered me to say: "Cursed are you in such misery," and in the Pater Noster at the words "Da nobis hodie" [Give us this day], they taught me to say *as a joke* "Donabisodie" [either a nonsense word or perhaps "give more hate"]. And in church they told me that I had to touch my private parts, and also that I should touch my whole torso, especially my breasts with maliciousness and pleasure, and many times I did the aforesaid things, and for the delight and pleasure that I felt inside of me I fell into pollution in that very church about twenty-five times.[49]

Even in the account of Maria Danellis, daughter of Gregorio, the same brazen description of bodily pleasures was retold: "I always desired different young men, as many as I would see, in church, outside of church, and everywhere, and I desired to commit carnal sins with all of them at all hours, and I could not free myself from that temptation." Once, while in bed, unable to sleep,

> suddenly the demon came in the form of a man, but in an ugly form. And black at first, he transformed himself into a very beautiful young girl dressed and adorned in the most beautiful things one could imagine. Then he transformed himself into a very handsome young man and he told me many things, and he showed me money, coins of gold, of silver, of every sort. And he wanted to give me each thing, as long as I would give him my soul. He touched all of my body with his hands, and with everything, and he used me sexually and put his member inside of me like husbands and wives do, but he did this only one time in the bed. And it seems to me that two other times he brought me to ugly, far-away countries where other times, that is twice, I had sexual intercourse with him in the way I described the first time. And this lasted for the space of three hours, nonstop. I consented to him because I had such strong temptations of the flesh that it was not possible to resist, and I had the *greatest pleasure.*[50]

Both in the true confessions of the use of spells and in those extorted through fear (because of the existence of a more structured vision), we find an enduring authentic component: extreme ease in retelling the sexual aspects of these cases. No form of censure seems to have obstructed the testimonies, which to us today appear obscene. Many fears came out in the confessions: the fear of being burned, the fear of being imprisoned, the fear and shame of being considered witches and having to remain isolated because of it, the discomfort in the face of misery and sickness. But in no instance did those interrogated show fear of being judged indecent.

It is often said that many obscene details were solicited by pathological Inquisitors: it may be that some were, but minute curiosity was at the very heart of the entire Inquisition, not merely in this area. A similar great precision is to be found in cases involving misuse of the confessional.[51] The evangelization of the countryside was preceded and accompanied by the clergy's moralization.[52] The devil Lucio Bello, in his false confession to Domenica di Faedis, said he wanted her as a wife, behaving just like many priests who in the confessional solicited sexual relations with penitents.[53] The sacrament of confession was an indispensable instrument in the process of evangelization and moralization of the countryside; and the Sixth Commandment, in the course of the seventeenth century, assumed a fundamental role there. The aim of such close attention to sexual detail seemed to be to obtain, even about sexual conduct, a wide range of information to improve and render more effective controls that were still uncertain and approximate.

The numerous Don Polidoros, Brother Giulio Missinos, and Brother Lodovicos spread through the Christian community had furnished material for reflection and became the source of confessional literature. Only after their intervention could confessions become "morbid"; the moralization of sexual practice was an indispensable condition of morbidity.

The unhappy Domenica di Faedis concluded her confession by asking for forgiveness. But a challenge underlay her words, calling into doubt the powers of the Inquisitor: "I ask pardon of God, of this Holy Tribunal and of Your Most Reverend Father and I pray that for the love of God, you will pardon my many sins, and free *if not my body at least my soul* from the hand of the demon [emphasis added]."

❧ Throughout the seventeenth and eighteenth centuries there was a process of pairing certain concepts: priests-faithful, soul-body, sin-guilt. Whether concerning spells or diabolical magic, the contrasting vision of priest and witch was marked by great tension, although it no longer had the character of a mortal clash, which it had had fifty years earlier. Rather, it seems that since norms had been defined to distinguish magic from nonmagic, the issue had become perfecting them, and, in turn, ritualizing their applications. In this phase, the function of mediator between clergy and laity actually fell to witches. Diabolic or thaumaturgical witches had to indicate and teach to everyone who was the antiwitch.[54] Their spells put into play a complex web of relationships, and therefore the witch's actions had extremely broad social potential.

First of all, it is evident that spells were handed down by married women through kin relationships: all the women, in fact, said they had learned spells from their mother, mother-in-law, or sister-in-law. Second, relations among women, not just relatives, but neighbors and fellow villagers, were fundamental, since each woman interrogated implicated two or three other women. In twenty-seven of the depositions, at least sixty to seventy women were named, in contrast to about a dozen men. Payment was not among the motives that induced these women to use spells, or at least it was not a noteworthy or sufficient motive: spells were lent and passed around like an exchange of help or information among good neighbors. Men believed in women's spells; some followed them, others sent for the women believed capable of casting them.

Many of these elements can be seen in the case that centered on Madalina del Conte. Why did Madalina confess everything to the parish priest and claim that her mother and sister-in-law would confess in their turn? Her entire conduct showed her to be very preoccupied with pleasing the priest: she confessed, she made others confess, she was repentant and assiduous in her penance. Her aim was to win the priest's trust and to convince him that she considered all those spells "superstitions."

Gioseffo and Bastiano del Conte, instead, resisted by every means possible, including the beatings given to Svalda and Madalina reported by the latter while at the priest's: the two men, in fact, saw their authority over the women of the house diminished, and hence their position in the social hierarchy of the village eroded.

The figure of the priest had a contrasting impact on Madalina and Gioseffo. Gioseffo, Bastiano, and Don Zorzi Salomon represented local authority, linked to relationships inside the community; the priest was a new element, the representative of an external, centralizing force. The women rushed to confess to him, clearly also out of fear. The Friulian Inquisition had always been rather mild,[55] but even there the echo of the great witch hunt remained a terrible, imminent threat, if nothing else.

Nonetheless, the priest's approach arouses the suspicion that the primary aim of the Holy Office was to inventory popular beliefs in order to clarify on which points and under which aspects the relationship with the supernatural was escaping the Church. Don Polidoro's primary objective was to control the situation subtly and to be brought up to date on the convictions most deeply rooted and widespread in the population. His meticulousness and precision were virtually those of an ethnographer: he recorded over and over again the same spells, the same formulas. He broke spells down into their constituent parts. If the woman hesitated in her account, Don Polidoro read other depositions to her and compared them. He had the testifiers verify their depositions before having them sign. He took care, moreover, always to have local people present while taking the depositions: if he was dealing with people from Giassico, the witnesses were always from Giassico. Often, other members of the community were present, more or less according to the case: Zannuta Peton's son, people who had begun the denunciation, and others. Even Madalina del Conte was a witness on various occasions; Zannuta Pillizuto and Don Polidoro's housekeeper were present at countless confessions. It seems highly probable that the witnesses in general, and the last two women named in particular, had a precise function of providing information and coordinating news, from priest to community and vice versa.

The priest acquired power from his ambivalent role; his threat decreased to the degree that one was willing to put aside some personal convictions regarding the supernatural. It was necessary to tell what one knew, what one had done, and also who knew or performed magic; then it was necessary to recognize that these activities were "superstitions" (this term recurs in all the denunciations) and that every activity of this type, that is, magical (good or bad), was a "matter for the Holy Office."

Once the sovereign authority of the Church was accepted, having learned what one must not do and promised what one would no longer do, the penitent woman was exonerated and purified of her guilt. The visit and the confession to the priest became, at this point, an element of strength, which permitted the obedient woman to present herself with new authority and new security to the community and to her family: in fact, the community lost its right to criticize her. The priest was transformed from an enemy to an ally; Madalina gained virtue and credibility from the priest, and the priest gained power through Madalina.

Madalina recovered her dignity at the cost of making herself a vigorous opponent of "superstition"; the priest, making use of her, penetrated the social network of the villages of Brazzano and Rutars. Madalina flushed out witches, denounced them, brought them to confess, served as witness. In this way she extended the authority of Don Polidoro, substituting him for the more ingenuous Don Zorzi Salomon, parish priest of the town. Madalina and the other potential witches, having confessed their crimes, all had an interest in making the authority of Don Polidoro prevail. Madalina, like the others, renounced her personal and natural capacities (linked to the potentialities of her body) in exchange for a reflective and dependent authority, but a more secure one, which guarded her from a bad reputation and from the uncertain and often conflictual familial and social relationships of women in peasant communities. A quarrel or unforeseen widowhood was enough to transform a reputation for good magic into one of malevolent witchcraft. In turn, Don Polidoro, through Madalina, was confirmed as an authority superior to the authorities of the community: his judgment about Madalina and Svalda became the only judgment that could raise them above the accusation of being witches. He did indeed affirm this against the opinion of Gioseffo, thus overstepping paternal and matrimonial authority, not to mention that of Don Zorzi Salomon, the parish priest who was too compromised by his relations with the community and perhaps guilty of the same "superstitions."

The ambiguity of the relationships between the women and the priest was due to the fact that they could become allies, as had been the case for Madalina. But these women were untrustworthy allies, for the magic that they possessed was difficult to expropriate: it was inside their bodies and could be used again, independently of the priest, at any time. It was a different power from that of the priest. Women were a continual threat, since, if the priest had the power to give life and death to the soul, women had the power to give life and death to the body: in the uncertain battle between soul and body, they could always intervene authoritatively in favor of the body.

❧ Let us move ahead one hundred years and observe the results of the battle between the clergy and the witches. In Aviano in 1740, we find Angela Roletti, a twenty-two-year-old woman, unmarried, daughter of Bartolomeo. The young woman, seriously ill, gave no fewer than three depositions. The development of her account, especially the crescendo of self-accusations from the first to the second deposition, testified to a long internal torment. Angela had, like Bartolomea Golizza, no fear that "they would burn her." Rather, she seemed driven by remorse: "I must present myself to testify . . . and to accuse my iniquities, committed against God and to the detriment of my soul."[56]

Two widows, Giuliana Chiaranda, sixty years old, a native of Marsure but living in Aviano, and Cattarina Paiara, about sixty years old, from St. Leonardo, had initiated her into witchcraft. About six years earlier, they taught her that "the Son of God had been generated after the Father. That God has not been, nor ever will be, eternal. That the demon is the creator of all visible things. That there was no purgatory. They taught me to abuse the Sacraments, sacred things, and to do injuries of all sorts to images of the Saints." While she was at Monte Reale, the widow Maria Schiavon, seventy years old, had taught her that "Virgin Mary was not â Virgin. That St. Joseph was the real father of Jesus Christ, and that our souls are mortal: and she made me learn this by extinguishing an oil lamp by saying: 'such too is our soul.'"

Chiaranda made her make a pact with the devil, "who appeared to me with a crown on his head, a scepter in his hand, that is, on a throne. . . . After having made the pact, the same woman taught me a thousand iniquities." She listed them in detail: strategies for foreseeing the future and "heretical propositions." "With the goal of perverting my . . . sisters, she said to them: do you believe that the things of the other life are real? Oh, how much better it is to take one's satisfaction in this world, than to wait for other things!"

She procured consecrated hosts for the two witches and pierced them with pins. Chiaranda possessed a small statue of the devil, which she as well as the others turned to in order to satisfy their desires.

> All, or almost all of my desires, I had with the people I wanted; most of the time, though, from the devil, who appeared in the semblance of such people; and this either by means of the statue or by demands made by me or by the aforesaid women from the devil. . . . I had sexual relations for a long time with people of all circumstances, and I conceived five times, and with the advice of the first woman I took different things in order to abort, as indeed, occurred. . . . I made two married women abort, about five years ago now, with little distance between one abortion and another. . . . The abortions were done in the following way: the two above-named women had stomach trouble, which I learned from the first evil woman. She sent me several times to the house of the aforenamed women with two glass containers filled with colored water, which had in it abrasive shavings of iron. The liquid was about the equivalent of two coins' worth of oil. And I told those same women to drink the liquid in those same containers as it was good for stomach trouble, but in fact it had been prepared to make them abort.

Such things took place "every single time I craved one of my satisfactions": the sabbat was not necessary, nor was the preseence of the demon—his statue was enough. The sabbat was only one detail among others: "I also used unguents about thirty times in order to go witching on Thursday nights. . . . I did that about thirty times with the *customary effect* of transporting my body to the witches' *usual recreations* [emphases added]." She then provided a list of the "instruments of maleficium": "various things, some sacred, some not."

On 6 November 1740, Angela, bedridden, had her spiritual father write a letter in which she asked again to be heard by the Inquisitor. On 2 December, the same Inquisitor of the dioceses of Aquileia and Concordia went to her house to receive her confession. Angela had her previous deposition read; then, with the repetitive tone of a litany and a *mea culpa*, she reviewed the already numerous self-accusations, confirmed them, and expanded on them. She claimed an additional number of acts of witchcraft and even took responsibility for her deeds, whereas in the preceding declaration she had laid the blame on Chiaranda.

> Where it says she taught me to approach the altar while not fasting, as I did more than once, it should say that I did it continually. Where I said I adored the devil more than 150 times, I should have said every night, for the six years that I was a witch. . . . Where I said: four children died, two males and the other two females. . . . because of the witchcraft of the aforesaid woman, I should have said, because of the witchcraft done by me, as Signora Elisa Detta, daughter of Signor dottor Oliva, fell ill because of my witchcraft.

At the end of the confession, Don Antonio Orivelli asked her if she had lied about anything else: "I have told everything which seemed culpable to me, and I have told the truth," she answered. The priest insisted and exhorted her to reflect again: "She remained a little in thought and then she said, as far as I remember, I have nothing else to say, beyond my first, spontaneous confession." Evidently Angela hesitated and the confessor noticed that, even driven by contrition, she had still not told everything. He asked "if she would have something else to confess to the Holy Office in order to exonerate her own conscience." Angela finally said:

> I must also confess for the relief of my conscience that after having made my first, spontaneous confession to the Holy Office, I left out Father Antonio Cigolotti. . . . who was the beginning and the origin of my Soul's ruin, because from the age of nine until thirteen he led me into sexual intercourse continually; he is a wizard and male witch; he composes spells and makes unguents to transport bodies. He has done eleven successive abortions, five to me and six to other

> girls and he has kept for himself eight fetus-corpses for use in spells. Even after my thirteenth year, many times here in Aviano he has had sexual relations with me.

Five other priests entered her house at nighttime, using her carnally and teaching her heresies. Among those, "Don Antonio Sartogo the young priest of Aviano is a wizard and witch. . . . He taught me that our soul is mortal. That God is not just: while he condemns those who merit rewards, he rewards those who merit condemnation. And that the Virgin Mary is not a virgin." Moreover, she and Giuliana Chiaranda had corrupted and made into witches a great number of women, whose names she listed, and they had also killed countless babies.

The confession went on and on, leaving out none of the possible crimes attributed to witches. Each act, each type of conduct was listed according to carefully codified canons and terminology. Angela estimated that the cause of her entire story was carnal corruption; nevertheless, her references to her body were quite discrete: "I have admitted that I made two other pacts with Satan, that is one with Lucifer only, who with my consent and with the said Chiaranda's persuasion, entered my shameful parts in order to have me try the stimulations of the flesh so that I would be more disposed to receive . . . the spirit of Satan, whom I agreed to receive seven times that night."

Times had changed: "the stimulations of the flesh" had replaced "evil deeds and pleasure" as Angela's vision of her crime. Now five corrupt priests entered and left her room as they liked to take their sexual pleasure; it was not she who went to the sabbat. But the distinction went deeper.

On 23 March, she testified for the third time. She was still sick in bed, but Don Giuseppe Simonetti from the Holy Office came to her, and Angela confirmed her second confession. "They are all true, those things which I said and now I ratify them all." As far as heresy was concerned, she said, "I did not hold, however, nor believe such things with firm conviction, but rather with the intention of displeasing God, and of pleasing the Demon and the companions of my excesses in order to thus have my sensual cravings satisfied."

It is true that many of Angela's heresies were formed from a sort of materialism, the negation of the mystery (the Virgin was not virgin, St. Joseph was the real father, Jesus Christ was not in the Host, God was not infinite, the Son was born after the Father), but no cosmogony was visible. Angela did not have her own organic interpretation of reality; she did not propose a world vision; she simply juxtaposed heretical elements that were circulating, without being a heretic. Less than two hundred years earlier, Menocchio had also declared that the Madonna was not a virgin and that St. Joseph was the real father.[57] But Menocchio was a man and Angela a woman, who was a priori denied the ability to conceptualize that was recognized in Menocchio. It was not merely this, however, that rendered very different the same position. Why did the devil suggest to Angela that the Madonna was not a Virgin and St. Joseph was the real father of Jesus Christ? Because he was "the spirit of fornication."

Between Menocchio's and Angela's declarations, the cult of the Madonna and St. Joseph had rehabilitated the lay family—something that was necessary so that a natural institution, so tied to the flesh as was matrimony, could fully become a sacrament.

The Madonna was always an unattainable model for women; she was the means of reintegrating Eve, the temptress. Accentuating the cult of the Holy Family implied accentuating Mary's contrasting virtues: Virgin and Mother. Having once admitted that sanctity could be achieved even in secular life, even in matrimony and not only in the priesthood, it became essential to reiterate that sexuality was intrinsically evil. Matrimony was the lesser of the evils,[58] acceptable only insofar as it was able to confirm that merit still remained with chastity.

Angela Roletti had no "firm belief"; rather, she rejected a model that did not leave any possibility for "the stimulations of the flesh," "intending to displease God and please the Demon and the companions of my excesses." She had been driven to this by her illness and by desperation: "in the final relapses she believed nothing of the truth of our Faith."

But let us examine the illness that confined Angela to bed.

> In fact, it has been a year and a half since I have been able to swallow anything, liquid or solid; nor have I been able to take the mercury, which more than once the doctors have tried out on me. One day, discussing this inability to swallow with the aforementioned woman, asking how I could live without eating, she answered me in obscure words. I understood, however, that that Demon, with whom I had made the pact, who is called the spirit of fornication, as she told me. . . . this above-named Demon was feeding me by administering food to me in his own time. I however have always abhorred,

> and I abhor even at present to be fed by the Devil. I said to the woman . . . that if this ever were true, I would immediately break with her and with the Demon by going to confess. In fact, a little while after having said this, that is about four days later, my throat was freed and I was swallowing just like before the sickness. But after about fifteen days, my throat closed again. . . . I chew every day, and I drink, but then I throw it all up, because I cannot swallow, as my servants know. . . . My throat shut after I put a piece of lime in my mouth, brought to me by the above-named woman, who after I ate it told me that I would never swallow again.[59]

She vomited; a knot tightened her throat; she could not swallow; all this was provoked by the "spirit of fornication." Angela searched in every way to escape her carnal desires, but soon she relapsed and the illness returned. She was afflicted by this illness for more than three years, although not continuously. The account of her sickness was punctuated by references to "thoughts of desperation," which the Devil suggested to her: all three confessions had a concern for the conscience, for self-examination and self-reflection, that was completely absent in the confessions of Domenica di Faedis, unhappy and psychologically disturbed, or of Maria Danellis, moved by "the greatest desire of the flesh." Of course, there were also psychological elements in these cases, but their fear came from outside—it was fear of the Inquisitor and of their fellow villagers. In Angela's case, rather, shame and a sense of guilt were developed from within, closing up her throat and ruining her stomach. Angela, far from fearing the Inquisitor, sent for him three times and made him bless and exorcise her with the Papal Agnus, the rosary, the Gospel of St. John, and "other sacred things"; she accused herself passionately and repented as much as she was able, but without success.

The clinical picture makes us think unequivocally of an illness that, one hundred years later, would be revealed as "natural" in women: hysteria. And Sigmund Freud stated that one of the most common symptoms of hysteria is a combination of anorexia and vomiting.[60]

Even Domenica di Faedis (like many others) gave signs that could be interpreted as madness: "she would beat her head against the wall and on the ground, with the danger of murdering herself. And she would have jumped [to her death] or something else, if she had not been held."[61] By jumping about, emotionally agitated and physically contorted, she fit the ecclesiastical cliché of a woman possessed. Angela, instead, languished in bed; her symptoms were different. One can see here a transition from a religious-ecclesiastical conception of demonic female sexuality to a scientific-medical conception of overabundant female sexuality.

The prerequisites for the neurotic type of madness that we see in Angela were lacking in the grotesque body of the Middle Ages. Sensuality and the womb were sources of joy and excess, which could be punished and contained by official morality. But no one was ashamed of them. That the female body had some normal and acceptable sexual propensities was a fact long accepted as obvious and certainly not reprehensible. In cases of seduction, it was believed that a man's promise of marriage, although purely verbal and private, was sufficient for a woman willingly to have sexual relations with him. Lies were considered rape. The consent of the woman did not interest the tribunal: even when the woman declared that she had consented, many times the charge of rape remained. The Inquisitor only wanted to know if there had been a promise or not.[62]

The control of women in peasant communities of premodern Europe was concerned with control of the birthrate and of relationships. In a stratified society, women transmitted social status together with life; they were the instruments through which the rigid, preconstructed social hierarchy was perpetuated. In the context of the network of social relations, aristocratic and feudal society had put the emphasis on the moment of exchange, that is, on marriage and its consequent alliances.

From 1600 to 1800, power gradually shifted from the periphery to the center, from the communities of the village to that of the state. Social mobility increased; the endogamy of the village and of the social stratum gave way; and as a result, blood was no longer a sure vehicle of social status. With the opening of the range of exchange, the quality of the merchandise became fundamental; thus, the crucial moment in the exchange of women shifted slowly, from marriage to sexual behavior (from birthrate to sexuality): virtue was the only guarantee of the quality of children.

It has been strongly argued that the structural transformations that were crucial for the modern era were based upon the fact that triennial crop rotation and technical innovations in agriculture put an end to famines; as a result, supplies no longer dropped below the level of subsistence. These changes are the most easily observable, but economic and matrimonial exchanges are integral parts of a system of relationships.[63] The birth of new networks of relationships was the source of an intricate interweaving of conflicts: a game was being played in which the parts were being redistributed and the rules reformulated.

The Church in Friuli (but also elsewhere) was able to control the reformulation of the rules in matrimonial exchanges by controlling women. This succeeded for two reasons: first, because the Church, with the Counter-Reformation, put all its energy into managing death and the fear of the afterlife; by definition, its adversaries were those who gave life.[64] The second reason was that among the new social classes that were taking power (artisan and mercantile classes, liberal and lay professionals), it was thought that an experimental and secular education was not suitable for women. Rather, an essentially religious one was required. In Catholic countries, the education of women was delegated to the Church; thus, through women the Church inserted itself into the fabric of social relations, all the more firmly in the areas where civil powers were less relevant.

Female neuroses seem to be so markedly different from male ones that a considerable part of these differences have been attributed to biological and natural diversities. But the distance between male and female culture in the seventeenth century had become as significant as that between social classes. The nature and the periodization of this phenomenon, for the most part, are still to be considered.

Through figures like Madalina, Svalda, and Angela, I have tried to provide a rough sketch of the contrasts between the clergy and women. The documents of the archbishop of Udine for the seventeenth and eighteenth centuries provide only some hints about the effects of evangelization on men: spells for seducing women diminished progressively from the sixteenth to the seventeenth century until they almost disappeared in the eighteenth. In the eighteenth century, men performed a great number of spells in order to obtain money, and in general the proceedings prepared against them were very brief; neither the Inquisitor nor the presumed male witch seemed to attach much importance to such cases. Men declared without difficulty that they had tried to give their spirit to the devil in exchange for money. But the devil, frequently invoked, never presented himself, and so they renounced him, more from distrust and his inefficacy in performing magic than out of respect for faith. The Inquisitor, for his part, did not believe that he had to insist, given the meager following that these practices had. In fact, none of the men involved named others; each tempted fate alone. For men, then, things had reached such a state that everything took place between a distrustful male witch, a reluctant devil, and an indifferent Inquisitor.[65]

## Notes

1. C. Lévi-Strauss, "Introduzione all'opera di Marcel Mauss," in M. Mauss, *Teoria generale della magia e altri saggi* (Turin, 1965), p. xviii. (This is the Italian translation of Mauss's *Sociologie et anthropologie* [Paris, 1950].)
2. Mauss, *Teoria generale,* p. 396.
3. Ibid., p. 23.
4. Ibid.
5. Lévi-Strauss, "Introduzione," p. xvii.
6. ACAU, S. Officio, busta 27, proc. 951, 1645.
7. ACAU, S. Officio, busta 27, proc. 946, 1645.
8. *Con* is from the Latin *cunnus* = cunt, vagina. [Editor's note: these spells have been particularly difficult to decipher because they are in the dialect of Friuli. I would like to thank Laura Giannetti and Antonietta Mattioni, both of whom went well beyond their own Friulian background, for trying to track down the meaning of these spells. In another article by Luisa Accati, "The Larceny of Desire: The Madonna in Seventeenth-Century Catholic Europe," in *Disciplines of Faith: Politics and Patriarchy,* ed. J. Obelkevich, L. Roper, and R. Samuel, trans. M. Eve and L. Roper (London, 1987), *bigonzo,* here translated as *yoke,* is translated as *wheelbarrow* (p. 78). It seems to have been, however, a curved piece of wood with heavy loads hung at either end and carried across the shoulders.]
9. The nettle spell consisted in bringing bread and salt to a nettle plant and saying, "Good day, good day, nettle, I have brought you some bread and salt"; in exchange, the nettle would carry away fever or sickness. There are various versions of the magical formula.
10. ACAU, S. Officio, busta 27, proc. 946, 1645.
11. Ibid. The spell for breasts had as its purpose warding off *la mastite,* an inflammation caused by the stagnation of milk in the breast tissues.
12. Ibid.
13. The term *madrazza* indicated an inflammation of the breasts or a painful reswelling of the breasts with milk.
14. ACAU, S. Officio, busta 27, proc. 946, 1645.
15. ACAU, S. Officio, busta 27, proc. 955, 1645.
16. ACAU, S. Officio, busta 27, proc. 946, 1645.
17. ACAU, S. Officio, busta 27, proc. 953, 1645.
18. ACAU, S. Officio, busta 27, proc. 950, 1645.
19. ACAU, S. Officio, busta 27, proc. 954, 1645.
20. ACAU, S. Officio, busta 27, proc. 945, 1645.
21. ACAU, S. Officio, busta 27, proc. 954, 1645.
22. ACAU, S. Officio, busta 27, proc. 955, 1645. *Vite di cividino* (cividin vines): vines that produce a wine called "cividin" or "zividin," an ancient variety from Friuli. "Cividin" derives from Cividale, even if this type of wine is found in different areas of Friuli (G. A. Pirona, E. Carletti, and G. B. Corgnali, *Il nuovo Pirona: Vocabolaria Friulano* [Udine, 1977], pp. 158, 1235).
23. ACAU, S. Officio, busta 27, proc. 954, 1645.
24. ACAU, S. Officio, busta 27, proc. 944, 1645.

25. ACAU, S. Officio, busta 27, proc. 945, 1645.

26. ACAU, S. Officio, busta 27, proc. 971, 1646.

27. ACAU, S. Officio, busta 27, proc. 945, 1645.

28. For the distinction between magic and religion, see Mauss, *Teoria generale,* pp. 17–19, and M. Gluckman, "Les rites de passage," in Gluckman, ed. *Essays on the Ritual of Social Relations* (Manchester, 1966), p. 37ff.

29. ACAU, S. Officio, busta 29, proc. 20 bis, 1648.

30. ACAU, S. Officio, busta 28, proc. 992, 1647.

31. Ibid.

32. Ibid.

33. M. Bakhtin, *L'oeuvre de François Rabelais et la culture populaire au Moyen Age et sous la Renaissance* (Paris, 1970), p. 315.

34. Menia of Rutars "said that as far as doing the spell on one's breasts with a man's member was concerned, she had never done it. But she had heard said that once it was taught by Primosa of Rutars to Giacoma, wife of Valentin Savalit, also from Rutars. That her mother-in-law Svalda . . . once did the spell on her breasts with a comb, where she made circles around them with signs of the cross three times, one after another, saying: 'In nomine Patris et Filij et Spiritus Sancti' " (ACAU, S. Officio, busta 27, proc. 955, 1645). Svalda learned this thirty years earlier from a certain Bastiano "who, when he did the spell on her inflamed breasts, used the male member." Madalina del Conte confirmed that Svalda and Menia had told her "that she did a certain spell, which was done when the woman took the male member and made some signs of the cross with it over the breasts for swelling" (ACAU, S. Officio, busta 27, proc. 946, 1645). The spell helped to make the milk flow from the breasts.

35. Bakhtin, *L'oeuvre de François Rabelais,* p. 34.

36. C. Lévi-Strauss, "L'efficacia simbolica," in *Antropologia strutturale* (Milan, 1966), p. 210ff. (*Anthropologie structurale* [Paris, 1958]).

37. M. Douglas, *Purezza e pericolo* (Bologna, 1972), p. 87 (*Purity and Danger: An Analysis of Pollution and Taboo* [New York, 1966], pp. 51–52).

38. She is called *Mater Castissima* (Most Chaste Mother) "because she was a garden closed to anything that could have offended her Purity, a garden always defended, always guarded" (St. Valfrè, *Divota istruzione* [Turin, 1694]).

39. For sanctity as the dominion of oneself, see J. Epstein, *Il giudaismo: Studio storico* (Milan, 1967); for sanctity as completeness and separation, see Douglas, *Purezza e pericolo.*

40. In Genesis, God created two women: a mother and a wife. The mother is in the image of God; she is in fact the feminine part of man and is the first mother of all men; to her as well as to the man is entrusted the duty of rendering the earth, the fish, and the birds their subjects. "And God created man in his image; he created him in the image of God; he created them, male and female" (Gen. 1: 27). The wife, instead, derived from the man and absolutely depended upon him. When, in fact, everything had been created, God said, "It is not good for the man to be alone; I will make him a helper like himself"; thus, from one of Adam's ribs he created the woman. "And the man said: 'She, finally, is bone of my bone and flesh of my flesh. She will be called woman because she has been drawn from man!' For this reason the man will leave his father and mother and will unite with his wife, and they will be one flesh" (Gen. 2: 18, 23–24). The woman-wife depends on the husband; the woman-mother, on God. For the Church, then, it is essential to insert itself between the mother and God in order to guarantee its hegemony over all that is sacred, male and female. Virginity in Deuteronomy is a norm that functions to control the wife. A woman must be a virgin until matrimony; if the husband does not find her to be a virgin, "then he will make the young girl leave through the entrance of his father's house, and the people of his

city will stone her, until she dies, because she has committed an act of infamy in Israel, prostituting herself in the house of her father" (Deut. 22: 21). The Church changed the norm exercised on the body into a norm exercised on the soul and transferred it from the figure of the wife to that of the mother.

41. C. Ginzburg, *Il formaggio e i vermi, il cosmo di un mugnaio del '500* (Turin, 1976), p. 146. (*The Cheese and the Worms: The Cosmos of a Sixteenth-Century Miller*, trans. J. and A. Tedeschi [Baltimore, 1980.])

42. ACAU, S. Officio, busta 29, proc. 18 bis, 1648; busta 28, proc. 997, 1647; busta 27, proc. 975, 1646. Concerning Domenica di Camillo, see C. Ginzburg, *I Benandanti* (Turin, 1966), p. 146.

43. On the concept of liminality, see V. Turner, *La foresta dei simboli* (Brescia, 1976), p. 123ff. (*The Forest of Symbols* [Ithaca, 1967]).

44. Bakhtin, *L'oeuvre de François Rabelais*, p. 213.

45. On the inspirational meaning of carnival, see N. Z. Davis, *Society and Culture in Early Modern France* (Stanford, 1975), pp. 147 and 103; P. Camporesi, *La maschera di Bertoldo* (Turin, 1976), p. 224; P. Camporesi, *Il paese della fame* (Bologna, 1978), p. 187ff.

46. ACAU, S. Officio, busta 48, proc. 997, 1647.

47. ACAU, S. Officio, busta 37, proc. 208, 1652.

48. Decidedly carnivalesque elements appeared in other cases, where along with the satire of religious functions, one discovers a joyous conception of the devil, not necessarily frightening or evil. Pasca, wife of Antonio, described to Don Polidoro a way to bless oneself in convoluted and jestful Latin, "which she had taught to different people for a joke" (ACAU, S. Officio, busta 27, proc. 955, 1645). Lucretia Panitiola, completely infatuated with a certain young man, asked for help from the devil, in order that he not leave her: "fearing that the demon would not appear to me . . . I recommended myself to God and then I called the devil" (ACAU, S. Officio, busta 29, proc. 1 bis, 1648).

49. ACAU, S. Officio, busta 48, proc. 997, 1647. Emphasis added.

50. ACAU, S. Officio, busta 27, proc. 975, 1646. Emphasis added.

51. "We must not forget that Christian preaching, making of sex that which, above all, had to be confessed, has always presented it as a disquieting enigma: not that which obstinately is shown, but that which is hidden everywhere, the insidious presence which risks remaining unheard, so much does it speak in a voice low and often unrecognizable" (M. Foucault, *La volunta di sapere* [Milan, 1978], p.35).

52. F. Chabod, *Lo stato e la vita religiosa a Milano all'epoca di Carlo V* (Turin, 1971), p. 231ff.

53. See, for example, ACAU, S. Officio, busta 28, proc. 999, 1640.

54. E. E. Evans-Pritchard, *Sorcellerie, oracles, et magic, chez les Azandé* (Paris, 1972), p. 189ff. (*Witchcraft, Oracles, and Magic among the Azande* [Oxford, 1937]).

55. Ginzburg, *Il formaggio e i vermi*, p. 81.

56. ACAU, S. Officio, busta 55, proc. 831 bis, 1740.

57. Ginzburg, *Il formaggio e i vermi*, p. 9.

58. P. Ariès, *L'enfant et la vie familiale sous l'Ancien Régime* (Paris, 1973), p. 398; see also C. Klapisch, "La 'Mattinata' médiévale d'Italie," a communication of the round table on the "Charivari" (Paris, April 1977), p. 13.

59. ACAU, S. Officio, busta 55, proc. 831 bis, 1740[?].

60. S. Freud, *The Basic Writings of Sigmund Freud*, trans. A. A. Brill (New York, 1938).

61. ACAU, S. Officio, busta 28, proc. 997, 1647.

62. In this respect, see S. Cavallo, "Fidanzamenti e divorzi in Ancien Régime: La diocesi di Torino," *Miscellanea storica ligure* 9 (1977): 5–50.

63. C. Lévi-Strauss, *Le strutture elementari della parentela* (Milan, 1969), pp. 76–77 (*Les structures elementaires de la parente* [Paris, 1967]).

64. "The popular comic tradition and the ascetic tendency are profoundly alien to each other. The former is in no way hostile to woman and does not judge her unfavorably . . . in this tradition, woman is essentially related to the ground (*bas*) both materially and bodily: she is the incarnation of the ground that degrades and regenerates simultaneously. She is as ambivalent as it is. She debases, brings down to earth, corporalizes, gives death; but, before all, she is *the principle of life, the womb*" (Bakhtin, *L'oeuvre de François Rabelais,* p. 240).

65. ACAU, S. Officio, buste 41–54, 1657–1740.

# 6 ☙ One Saint Less: The Story of Angela Mellini, a Bolognese Seamstress (1667–17[?])

*by Luisa Ciammitti*

> Angela Maria Mellini . . . is about thirty-four years old, of ordinary stature for a woman; she is an Ursuline nun; lower class, with a pretty face, rose and white skin tone, hair which tends toward brown, grayish eyes, a rounded face, her mouth protruding a little. She wears black, with a small collar, the ordinary black shoes of an Ursuline, and she must be immaculate, because as she told me . . . Father Giovanni Battista her confessor watches over her because he does not want to see anything in her that is not clean and pure.[1]

In this attentive and detailed manner, Elisabetta Maria Zani described her old friend and confidant to the Inquisitor of the Holy Office on 1 October 1698. The daughter of a manual laborer of the Albergati family, Elisabetta, thirty-four and unmarried, grew up with Angela, about whom it was said that "she sewed and knitted." Both of them lived with their respective parents in the same building in Via Sarogozza. At a certain point, however, their friendship dissolved because of the intense spiritual relationship that had grown up between Angela and their common confessor, the Franciscan Giovanni Battista Ruggieri: Elisabetta had had to leave him because "all his attention" was for Angela.[2] But six years later, "enlightened" about their strange relationship by a Dominican, she had decided to "unburden her conscience," denouncing the two to the Holy Office. One confessor, to whom she had previously recounted the secrets told to her by her friend, had limited himself to scolding Angela; another had expressed

---

"Una santa di meno: Storia di Angela Mellini, cucitrice bolognese (1677–17[?]," *Quaderni Storici,* no. 41 (1979): 603–39. Translated by Margaret A. Gallucci.

doubt that he could involve himself in "the affairs of the Molinos"[3] and had not pressed her to lodge a denunciation. On the basis of Zani's account, the General Inquisitor of Bologna accused Angela Maria Mellini of "affected sanctity," together with her spiritual fathers, Giovanni Battista Ruggieri and Evangelista Biffi, of the Order of Saint Jerome and Prior of San Barbaziano.

On 22 October 1698, Angela, officially summoned, presented herself before the Inquisitor. She stated that she did not know what the Holy Office was concerned about. When the complaint was explained to her in general terms,[4] she affirmed that she knew no one guilty of the sins described, but she expressed the desire to recount some matters that she had spoken about with her spiritual father.

Then she began a long, detailed account, sometimes interrupted by the Inquisitor's questions, but more often by Angela herself, who, unaccustomed to returning home late in the evening, asked that the deposition be interrupted and begun again on the following morning or after lunch. In the course of the five months of the trial, she recounted with precision and order the events of her spiritual life, beginning with her meeting with Father Ruggieri. The entire time she maintained the attitude of someone who knew she had done nothing evil; she responded with certainty or, if uncertain, she asked to be allowed to think "a short time." She rectified what she felt were Elizabetta's erroneous interpretations; she denied conversations that never took place, "when it was not for loss of memory"; she exposed the euphemisms used by the Inquisitor. In fact, when the Inquisitors asked her if she knew any confessor who said to a penitent, "Oh my dear N., you have done well to come visit me," she responded, "Me, I know nothing whatsoever about this; does that N. mean Angela?"[5]

She promised to bring a spiritual diary, which she herself had written on the orders of Father Ruggieri. Two years earlier, in fact, Angela, who already knew how to read, had learned to write.[6] Another confessor, Evangelista Biffi, had been her teacher. "Three or four months before he left Bologna," recounted Angela,

> he asked me in the confessional if I knew how to write; and after I told him no, he told me that I must learn how and he gave me a sample of letters on a page and a pen. The reason for this was because he said that if he left Bologna he wanted to learn my spiritual progress from me and how I was following in the path of the Lord,

> because his desire was to help me in spirit and body, that is in the temporal concerns necessary to live, knowing that I had an ill mother and that I did not feel that well. And after he gave me the first sample he gave me another page with letters so that I learned better.[7]

Angela, however, was not quick enough to deliver the diary herself: a search that had been immediately ordered located "a small notebook of 24 pages bound *in quarto*. . . . a small book *in sedici* of nine pages," plus some letters and various notes. These were turned over to the Inquisitor.[8]

❧ In the pages of the diary, painstakingly written in her own hand, Angela recounted her spiritual story.[9] She began with the beginning when, while reciting silent prayers on the Passion, the face of Christ, pale and bathed in blood, had appeared to her; she had fallen to the ground, overcome by compassion and sorrow. Recovering her senses, she had seen women around her who were helping her. With eyes lowered, she remained "internally peaceful,"[10] feeling no physical pain but "melted" and "impassioned" for the Passion of Jesus. Her conviction that this had occurred "because she had been admitted to Grace" was immediately opposed by the opinion of her confessor, the Dominican Raimondo Bonacorsi, who urged her not to continue with such silent prayers as long as similar phenomena persisted. The duty of obeying her own spiritual father had thrown her into "great sadness," so much so that each time she entered church she felt "something within me which told me that I should take another path; that that one was not mine; and when I went to confession, I felt an affliction that passed through the depths of my soul."[11]

The fear of being tricked by the devil accompanied the certainty that Jesus wanted to give her a spiritual direction "more to his desire."[12] One morning she had entered the Church of Santo Spirito in this state of mind and had confessed to a priest (Giovanni Battista Ruggieri, as will become clear later) "the suffering that I bore for having nothing that involved my heart and for not knowing in any way how to express myself in order to make myself understood."[13] He had asked her then to become his penitent for a period of time. Her other spiritual father, Domenico Bonacorsi, in answer to her first request to replace him for a time, "was unhappy or showed some remorse . . . and closed the confessional window"; but the second time he closed the window "with anger."[14]

The new spiritual direction, deeper in understanding but also more disciplined than the preceding one, immediately proved fruitful for Angela. Jesus, in fact, had begun more often to manifest through her his own sorrow for the sins of the world, and at the same time his satisfaction for a soul like hers, which had chosen to follow him and to suffer with him. To the exhortation which the Son of God had addressed to her, "Do not concern yourself with the world, nor with its pastimes, because they pass like the wind," Angela had answered promptly, trying to be "always more and more detached from things of the world."[15] Obeying the requests of Father Ruggieri, she had then begun to write about "the way of prayer"[16] and the graces with which she had been favored, hoping to thus do the will of God.

❧ The notary Francesco Moruzi, who compiled the case, enclosed in the dossier of the trial the material that had been seized, numbering it and describing it as "rough script with poorly formed letters like those of beginners learning to write."[17]

Angela's writing, which in the first pages is ink-splotched and very uncertain, little by little becomes more sure and legible. The lines, packed together at the beginning, become more distanced and upright (see figs. 1 and 2). The difficulty of the task that she undertook is immediately clear, not only in the form, but in the evidence of the terrible effort and control that are visible on every page and that at times constrained her to omit some things.[18] There was never a sense of abandon: to write was for Angela a duty and an act of thanks to God. She herself, moreover, stated immediately with great simplicity: "Your Reverence commands me to write and knows that I do not know how to write and that I am not able to do so without making many mistakes and blunders. That he loves me or not is of little importance: it is enough to satisfy[?] my Jesus; I am happy both because of my faith and because I rely totally on Jesus and Mary. Amen."[19]

The errors in a spelling that was carefully worked out on the basis of pronunciation do not conceal that the vocabulary was that of someone who read. Very probably, reading was easier and more familiar to her than writing. In fact, she used a literary vocabulary with terms like "tribulation," "sorrowful," "effects," "operations," "understand," and "discern" (even if the words were frequently misspelled). She used rhetorical flourishes of the type, "on one hand I saw my weakness, on the other divine goodness";[20] "I cannot but commit many mistakes and blunders"; and "I pray to You my loving Jesus to lend me the

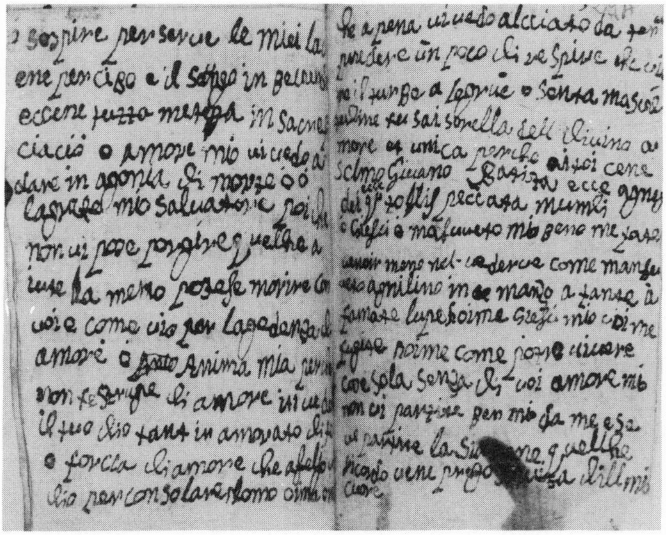

**Fig. 1.** *Angela Mellini's handwriting as shown in her diary. Biblioteca Comunale di Bologna (Archiginnasio), MS B. 1883,* Diario scritto da Angela Mellini, *cols. 12v, 13r.*

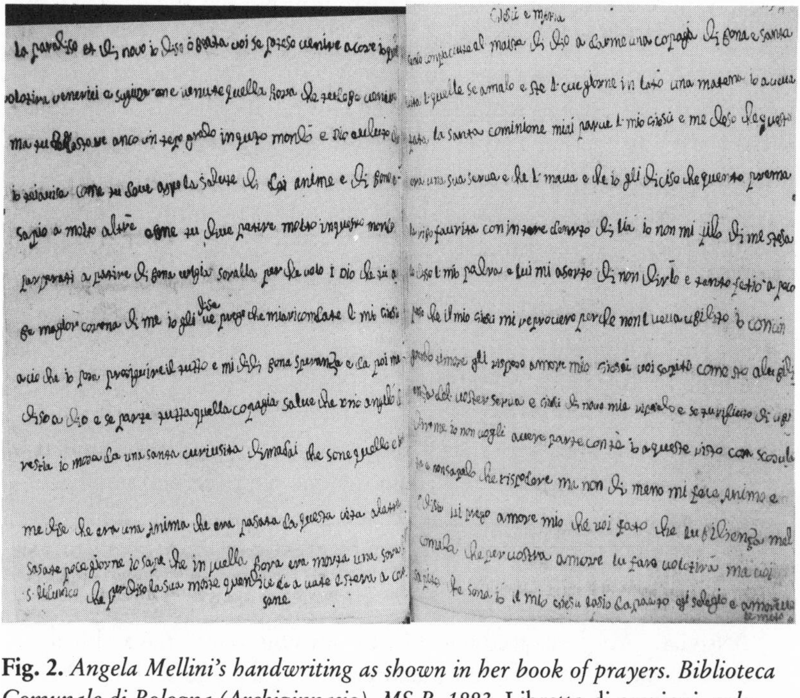

**Fig. 2.** *Angela Mellini's handwriting as shown in her book of prayers. Biblioteca Comunale di Bologna (Archiginnasio), MS B. 1883,* Libretto di orazioni, *cols. 4v, 5r.*

lance that wounded you in the side to write at least a few of the many things that you have wrought in me, unworthy creature."[21] Other times her usages were more surprising and unusual: "O holy and blessed suffering, you are the telescope which makes the beautiful face of Jesus which is far away near."[22] Never, however, did references to the animal world appear in her writings.

The practice of silent prayer, linked also to Angela's belonging to the order of the Ursulines,[23] added to her vocabulary modes and terms of scenic representation used in spiritual exercises: "I set out to do a bit of silent prayer and I prepared myself to go find my Jesus in the garden and being there I saw my dear Jesus with his face pale."[24]

The "small book of nine pages," confiscated with her diary, which Angela said she had written for herself during the previous summer and had not shown to anyone, was completely dedicated to prayer and spiritual exercises. There she strictly followed the technique of the mental representation of episodes of Christ's Passion, supposing that she had been present at the unfolding of these events: "O my beloved Jesus I went there looking for you and I did not find you there. Where are you my husband? Are you here in the garden? Will I see my love himself here? And how? With his knees on the ground and his face pale—eyes raised to heaven with hands clasped and with a breath blood gushes from his veins to fall upon the barren earth. Where are you eternal Father, have you not seen your child?"[25] The moments in which God manifests himself through her were introduced by expressions such as, "I felt inspired within me"; "my spirit ravished me"; "there came to me in revery"; and "an inner voice called me."

At times it seems that we can identify fairly precisely the echoes of Angela's reading in her writings. Compare, for example, the voices of Catherine of Siena and Angela in their dialogues with Christ:

> CATHERINE: "And who calls for the salvation of Catherine so that Christ would not suffer? . . . I am the one who sins and you have penance to do? . . . And what do you gain from it? . . . Will your holiness perhaps increase? Will you be greater or more powerful? Certainly not."[26]

> ANGELA: "My Jesus told me: . . . I want you to love me and feel close to me. To this request I answered:—when you will have been loved will you be more blessed? Certainly not."[27]

On other occasions, although there are not precise references, it is still possible to track down similar situations and words. Caterina de' Vigri, tormented by diabolical apparitions that attempted to weaken her obedience to her prior, sought refuge in the comfort of prayer, "but she remained in great sadness."[28] Angela, bound in turn by obedience to a spiritual direction that she considered not appropriate to her situation, but fearing also that it could be a trick of the Enemy, declared, "under the direction of the Reverend Father Rimondo Bonacursi . . . I suffered a great deal and I found myself in great sadness."[29]

❧ We possess information about only two of the books that Angela had clearly read. During the trial Angela recounted that, at the moment of accepting her as his spiritual daughter, Father Ruggieri had given her a summary of the life of sister Cecilia Nobili "with several exercises in doing things with the will of doing them always in the presence of the Lord; and there were ejaculatory prayers on the passion of Christ."[30] She had lost this book. The other one, however, whose author she did not remember, was given to her before communion: "there were ejaculatory prayers for the holy days of many saints."[31] After communion she returned the book to the confessor or to a cleric.

More than one hundred fifty years earlier, a Sister Cecilia Nobili had wandered the same streets that Angela traveled every day. Vicar of the monastery of Santa Maria della Concezione, Sister Cecilia guided, together with Ginevra dell'Armi, a group of women belonging to the Bolognese aristocracy, spiritual daughters of Don Leone Bartolini.[32] Ginevra, wife of Giovanni dall'Armi, lived on Via Asse. Not far away, in the parish church of San Marino, set on the old Via de' Gombruti, now Via di Porta Nuova, Don Leone Bartolini officiated from 1560; he was also confessor in the convent of Santa Maria Nuova and della Concezione.

Angela Maria Mellini lived from 1691 in the parish of San Marino, in a house situated on the corner between Via de' Gombruti and Via Asse, but frequented the closer Church of Santo Spirito, opened on 8 May 1647. Father Ruggieri officiated there; he was also the special confessor of Santa Maria Nuova and Santa Maria della Concezione.

The coincidence is surprising. It has not been possible to discover any biographical details about this Cecilia Nobili, who, from the exchange of letters with Bartoloni, also appears to have been directed to an intense spiritual life.[33] The actual Cecilia Nobili about whose life Angela read was closer in time, even if farther away in space. That book pertained to a Cecilia Nobili, a lay sister in the monastery of San Giovanni di Nocera Umbra, who died on 24 July 1665, at the age of twenty-five. One of her confessors, Michelangelo Michelangeli, having "recognized in her a compendium of many Christian virtues, an epitome of sanctity, an image of perfection and a study of it," decided to recount "in . . . summary the sketch" of her life. He used notes taken on the orders of her other confessor, Father Vitelleschi, and an autobiography that Cecilia had written "on the insistence of one of her friends" in which she had also spoken of "aims, intentions, and desires which one can have in all actions, and these together with some devotions were printed in Rome in 1664." It is improbable that Angela had seen this latter work.[34] In the trial, she said that she had read "a summary of the life of Cecilia Nobili," and Michelangelo spoke precisely of a "summary." Father Ruggieri's suggestion to Angela Mellini that she read the life of Cecilia Nobili di Nocera Umbra would, in any case, have stirred her memory of the Bolognese Cecilia Nobili.

There are precise similarities between some paragraphs of Cecilia's life, cited by Michelangeli, and Angela's writings. For example:

> Sister Cecilia wrote in obedience to her confessor who ordered her to do so. She, however, felt a great repugnance in writing such things, since she would have more willingly written about her shortcomings and sins, and after she had modestly asked that he be content not to order her to do such a thing she gave in to obedience.[35]

Angela wrote:

> Jesus, Mary and Joseph, I would like that just as you have ordered me and given me full license to write about the way of prayer and the graces that the Lord showed me; that you would give me license to tell in detail and with clarity my great sins and my evil life, which would give me the greatest consolation. . . . Blessed be God forever who has waited for me so long and with all my heart I beseech him to give me the grace that I may write this account which my confessors commanded of me with every clarity and truth.[36]

I shall touch upon other analogies later. These should not make us think that Angela merely read the biography of Cecilia and passively incorporated it. Yet, on the other hand, the intensity of Angela's words should not mislead us. That intensity appears to be so great because her words come to us directly, while those of Cecilia passed through her intermediary, Michelangeli. In this sense, the comparison between the two is not entirely valid. But clearly Angela, too, walked alone on the chosen path. Through silent prayer and reading the lives of the saints, in fact, she learned a form of self-analysis that permitted her both to verbalize her own states of mind ("and one time I told him that I found myself impassioned in spirit, other times distracted . . .")[37] and wisely to control her own gestures (or at least the description of her gestures) based on their "origins." One day, for example, when she was dejected on account of her distance from her spiritual father, "moved by suffering I ran with open arms towards the crucifix which I picked up and I clasped him to my breast and I washed his most sacred body with my tears saying: 'O my love, the beloved bridegroom of my soul, I beg you to return my father if it pleases you. . . .' Feeling my spirit restored, I stopped with my mouth clasped to the wound on his side and my heart told me: 'Do not doubt.'"[38]

She knew how to describe the mysterious effects of the manifestation of divinity in her:

> It sent me into the agonies of death . . . [when] I spoke with him [the confessor] or thinking about the anguish that my Jesus suffered or when I was about to begin I heard it said "here is the lamb of God" and I heard music and I saw my Jesus on the cross . . . in admiring the heavens and other similar things my spirit marveled and I remained as if immobile and I remained without saying anything and many times I was not able to move from place to place and not even any part of my body, or my hands not even one finger.

She distinguished: "These are things in general. I will say some things more in particular."[39] Angela knew the difference between emotional perceptions and intellectual ones: "Love makes me experience the truth of sufferings through the senses, now it beats, now it purges, now it hurts and now all sorts of torments are felt."[40] But she also said, "One never sees things with the eyes of the body, but everything is seen intellectually."[41]

❧ Such intense introspection did not annul Angela's perception of her body, which also occurred on various levels. The first was the one closest to "human fragility": "the rebellion of senses."[42] The "temptation to commit a mortal sin with the said Father Giovanni Battista Ruggieri in matters of the flesh" had manifested itself to her for seven or eight days with "great heat in all the parts of my body and particularly of movements in my genitals and these movements and rebellions of flesh I experienced especially when I saw the said Father Ruggieri, indeed, in looking toward the confessional or where he was standing, and particularly when I was in the confessional before him I felt greatly spurred on by temptation toward the said priest."

She had spoken to Father Ruggieri about it, but "I did not tell him he was the person that I was referring to."[43] Shrewdly Angela recounted that

> inflamed by a sexual fire, . . . I could not prevent myself from speaking with him. One morning after I had spoken with him, I felt thrown again into such profound misery that I went before the most sacred sacrament and I cried with abandon and I uttered many sighs and I prayed to Jesus and Mary. While I remained there suffering I heard a voice inside me which told me: "Be tranquil, daughter." I calmed down and I went as if outside myself and I saw the most sacred Mother of God come toward me and she said: "Tell me what has afflicted you." And I answered: "The fear that I will not be able to avoid a deed that will displease your Son and you."

Mary freed her forever from similar torments, accepting her as a daughter with a true rite of investiture, saying: "'I accept you.' And she took a white veil from underneath her cloak and she put it on my head and said: 'Be certain that you will no longer have this temptation.' "[44] But Angela's perception of her own body—similar to that of her soul—occurred in different stages and on different levels: besides the "rebellions of the senses," a real threat if she chose chastity, there was the difficulty of enduring the physical demands that came from God. As had happened to other mystics, for Angela, too, the passion of Christ became one of the fundamental experiences of the life of her body. It was an aspect of that life where introspection and physical activity proceeded in a parallel manner and mutually reinforced each other.

"My soul was consumed by love and my body was consumed by pain," Angela recounted when Jesus removed the crown of thorns and placed it on her head, pressing down hard. In response to her groans of suffering, he had asked her (like a beloved bride) to allow him to do it, because he wanted to let her feel his agonies. "If this is not enough, here is my body and my soul and all of me in your hands," Angela had exclaimed, and immediately she had seen "my Jesus exposed my breast and opened my ribs and took my heart and in place of it he put all the instruments of his sacred passion."[45] The anguish that Christ had given her, insupportable to a human body, had forced her to bed for fifteen days. Moreover, for the five years that followed, until, that is, the moment she began writing the diary, the anguish had recurred on several occasions. After she had had her sister Margherita look at her, as Father Ruggieri had advised, she discovered that "at her ribs near her heart . . . she had two small marks of the color of iron and dark tobacco like the heads of two nails." Only communion relieved her from the excruciating pain that prevented her from breathing. To better explain what she felt, in September 1697, Angela had drawn her heart on a piece of paper, and one morning she had brought to Father Ruggieri "a scrawl on a half page of paper folded four times . . . and a small design on a piece of paper written in her own hand." But since the friar did not understand many things, Angela had provided a detailed explanation of each of the design's particulars in the confessional.

These documents are also enclosed in the trial proceedings: Father Ruggieri, in fact, had delivered them to the Inquisitor (see fig. 3):

> These three small points are located on my ribs—the cross is a light reddish color, which I had never realized I had until last Sunday, the first day of February 1697: This gave me pain there, which was a different pain from those I feel continuously. Because of this latter pain I was moved to look to see if there was some sort of injury there, that I had to treat. The mark where the cross is is both circular and dark but not black, and the size of a small coin. The width of the cross is about that of a thread, and it pricks the heart, on which I cannot bear any piece of clothing without great pain to the bare breast. The transversal line signifies the agony which passes from one side to the other. The lance signifies a lance of anguish which pierces my heart, the nails signify that my heart in all its sections is pierced with nails. The hammer signifies the blows which I feel in my heart, as if I felt it hammering on the above-mentioned nails. The cross inside signifies a place inside in the middle which repre-

> sents the agony which I feel there, which opened my heart in the form of a cross. The little punctures signify a precious crown of thorns which surround and prick my heart.[46]

❧ Only a few years earlier in Paray-le-Monial, a small town in France, another woman, Margherita Maria Alocoque, of the order of the Visitandines, had received from Christ first the revelation of his Sacred Heart, then the order to disseminate the cult with the help of the priest, Bl. Claude de la Colombière, the superior of the local community of Jesuits. After initial disagreements the penitent and her spiritual father had struggled together to realize Jesus' request, until on 21 June 1686 the entire community of Paray-le-Monial celebrated the feast of the Sacred Heart. It was only the beginning of a cult,[47] which had behind it a long tradition.

The temporal closeness of Margherita and Angela prevents positing a direct connection.[48] A possible common source is provided, however, by the writings of Francis de Sales, founder of the order of the Visitandines, who was probably read by Mellini, as we shall see later.

There is, in any case, a difference between Margherita and Angela: while the former spoke of Christ's heart, the latter represented her own heart with the instruments of Christ's Passion. The technique used by Angela is one learned from spiritual exercises. Perhaps she had even seen an image of the Sacred Heart, but undoubtedly the experience of reading the life of Cecilia Nobili had made a strong impression on her: Cecilia too, Michelangeli recounted, suffered terrible pains "to her ribs"; the pain in her heart, about which she often spoke, had lasted a long time. Once she showed the confessor "a formed figure of a heart pierced with arrows, saying: "Thus my heart seems to me. I have felt it like this or in a similar form many times."[49]

The source of the pain became clear at Cecilia's death when the "surgeon" was called to embalm her. He thought he had to perform a simple autopsy. The operation began in the presence of some nuns, the abbess, and Father Michelangeli, who described it thus:

> Before he cut into the bones of the breast, some [sisters] looked at the heart, which was seen under the arch of the ribs. . . . The abbess who remained standing and held a light in her hand, saw a stream of blood flow out and after she alerted me and the surgeon, he marveled at it and said: "I have not cut the heart with my instruments; I

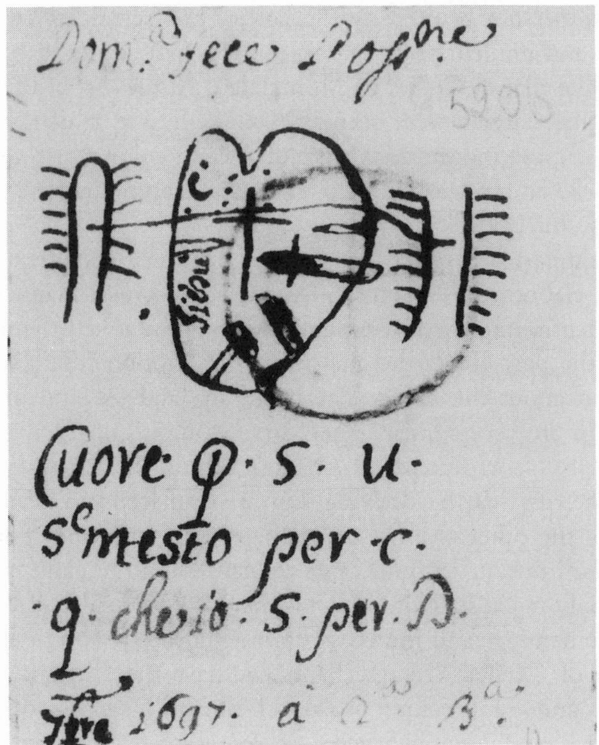

**Fig. 3.** *Angela Mellini's diagram of the wounds in her heart. Biblioteca Comunale di Bologna (Archiginnasio), MS B. 1883, between cols. 520–21.*

> do not know, then, how blood can flow out, but now we will clear this up." And so diligently having opened the chest, a burnt lung was found attached to the ribs. Then taking out the heart three wounds were seen on the exterior part toward the breast in this triangular form. The first two were in a straight line, as if they had been made by a tip of a lance and the other at the bottom like a blunt nail.

The surgeon, more and more astonished, finally opened the heart and "saw in one part and in the other two orders of flesh, that is, one on each side, worked with so much craftsmanship, that we knew God to be the craftsman. They both were attached to the shaft of the heart, and the shaft was perfectly round. . . . The whip was worked with such beautiful interlacings almost as if so many tiny strings were all sewn together, that you could not see anything more marvelous."

One of these, not bruised by the lancet, had remained "whole and beautiful and immediately the surgeon, on first seeing it, said it was ordered like that of Chiara da Montefalco. At the top of the heart itself two half circles were seen one on each side which were as if painted . . . and those points were of a violet color which tended toward black, and it was believed that they represented the crown of thorns of Our Lord."[50]

The similarity between the two descriptions is evident. Angela, however, elaborated her symptoms in a less technical manner, immediately mentioning the instruments that had provoked them and neglecting the part about the anatomical description (the shaft of the heart) and about the order. The beginning and the end of the two paragraphs are very similar. The "three wounds" of Cecilia attached "to the ribs" correspond to Angela's "these three points," which "pierce the ribs." In the drawing they are displaced in a diagonal, one on top of the other (see fig. 3): perhaps Angela did not know what "triangular" meant. In both cases the lance and the nails appear, although only in the case of Cecilia is there the particular of the "blunt nail"; the hammer and the cross do not, however, appear in the description of Cecilia. On one hand, we have the "little punctures," which "signify a precious crown of thorns"; on the other, "the points," which, "it was believed, . . . represented the crown of thorns of Our Lord." Even the colors are not dissimilar: in Cecilia, "points of a violet color which tended toward black"; in Angela, "a dark mark but not black." Another time Angela had spoken of "the color of iron and dark tobacco."[51]

The story of Christ's Passion and its instruments was for Angela, then, of help in interpreting and representing the symptoms of her own sufferings. Similarly, for Michelangeli, a sign of Cecilia's uniqueness was the fact that the surgeon "found" an order similar to that of Chiara da Montefalco. Thus, Angela used the language taken from books and prayer to decipher her own intellectual and corporeal states. It seems to me, in fact, that in this case, in contrast to others, the pain that Angela felt in her heart was real: the story simply offered an explanation in terms consistent with the rest of her life.

❧ In church on Christmas Day 1692 in spiritual meditation, Angela had seen the Virgin "with her son in her arms, who with a loving face, kissed and held him." Suddenly, Angela recounted, "I saw that my little Jesus extended his tiny hands toward me. I was afraid: on the one hand I felt my hands open and on the other I felt death. I suspended all fear and said: 'O my most sweet mother let me hold your son.' And Mary extended her arms and I took him in mine." Aware of the privilege that had been conceded to her, Angela had immediately made some requests of Jesus. Among other things, she asked for the return of her spiritual father, who had been transferred to Genoa. From his heart a positive response had come to her. After a few minutes, "the Virgin Mary asked me for her son saying: 'Enough for now, let me see my son.' " But Jesus at this point had shown love for her, just like children do: "he turned away instead toward his mother pretending to want to go, and then he turned around towards me and *comte*[?] *poverede*[?] my dear little child and then he returned to the arms of my most holy mother. I leave to your R[everence] to judge how great was the happiness of my heart and the joy of my spirit."

Leaving her, Jesus had left a flame of love ignited in her heart, which, consuming her "day and night on account of the intense heat," constrained her to wear her clothes unbuttoned, although it was "the coldest part of the season," and to hide herself from the eyes of her relatives in the most remote corners of her house. "Oh my Jesus, how many sighs, oh how many tears, oh how many footsteps, oh how many tremors in my body, oh how many times I opened my arms, oh how many cries I sent for love of my Jesus." And, not being able to talk, "she roared like the animals," and "hot tears like flames" poured from her eyes.[52]

The appearance of the Madonna and the holding of the baby Jesus in one's arms on Christmas night recur often in biographies of mystics. Much earlier in the Bolognese convent of Corpus Domini, Caterina de Vigri "on the vigil of Christmas" had asked and obtained permission from the abbess to remain all night in church to pray. Suddenly, "the glorious Virgin appeared to her with her most elect son in her arms, and he was swaddled exactly as the others are when they are born." The Virgin herself "placed him in her arms." Caterina, knowing well "that this was the true son of the eternal father, took him in her arms, laying her face upon that of the most beloved infant Christ Jesus. And with so much sweetness and tenderness that everything seemed to melt like wax in a flame." Commenting on this extraordinary privilege, Caterina—like Angela—said, "But I leave this to the judgment of the listeners."[53]

❧ Faced with the quantity of exceptional behavior manifested by his penitent, Father Ruggieri knew that he would have to exercise a role of guidance and control, carefully balancing the two. The rules forced him to put Angela to the test. One day, for example, when giving her communion, he gave her two hosts and then asked her: "All right, now that you have had two pieces of the host, will you have had more Lord than other people who had only one piece, since I, having a host, have had more Lord than you have had in two pieces[?]" But, in recounting this to the Inquisitor, Father Ruggieri suddenly understood that the control he had exercised over Angela was now exercised over him by his interrogators. Frightened, he explained in detail: "I told her this not because I believed it nor have I ever believed that in the pieces or larger hosts there is more Lord than in the lesser or smaller hosts, because I know that there is as much of the Lord in one as in the other even in a fragment, as Saint Thomas says." But Angela, too, had given the correct response: "Indeed," he added, "she explained to me that in whatever portion of a consecrated host, even if it was as little as a droplet of water, there was all the Lord." Father Ruggieri had seen in all this a confirmation of his penitent's orthodoxy, and even a possible sign of sanctity: "You have thought like a theologian because you have answered like Saint Thomas in his discourse, and I said to myself that there was in these deeds of the said Angelina something of the Lord who wanted to show now and on other occasions that this creature was graced by him."[54]

The fear that a heresy could be hidden in the behavior of his penitent arose in Father Ruggieri only when confronting her physical manifestations of sanctity. Angela, in fact, besides suffering the agonies discussed earlier, often, after receiving communion, remained as still as a statue, without speaking. One day, "seeing her remain in this way lost in thought," he had commanded her in the name of God to answer him and to tell him how communion had gone. Only then, "as if she had returned to her senses and woke up," Angela had answered that it had gone well, but she was not able to say the Pater Noster "because she felt very tired." From then on he forced her to recite the rosary with him for three reasons: "first, because she doubted that she could speak in that state of mind as I had heard said about the followers of the Molinos who were not able to say the Our Father and Hail Mary; second, to thank God who had deigned to come into our souls in the sacrament of the Eucharist; and third, because we were humble and lowly creatures and in this way I believed

I would understand if these agonies that the said Angela suffered, and the way she remained so frozen and immobile were diabolical or else the work of the Lord."[55]

During the search of Angela's house, no books or writings of the Molinos were found. Moreover, the Holy Office did not share the fear expressed by Father Ruggieri, nor did it try to learn more about the other book read by Angela. Elisabetta Zani, in her denunciation, had tried to throw grave suspicions on the exchange of a book between Mellini and Father Ruggieri, saying that the priest was very possessive of it, because he entrusted it only to Angela and did not want her to show it to anyone. She could only say that the book was big like Bellarmino's *Dottrina.* But Angela had tranquilly specified that the matter concerned a book containing "ejaculatory prayers for several saints' holy days" and that it was given to her so that she could prepare herself for communion.[56] For the Inquisitor that was sufficient explanation.

❧ Each page of the diary opens and closes with an ejaculatory prayer. Angela had also read some ejaculatory prayers in the life of Cecelia Nobili. Yet beyond the mechanical recitation of this type of prayer, Angela seemed to know something more. In a letter dictated to father Ruggieri in the confessional, speaking about the "effects" caused in her by her martyred heart, Angela wrote:

> In the most intense moments of love I experience more pains and I confess that . . . the effects then are many and one is that it makes me sigh, the other that it makes me breathe in deeply. As to the sighing, I so long for my beloved Jesus, that I cannot see his beautiful face: and the sighs are hot like the flames of a fire, as if they were loving exclamations that flow from my eyes, tears, I would not say of blood, because God does not permit it, but indeed of hot water, as if water had been on fire. Other sighs resound in my heart and I am not able to breathe without pain and I remain afflicted.[57]

There are many similarities between these "effects" on Angela's heart and the technical definition of ejaculatory prayers as "breaths" or "sighs to God."[58] For example, Francis de Sales, in *Introduction to the Devout Life,* said, "Man withdraws into God because he aspires to him and he aspires to withdraw himself there. . . . Aspire to God often then, Filotea, with brief but ardent explosions of your heart, admire his beauty, invoke his help . . . thus ejaculatory prayers are made . . . and this exercise is not at all out of place since one may intersperse them among all our anxieties and worries without any disturbance."[59] In another work, *Maniera divota di celebrare con frutto il SS. sacrificio della messa,* he said, concerning chastity, "Keep in mind that your holy laws obligate you to not live, breathe, or aspire except for your celestial bridegroom."[60]

All of Francis de Sales's works were addressed to people who were not able to follow God by taking vows. The order of the Visitandines[61] had been appropriately created for virgins and widows who were not able or who did not want to enter a convent: its spirit was very near that of the Company of Saint Ursula, to which Angela belonged. We can surmise that among the texts that Father Ruggieri gave to Angela to read were the writings of Francis de Sales. In this manner, Molinist attitudes could have reached her, since, in fact, the writings of Francis de Sales were accused of promulgating these ideas at the end of the seventeenth century. The *Maniera devota,* then, could be the book whose name Angela did not remember, which she used to prepare herself for Mass and the Eucharist. Nevertheless, she remembered its dimensions perfectly: "height about three fingers, width about five fingers, and length about eight fingers." Both the 1663 edition of *Maniera devota* and the 1668 edition of *Introduction to the Devout Life,* preserved in the Communal Library of Bologna, correspond to these dimensions. Upon opening the latter book, the name of the owner appears: Angela Ungarelli. (It is not "signora Anna Unualeli," whose death Angela foresaw on a page of her diary.)[62]

Concerning the other "effect" of which Angela spoke, the "breathing in," it is true that we find traces of Sales's spirituality here, but they are completely overwhelmed by explicit and sensual declarations of love: "Your reverence knows that as to aspiring I aspire to the highest good, and clasping my arms together I cry sweetly: love, love, my love Jesus, and I hope to see nude the desired good, and I am so in love that I sing, laugh, cry and am silent." Realizing the powerful sensual charge, Angela added, "This love is so pure that I place myself in Jesus' heart like children do at the breast of their mother breastfeeding, and thus I rest."[63] As we shall also see later, the theme of breast-feeding always took on strongly sensual connotations for her, which do not at all exclude a feeling of spiritual love toward God but rather, by combining with it, increase it.

❧ But the Inquisitor showed no particular interest in the pains in her heart, which Angela explained by means of the instruments of the Passion, or in the effects of prayer, or in the fears of Molinist heresy manifested by Father Ruggieri. After a while, all the questions were addressed to one point: to delineate what special relationship had been created between penitent and confessor. Confirming in part what was denounced by Elisabetta, Angela recounted how one day, speaking with Father Ruggieri, she had had the clear intuition that he regularly had the tendency to fall into mortal sin. The fear that the devil had come to her placing "evil concepts against this good creature"[64] made her cry. Yet the more she tried to resist, the more the awareness of his sin grew, to the point of realizing each time the precise moment at which it occurred, because a terrible weight tugged at her heart. The fear of overstepping her place prevented her from speaking, although she strongly felt the impulse to do so. In a desperate attempt to make herself understood, "I told him indirectly, but in vain." Father Ruggieri advised her to pray for aid so that she could explain clearly. During those prayers, Jesus, angry, had scolded her and had explained to her precisely what sin was involved. Shame, confusion, and fear were stirred up in her heart, and she had immediately spat in Christ's face, thinking the whole thing might be a temptation. To this he had replied that he feared neither her threats nor her spit, and had urged her to know how to suffer a little shame for his love. Thus, the following morning, after she had futilely tried to speak to Father Ruggieri in an indirect way, overcoming the reticence of both, Angela had explicitly declared that it concerned a sin against chastity.[65] Seeing himself exposed, Father Ruggieri had exclaimed, "You are a gypsy!"

From that moment on, her suffering and repugnance for the sin had driven Angela to keep closer track of her confessor: each morning she questioned him about this matter; each evening she forced him to recite five Paters and five Aves, in memory of Christ's wounds, but to do it with his arms open "so that the enemy does not tempt him to offend him with that sin." If, however, he had still fallen into sin, he would have to confess: "Then I said to him that I wanted him to be a saint," Angela concluded, addressing herself to the Inquisitor.[66]

In the course of his depositions, Father Ruggieri gave substantially the same testimony, showing how, in addition to an attitude of prudence toward his penitent, he had slowly developed the conviction that the Lord "wanted to show now and on other occasions that the said creature was graced by him." Many times Angela had stupefied him with predictions of the future; even more important, her inflexibility had given him the desire to resist his temptations and to try to overcome his own difficulties as a man facing the obligation of chastity. But let us follow his own words at one of these terrible moments:

> Really, it seemed to me that in my room there were demons and that she was dressed as if she were Saint Catherine of Siena with a bunch of rods in her hand and she went around my bed chasing away the said demons; and truly two or three times at night while I was in bed it distinctly seemed to me, while I was under attack by impure thoughts, that I saw these demons in my room and that she, Angelina, dressed as a nun with the rods chased them away from my bed. And at that time I thought that in fact the said Angela commended me to God and to the most sacred Virgin and to Saint Catherine of Siena who was her counsel and I in that instance said the rosary and in that way I slept.

In facing these difficulties, Giovanni Battista needed to remove from Angela her characteristics as a woman who was not bound by religious vows, giving her nun's clothes, at least, if not those of Catherine of Siena. But, seeing that he did not make much progress in overcoming his sins, Angela often threatened to abandon him. He, then, begging her to pity him and to help him, dissuaded her: perhaps he added that it was the devil who suggested drastic measures that would hurt them both.[67] Every act of confession concluded with the benediction imparted first by Father Ruggieri to Angela, then vice versa. She knew how to do this in Latin: "Benedictio Dei Omnipotentis Patris, et Filii et Spiritus Sancti et Beatissima Verginis Santissimi Rosarii et nostri Angeli custodis, et omnium sanctorum et sanctarum descendat super nos et maneat semper." Father Ruggieri himself recounted: "She kept her hand raised moving it in the manner of the priests when they give the benediction, and I saw this through the holes of the confessional grate and I answered her 'let it be so' or else 'let it be done' or 'amen': and if I did not always say it with my mouth I said it with my heart."[68]

Even this gesture, totally outside the norm, had not been an arbitrary one on the part of the woman. Confronting the internal voice that ordered her to bless the confessor, Angela had felt dismay. And, immediately posing resistance, she had replied that one cannot bless the person from whom one expects the blessing. But the Son of God had assured her and freed her from the temptations that could spring from a similar request. At times, however, she shirked this duty and followed it only if Father Ruggieri imposed it on her in virtue of obedience. Moreover—Angela stated—in those moments it seemed to her that the Virgin was over her, and, "It has always been my belief that it was the Blessed Virgin who blessed him, and not me who proffered the words for obedience to God and to Father Ruggieri, because I knew I was a worm."[69]

But the demand to bless Father Ruggieri had come after another one, equally painful and difficult to accept. One day, in fact, she felt "inspired internally" to let herself be called mother (*madre*) by him.[70] To this she had answered that it was sufficient for her to be a good "daughter" (*figliola*). But after several days Father Ruggieri repeated the request to her. In the face of his insistence she despaired: with "loving exclamations" and "hot tears" she turned to the Virgin Mary, saying that to her alone belonged the name of mother and the being of mother. But the internal voice answered her that if the Madonna, who is just, is not outraged at being the mother of all sinners, how much more a female sinner was able to be a mother to a male sinner. From then on the confessor had taken to calling her at times "Mother" (*Madre*), at times "*Mamma*,"[71] names both were accustomed to using for the Blessed Virgin. Along with the mother full of authority, Angela became the tender mother: "One evening, around four o'clock, while I was working, I felt something in my heart as if the said Father Ruggieri was saying there—'Good evening *mamma* or mother' and I with my mouth answered him—'Good evening, my son, be good.' "[72]

❧ The journey followed by confessor and penitent traces exactly the developmental curve described by H. Brémond in regard to other mystics:[73] moving from an unsatisfying, agonizing spiritual guidance to a profound link with the "awaited director." In the beginning it was he who commanded; then imperceptibly he began to modify his relationship to Angela, until from "teacher" he moved to "disciple"; that is, a soul to assist and to elevate to divine grace. "Then I told him that I wanted him a saint," Angela had said at the moment in which she had begun to fight against his sins. A complete reversal of roles had occurred: from spiritual daughter in need of guidance and control, Angela had become spiritual mother of her confessor, who trusted her completely.

In terms of spiritual maternity, for Angela it was not a question of simply accepting the name of mother but of effectively becoming one. To the Inquisitor's impersonal question on the basis of Elisabetta Zani's account, "Do you know whether any person said that she had given birth in spirit to a certain spiritual father who felt filial love, or that she felt something awkward or heavy in her ribs?" Angela had immediately responded by referring the question to herself:

> I know well that I will have said that I felt impressed on my soul the said Father Ruggieri, as a son; indeed I remember that, having gone into the sepulchre of Santo Stefano in the first year, before the said father went to Genoa . . . he having asked me to pray to God for him, in entering the Holy Sepulchre I felt a heaviness in my soul, which tugged my heart sensibly and I seemed to feel him impressed on my soul like a son. And in leaving I felt delivered of that weight on my soul, and I think that I said all this to the priest himself in the confessional. But I do not remember what he answered me, but I believe he said "Be humble."

Unsatisfied, the Inquisitor pressed her, insisting on the physicality of the event: "Do you know whether anyone said that she suffered many pains and that in this manner she gave birth in spirit to a certain spiritual father and moreover that she confirmed that he was her son and she was his mother?" Angela answered, "About this father I know nothing new, and I do not know that I said it nor that I experienced it, because I do not remember."[74] But at another time she spontaneously recounted that, after a procession in a parish near Baraccano, she commended her soul and that of Father Ruggieri to the Lord:

> While praying I felt myself conceive or have enter into my soul the said Father Ruggieri like a tiny son three or four months old. I felt so much fervor in my soul that I felt it physically in my left breast, as if truly I breast fed him like a mother, and it seemed to me, indeed I felt sensibly, how he pulled and sucked the milk from my breast. And in that instant I felt also a fervor of love toward God, and going to see the tapestries in the parish, when I saw any image of the blessed Virgin or when she breast fed her son, or she caressed him when he was a one-year-old or she held him in her arms like a sorrowful mother, I was moved by pity, feeling my soul enraptured for love of God: and because of this tenderness I could not help crying with abandon.[75]

At the same time, it is evident that Angela denied every purely physical foundation of her maternity. She did not say—as the Inquisitor tried to suggest to her—that she *gave birth amidst many pains* but that she felt the baby *impressed on* her soul and that she felt it *enter* her soul. It was not, then, a question of a birth, but rather a conception; to give birth at such a point would have signified accepting completely the gravity of the annunciation.

For a single woman prohibited by social norms from the legitimacy of biological maternity, its physical and mental representation could only be the virginal one of the Madonna, known through sculpture and painted images in churches. Breast-feeding, infancy, and agonies linked to a son were well known in this manner to Angela, who, "because of this tenderness . . . could not help crying with abandon."

This consuming experience of maternity in which the physical pleasure of feeling the baby pull the milk from the breast—"it seemed to me, indeed I felt sensibly, how he pulled"—was mixed with the fervor of love for God. All this creates a strong desire to know something more about Angela's life.

❧ Angela Maria Mellini—whose father was dead at the time of the trial—was the daughter of Giacomo, seller of distilled liquors, fruit, and grilled meats. Apparently nothing remained from this activity, which he had perhaps performed as a peddler. An illness had made him bedridden in the last years of his life.[76] His wife, Francesca Elmi, was often sick as well and unable to move. Angela spoke about her many times in her letters to Evangelista Biffi.[77] After they had lived in the parish of Santa Caterina di Saragozza, the Mellinis moved, going to live—around 1691—in Via de' Gombruti.[78]

The other members of her family were her sister, Margherita (dead at the time of the trial),[79] and her brother, Domenico.[80] About this latter, unfortunately, we know nothing except his name. Probably he did not live with his mother and sister Angela or contribute in any way to their maintenance. Angela, in fact, spoke often of her poverty and of the charity she received. At times she was forced to beg in front of churches for her sick mother, but she did it willingly to mortify her pride. After her father's death, she was the only one in her family who worked: her trade was to sew and to spin. We do not know for whom she worked except for one person: Father Ruggieri. Every Thursday he went to pick up his things. In fact, Angela herself stated to the Inquisitor that she mended for him or did his socks, his buttons, "or other necessary items, he giving me what I had earned as payment: indeed recently I made him a shirt which he had to pay me for, as well as an ivory comb."[81]

Elisabetta Zani's account was more detailed, and above all full of malevolent insinuations:

> She kept track of all his affairs, that is, his shirts, suits, socks. She brought him fresh eggs, he having given her some hens to keep. Many times he bought her shoes when he bought his own, a pair for him and a pair for her, because they were already saying that they two were as one. Moreover, when she was sick, the said father Giovanni Battista not only went to visit her, but he with his own hands fed her, changed her position in bed, and cried with abandon in her presence. He provided a doctor, medicine, and other necessary things for her. And I know all these things from Angela Maria herself, who on various occasions and times recounted them to me.[82]

In contrast to the clarity of Angela, who neatly distinguished between work relationships and spiritual relationships, Father Ruggieri tended to mix everything together. Asked, in fact, if he knew anyone who in the confessional had called a woman *mamma,* he answered that he himself had done it toward Angela Mellini, begging her to commend him to God as a son: "In that instance I also sent her my clothes so that she could mend them as a mother does for her son."[83] Later he added: "She told me that she felt as if she had conceived in her heart a son and that she breast-fed him and that it seemed to her in her mind that this son whom she breast-fed was I: and I told her that it was clear that the Lord wanted her to help me with her prayers and spiritual assistance as a mother does breast-feeding her son, and that therefore she should continue to commend me to the Lord."[84]

On one hand, the "fresh eggs," the "milk of the prayers," the shirts, the socks, the buttons, the combs; on the other, the shoes for both, the doctor, the tears. There was a union of reciprocal material and spiritual assistance. A similar thing had also happened with her other confessor, Father Evangelista Biffi, but on a different level. He, as we have seen, taught her to write because, if he left Bologna, he wanted to know about "[her] spiritual progress" and how she "was following in the path of the Lord."[85] Father Biffi also helped fill Angela's temporal needs, allowing her to collect money for masses that he would later celebrate. That money Angela kept for herself. Once she succeeded in collecting enough that she was immediately able to pay the rent on her house.[86] Before he left Bologna, Father Biffi had helped her in other ways also, with "two *stara* of flour from the Certosa, a *quartarola* from the Malvasia, two *quartiroli* from the office of the poor." He had paid her besides "one *genovina* for rent," and "once during Lent," Angela explained, "he asked me in the confessional if I had anything to eat, and then he brought me a handkerchief with chestnuts, nuts, and bread."[87] The unfailing Elisabetta had reported that "the same father prior . . . made many charitable gifts to her house, now some broth, now some fish, and he gave her the alms of others. Once he had offered her two *doble* so that he could help her in her needs, but she had not wanted to accept them."[88]

Father Biffi's interest in Angela was conceived following one of her confessions. Having asked her if she did penances and observed abstinence, Angela had answered negatively, "but I suffered a pain on the left side of my ribs and also a pain in my side and I have an ill mother and I am poor and these are my penances and crosses."[89] Evangelista Biffi had then asked her for permission to speak with Father Ruggieri. Following this conversation he had become her second spiritual father. Together the two priests spoke about her progress along the path of the Lord.

Biffi had offered her a real possibility for the future, proposing that she become a nun in Cremona, where he had become prior of San Sigismondo.[90] Angela responded in a letter: "You know before you left Bologna what you said to me about coming to Cremona: and I answered that if my mother died I would come immediately and I beg you if you still have that opinion and there is a place that you advise me how I should proceed."[91] But in an undated letter, which Father Ruggieri wrote on behalf of Angela to Teresa Biffi, Evangelista's sister, there appears, cryptically: "I do not know if it comes from me or from God, that in respect to the request your most reverend brother made to me, I find myself so distracted and confused that I do not know how to answer concerning his good and holy thought. For as you know better than me the love of God controls and if it does it works great things. Good-bye . . . and I beg you to pity me because I do not know how to write."[92]

There is no information that would clarify what request is referred to in the letter. Yet it is very probable that the decision about which Angela found herself "distracted and confused" was that of becoming a nun in Cremona. What had happened? We can set out various hypotheses. The most simple, but also the least probable, is that Angela had changed her mind, no longer accepting the letter written in her hand. Or else we can posit that Father Ruggieri was not in agreement with that decision, which would have sent his spiritual mother far away. Finally (and this is the most likely conjecture), we can hypothesize that there were already rumors about the trial, but it was not possible to inform Father Biffi in a more precise manner. His last letter bore the date 23 September 1698. Elisabetta's denunciation came only seven days later.

❧ What material and social possibilities did a woman like Angela Mellini have at the end of the seventeenth century, deprived as she was of any institutional protection? In other words, what could a woman alone, and a poor one at that, do in a society in which institutions were a form of self-defense and at the same time a support for others?

With her mother's death, believed at the time to be imminent, Angela would have been truly alone, deprived of every bond of kinship. Deep and complex bonds existed for her only with Father Ruggieri, but it was precisely the licitness of these which was questioned and rejected at the trial. Beyond this close relationship, the exchange of letters with Father Biffi demonstrates both his role as spiritual father writing to his "daughter in Christ" and her role as liaison and often guide, once she had learned to write. In fact, both the power gained through writing and the particular intensity of her spiritual life are features that differentiated Angela from her acquaintances, all similar to her in social and economic background. These women were primarily single or widowed. We already know Elisabetta Zani. Her rancor toward Angela must have been closely linked to her absolute dependence on her. During the trial, in fact, the accused admitted that she had recounted many of the things testified by Elisabetta "because she was my friend and I guided her to the spiritual life, with the help of the Lord. She called me, in fact, by the name spiritual mother. Indeed she did not do anything which she did not discuss with me and we had a great understanding between us." And she concluded: "But it would be about six or seven years since I have confided in her because I realized that she went to Father Bonacorsi to tell him everything; indeed I then had the suspicion that she told Father Certani too, because she made a remark to me once which I had confessed to him."[93]

In addition to Elisabetta, the letters also introduce us to Maria, who, having recently lost her mother, was advised by Father Biffi to "go to the houses of honest people to be a domestic servant for a fixed period of time";[94] a "good widow who had been the wife of a soldier";[95] and Susanna Solfanara, daughter of a ragman. The latter worried Father Biffi a great deal, and he strongly entreated Angela to help her obtain the habit of the Ursulines.[96] Annina was the Renoaldi family's domestic servant. About Marina we know only her name.

The thirty-four-year-old Maddalena Cavina, in contrast, was not part of this group of Father Ruggieri's ex-penitents, but like Angela frequented the Church of Spirito Santo, where she confessed to Father Alessandro, who was "a little old man."[97] Maddalena, unmarried and fatherless, was a manual laborer and spinner at the convent of the Sisters of Santa Maria Nuova. She lived near the Church of San Francesco, very close to Angela's house, and testified that the sisters of the convent held a favorable opinion of Father Ruggieri. From her testimony we learn that Angela, twice in the same week in July 1698, had gone to the convent of Santa Maria Nuova—where Father Ruggieri was special confessor—to beg for her sick mother. The porter Maria Archangela Bonaveri ("as young as me," the accused had defined her)[98] had said to Maddalena that "Angelina was a good daughter and a little saint." Maddalena concluded her deposition by adding, "I do not know really how she knew that she was a little saint."[99] About Angela's goodness and sanctity, in fact, she said that she knew nothing. The only report of sanctity from a neighbor was noted by Elisabetta Zani, whe remembered meeting a woman (whose name is unknown) in the hospital; the woman began to speak of Mellini, saying that she was "a great soul" because she continually went to confession and took communion.

Angela Maria Mellini, then, did not have any particular reputation for sanctity, even in her neighborhood. The people who more often met her in church admired the constancy with which she frequented the sacraments, but not much else. The more "technical" language used by Archangela Bonaveri was perhaps related to the possibility that she had spoken with Father Ruggieri about the details of Angela's spiritual life. But the diminutive "little saint" removed every indication of true sanctity from her statement. What interested Angela, however, was not public recognition of her uniqueness, but rather understanding each time what was made manifest "inside her" and succeeding then in expressing the "effects" to her spiritual fathers. Her "inclination to good" was a choice that concerned above all herself and, immediately after, Father Ruggieri. To Archangela Bonaveri, who spoke to her about the qualities of her confessor, she had answered by asking her to pray to the Lord so that "He make him a saint, because I would like to be a saint myself first, then him, then all the creatures of the world." Immediately afterward, fearing perhaps that she had gone too far, she added that she was "a piece of dirt enveloped in two rags."[100]

Yet beyond Angela's good relations with her neighbors, which also offered her the role of guide, and as a result a limited moral power, the problem of her own sustenance remained paramount to her. The absence of a father, brother, or husband, and, after the trial, of the economic contribution of her confessors clouded her future. In a paragraph that is difficult to decipher, Angela seemed to hint at an attempt by her relatives to marry her:

> For seven years I have battled the numerous and varied evil attempts and lies[?] of relatives who prevented the good that I desired and of a man who is a wolf who wanted to steal the sheep of Jesus Christ. But it is not due to my virtue that I have remained chaste, for I tell you I have been inclined to that good since I was a child. Having naturally a compassionate heart when I heard the passion of Christ recounted, it destroyed the depths of my body with the great compassion and love which I felt for that suffering.[101]

Adhering to this explicit declaration, Angela had consciously chosen her destiny. In her analysis of her life, the motives for such a choice did not depend in any way on the external world but were tied solely to her own compassionate nature, and the only events that mattered for her were from a far distant past: the Passion of Christ. Even learning to write was not of any use to her for human time, from which in any case she had been excluded. For her it was an instrument useful for the long term: eternity.

Father Biffi—as noted—worried by the solitude and difficulties that awaited her, offered her the solution that he believed most suited her, different and more fitting than those suggested for Maria or Susanna Solfanara: to become a nun. Yet, this implied an investment that Angela alone would not have been able to afford, given her extreme indigence. It was costly to become a bride of Christ, even if less so than becoming the bride of a man.[102] A review of nuns' dowries during the period 1698–1710 (the years in which Angela could have taken vows) demonstrates that the price paid by poor "old maids" coming from charitable institutions was around twelve hundred lire for "lay sisters" and around eighteen hundred lire for "regular sisters." To this it was necessary to add the expenses of consecration, about one hundred fifty to two hundred lire.[103] But between the status of wife and nun existed a third possibility: the Tertiaries, or Third Orders. Like every other "inscription" in an institutionalized association, even these had a price, but it was more reasonable. Susanna Solfanara, in fact, paid one hundred lire as dowry at the moment she received the habit of an Ursuline.[104] To this must be added the expenses of the consecration: rosaries, candles, crucifixes.

On a material level, the Company of Saint Ursula[105] assured its initiates economic assistance in case of poverty and, at their death, a funeral accompanied by other Ursulines. It was as much as a natal or adopted family could do to provide these guarantees, which were crucial for women who, unmarried or widowed, were in precarious institutional situations. The assurance of a funeral was very important, because it removed the specter of a solitary death in complete isolation.[106] The Ursulines took a vow of chastity, but they remained with their families and undertook to teach Christian doctrine in their neighborhoods.[107]

This was one of the more interesting ways in which the Counter-Reformation church faced the problem of both institutional placement for the unmarried woman and, at the same time, the penetration of the family and the neighborhood.[108] To these women, "freer" than both married women and nuns, was entrusted part of the transmission of the culture of the catechism. To this end they learned to read: one of the things that distinguished the origin of the Ursulines was precisely the miracle of women who learned to read. This was the case for Angela Merici, the founder, as it was for Osanna Andreasi, who was inspired by her.

By belonging to the Company, the Ursulines recuperated in a single stroke all the roles denied to them or diminished by the society of men: they were, indeed, *daughters* and *brides* of Christ, *sisters* of other Ursulines, *daughters* for the bishop and for the mother prioress. Here was reconstituted a family to which they "belonged." This permitted them correctly to redirect their "liberty" from the normal bonds of family, "without danger of being deceived and tricked by their own Senses, by the World or by the Devil, as at times are those who want to live in their own way." In fact, the deeds done in observance of the Rule of the Order "are more sure and of much greater merit than those which are done of one's own free will, according to one's own desires and without any direction, which many times are indiscreet, dangerous, and without merit."[109] Naturally, their model was the Madonna. Clothes of "cheap cloth, serge or *sarza*, black in color,"[110] the absence of any ornament, a small leather belt, and black shoes identified them.

❧ "She wears black, with a small collar, the ordinary black shoes of an Ursuline . . ."[111] thus, Elisabetta Zani described Angela. Between the condition of wife, which she had apparently refused, and that of nun, which she had not been able to reach, Angela had "chosen" that of an Ursuline. It was, after all, perfectly suited to her situation—as, in fact, the *Regole* stated: "The Company was instituted for the individual benefit of those virgins who desire to serve God in a Virginal state, and cannot or do not want to accept another state."[112] It specified, furthermore, that whoever entered it had to have had "as her goal the health of her soul, and not overcoming poverty,[113] hoping for temporal gain. She possesses some patrimony to sustain herself, or with her own industry is inclined to earn her board for herself or has someone who helps her out of charity."[114] Among the more important duties, beyond teaching Christian doctrines and helping at Christian gatherings, were knowing how to do silent prayer and spiritual exercises.[115] But Angela—as we have seen—had decided to do much more. Too much, according to the opinion of the Holy Office. After Rome's decision arrived on 17 April 1699, the charges against her remained, but she was released. Various penances were imposed on her, and her spiritual father Giovanni Battista was sent away. He in his turn was reprimanded above all for having spoken confidentially with a woman about problems regarding his own chastity. He asked forgiveness and said that he had done it "blinded by the desire of helping my soul, which help I thought I obtained through the prayers of the said Angelina, who I believed was good, and prayed to God for me."[116]

In short, for Angela—and consequently for Father Ruggieri as well—the trial could have had a positive outcome. It could have served as the necessary, normal step for a day of reckoning with the institution of the Church on earth. It had been thus for many women—and many spiritual fathers—recognized as saints afterward by the official Church. Margherita Maria Alacoque and the priest of la Colombière are examples. But for Angela and for Cecilia, something had not worked. The buttonmaker and lay sister had not been accepted. Why?

In Cecilia, who had learned to read because of her desire to savor, on her own, the lives of the saints, Angela had certainly found many things to empathize with, perhaps more than in Caterina de' Vigri or Catherine of Siena. Cecilia, having lost both parents (perhaps poor farmers, even though Michelangeli went to lengths to demonstrate a higher social status supported at least by her surname), had, after much persistence, obtained permission from her brother to become a nun. He, however, had granted her a dowry so small that it forced her to become a lay sister, "while she was capable of becoming a nun." For a long time, this fact had been a source of temptation for her, because the devil suggested to her "that her brother, in the interest of not paying as much dowry as one gives to nuns, had put her into that state not caring for her suffering and loss: while in order to help another of her brothers he had not found it a problem to spend a great deal, for her he had found nothing."[117]

For Cecilia, no mere passing acquaintance of Angela, I want to report only one proof of her sanctity. It was the one nearest to the space in which the life of a woman was lived—the kitchen—and, therefore, the most difficult: "They gave her eggs for the main course, she cooked them in the pot, she pretended to put in sweet herbs, but in place of them she put in chicory or other bitter herbs and she made the sauce from them and cooked them together with the eggs. But in the end it turned out very gentle to the taste. She cooked them on the coals without salt."[118] Ironically, those very herbs which she had loved so much that she went without them for the love of God were among the "sweet ones" that were used to fill the cavities of her dead body and cause it to decay. (The mixture was provided by a doctor from Foligno; the herbs came from Nocera.) Even the painter, also called from Foligno to paint her portrait, failed to make the picture resemble her.[119] Cecilia's was a story of failures, even if apparently others', not hers. But in Angela's case, who had failed? Not even the Holy Office passed judgment: apparently the only error was the priest's for having talked with a woman about chastity.

Angela, in reaching too high—to sanctity—had created a higher level of female marginalization. Wives, nuns, and prostitutes were all included in their way on the rolls of the community; the poor "old maids," to "preserve their honor," were helped to enter the Conservatori, and even "normal" Ursulines were less marginal than was Angela. Her quest for sanctity made her a true weak link in the fragile chain of women's choices. After the trial, it is difficult to follow her. Certainly, at her mother's death she moved: in fact, she was not entered in the register of deceased members of the parish of San Marino. The last trace we have of her is contained in a document datable between 1707 and 1717.[120] It was a list of poor Ursulines who regularly received charitable donations. Among them is one "Angiola Mellini."

## Notes

1. Biblioteca comunale di Bologna (hereafter BCB), MS. 1883. Trial "contra Angelam M. Mellini, ursolinam Bononiensem, P.D. Joannem Baptistam Ruggieri Ianuensem, ordinis clericos minores, P.D. Evangelistam Biffi, ordinis s. Hieronimi, priorem sancti Barbatiani," fol. 492v. The citations that follow which contain only a folio number refer to this trial.

2. Fol. 489r.

3. Fol. 492r.

4. In addition to those who offended God in various ways, it was preoccupied "with those who commit any evil deeds under the cover of holiness and act as if they were saints" (fol. 494r). I am preparing a study on a series of seventeenth-century trials for "affected sanctity." The case of Angela Mellini is a preview. On the problem of "affected sanctity," see G. Bona, *De discretione spirituum* (Rome, 1672), chap. 7. A list of cases appears in M. Summers, *The Physical Phenomena of Mysticism* (London, 1950), p. 204ff. On the connections with Quietism frequently encountered in the second half of the seventeenth century, see M. Petrochi, *Il quietismo italiano del seicento* (Rome, 1948).

5. Fol. 512v.

6. F. Furet and J. Ozouf, *Lire et écrire: L'alphabetisation des français de Calvin a Jules Ferry* (Paris, 1977), p. 199ff.

7. Fol. 501r. Evangelista Biffi had left Bologna on 6 January 1698. Angela, then, had learned to write at the end of the preceding summer, at thirty-three.

8. Fol. 499v.

9. Angela stated that she began to write what I label her diary about a year before: "It contains feelings and events which came to me during mass and holy communion." (fol. 501v). Father Ruggieri had given her a small notebook after 4 September 1697, the day on which Angela had shown him the drawing of her martyred heart, detailing to him in the confessional the explanation of every feature sketched. In transcribing the diary, I intend to document on one hand Angela's relationship with writing, and on the other what Angela wanted to say through writing. On certain points, however, these two goals clash because writing was a means of expression that Angela had mastered imperfectly.

10. Diario, fol. 2v. This document was included in the trial proceedings but was numbered independently. The written pages are 17 through 24.

11. Ibid., fol. 3r.

12. Ibid., fol. 2v.

13. Ibid., fol. 3r.

14. Fol. 495v.

15. Diario, fol. 5r–v.

16. Ibid., fol. 1v.

17. Fol. 499v.

18. "My spirit was enraptured and my Jesus appeared to me with a crown of thorns on his head; he said many things which I omit for brevity." Diario, fol. 9v.

19. Ibid., fol. 2r. [Editor's note: The question mark is Ciammitti's because she

was not sure what her reading of *contitare* in the text meant. I have hazarded a guess that it was a variant spelling of *contentare,* but obviously the question mark still applies. In fact, the rather strange "That he loves me or not is of little importance . . ." might also be changed to the more likely sounding "To myself I am of little importance . . ." simply by dividing the often-run-together words slightly differently.]

20. Ibid., fol. 1v.

21. Ibid., fol. 9v.

22. Ibid., fol. 10v.

23. G. Boncampagni, *Regole della Compagnia di S. Orsola, già eretta in Bologna l'anno MDCVI da Mons. Alfonso Paleotti arcivescovo* (Bologna, 1702), p. 20.

24. Diario, fol. 2r. [Editor's note: The last fragment is Ciammitti's tentative reading of a fragmentary line.]

25. Libretto di orazioni, fols. 3v–4r.

26. G. B. Manzini, *Dell'officio della settimana santa, affetti devoti* (Bologna, 1635), p. 11.

27. Diario, fol. 5r–v. [Editor's note: The *certo che no* that translates as "certainly not" has more emphasis in Italian because of the placement of the words.]

28. *Il libro della beata Caterina Bolognese, dell'ordine serafico di s. Francesco quale essa lasci scritto di sua mano* (n.p., n.d.), fol. B3.

29. Diario, fol. 3r.

30. Fol. 495v. [Editor's note: Ejaculatory prayers are brief prayers of explosive feeling.]

31. Fol. 511 v.

32. G. Zarri, *Il carteggio tra don Leone Bartolini e un gruppo di gentildonne bolognesi negli anni del Concilio di Trento (1545–1563),* reprinted from *Archivio Italiano per la storia della Pietà,* vol. 7, pp. 337–885.

33. Ibid., pp. 709–11.

34. The echoes of Cecilia's autopsy in Angela's diary, as we shall see later, demonstrate that she had read M. Michelangeli's biography, *Vita della serva di Dio Cecilia Nobili da Nocera, conversa nel monastero di S. Giovanni di detta città dell'ordine di Santa Chiara* (Rome, 1673). I was unable to see the 1664 edition of the autobiography; I saw the 1786 edition, printed in Foligno and conserved in the Biblioteca Comunale di Foligno: *Pratica utilissima per acquistar merito in tutte le azioni, composta dalla venerabile serva di Dio suor Cecilia Nobili da Nocera . . . , col compendio della vita di lei, il modo per arrivare presto alla perfezione e alcuni divoti Esercizi.* In it the 1783 edition printed in Rome is mentioned as well. On Cecilia Nobili, see also G. B. Gemmi, *Vita della suor Cecilia Nobili* (Rome, 1734).

35. Michelangeli, *Vita,* pp. 138–39.

36. MS. 1883, a loose sheet numbered by the notary fol. 5–4v.

37. Fol. 496v.

38. Diario, fols. 11v, 12r.

39. Ibid., fol. 4r.

40. Lettera a padre Biffi, dated 2/13/1698.

41. Diario, fol. 5v.

42. Fol. 506r.

43. Ibid.

44. Diario, fols. 10v–11r.

45. Diario, fol. 10r.

46. Fols. 520–21.

47. The cult was approved by the Congregazione dei Riti on 6 February 1765, under the papacy of Clement XIII.

48. Margherita died in 1690.
49. Michelangeli, *Vita*, pp. 35–36.
50. Ibid., pp. 52–54.
51. Fol. 518v.
52. Diario, fols. 7v, 8r–v.
53. *Il libro della beata*, fol. D VII r–v.
54. Fol. 525r.
55. Fol. 520v.
56. Fol. 511v.
57. The sheet, enclosed in the trial dossier, is between folios 520 and 521.
58. See *Dictionnaire de spiritualité*, s.v. "aspirations" and "jaculatorie."
59. F. de Sales, *Introduzione alla vita devota* (Venice, 1808), pp. 112–13.
60. F. de Sales, *Maniera divota di celebrare con frutto il SS. sacrificio della messa* (Milan, 1663), p. 130.
61. The order of the Visitandines originated in Paray-le-Monial in 1610 on the initiative of Giovanna Francesca di Chantal and Francis de Sales, her spiritual father.
62. Diario, fol. 13v. The copy of the *Introduzione alla vita devota* cited is signed 2.Y.V.101., but the note of ownership is in a later hand.
63. Sheet between fols. 520 and 521.
64. Diario, fol. 14r.
65. In her diary, Angela never explicitly named the sin, which is instead mentioned by the notary.
66. Fol. 510r.
67. Fol. 525v.
68. Fol. 505r.
69. Fol. 505v.
70. Diario, fol. 15v.
71. Fol. 504v.
72. Fol. 511r.
73. See H. Brémond, *Histoire littéraire du sentiment religieux en France*, vol. 2 (Paris, 1930), pp. 38–40.
74. Fol. 511r–v.
75. Fol. 512r.
76. "Angelina has other things to do, she has to attend to her father who is ill" (fol. 492v). I was unable to find the date of Giacomo Mellini's death: he appears neither in the register of the deceased members of the parish of Santa Caterina di Saragozza nor among those of San Marino.
77. In a letter to Father Biffi, dated 18 June 1698, she said: "I beg you to pity me if I have delayed my response because I find myself burdened from head to foot with crosses. . . . I keep my poor M[other] in bed having received communion for those who are about to die." In another, undated letter: "My mother has taken a turn for the worse again with fever as before." Francesca Elmi died on 29 June 1701, as is recorded in the register of the dead of San Marino.
78. This occurred after 1690, as I reconstruct events from the depositions of Elisabetta Zani. It is probable that Father Ruggieri himself had helped Angela find the new house. Situated in Via de' Gombruti, it is perhaps the same one that appeared as property of the sisters of S. Maria Nuova, where G. B. Ruggieri was special confessor. The nuns obtained it with a deed of exchange from Angelo Michele Brugnoli on 10 May 1690. Unfortunately, the space designated for the name of the tenant was left blank. At the moment of the drawing up of the notorial act, Sister Archangela Bonaveri was also present, as we shall see later on (Archivio di Stato di Bologna, busta 47/614,

"Scritture spettanti alla casa nella via de' Gombruti e mezza casa dalla parte di dietro dirimpetto dei SS. Locatelli nella strada di S. Marino").

79. Fol. 518v.

80. All the letters that E. Biffi addressed to Angela were sent to Domenico Mellini; this was the only time that Angela named him (fol. 502v).

81. Fol. 502r.

82. Fol. 493r.

83. Fol. 526r.

84. Fol. 529r.

85. Fol. 501v.

86. "I thank you for the charity of the five masses whose alms I used to pay the rent on the house and I settled it so that I do not owe anything" (Undated letter). "There are seven masses to celebrate and I will keep three if God provides enough with the others" (Letter dated 18 June 1698). In his turn, E. Biffi wrote: "I am set to celebrate nine masses. . . . When I will have the opportunity to celebrate other masses, I will tell you" (Letter dated 9 July 1698).

87. Fol. 501v.

88. Fol. 491v.

89. Fol. 501v.

90. Elisabetta specified the exact date on which Angela had recounted Biffi's offer to her: 23 April 1698, the day of her mother's death (fol. 491v).

91. Letter dated 18 June 1698, only three months before the trial.

92. Letter, numbered by the notary, fol. 40.

93. Fol. 510v.

94. Letter dated 9 July 1698.

95. Undated letter.

96. Letter dated 13 February 1698.

97. Fol. 514v.

98. Fol. 513v.

99. Fol. 515v.

100. Fol. 514r.

101. Numbered by the notary fol. 5a-4.

102. See R. Trexler, "Le célibat à la fin du Moyen Age: Les religieuses de Florence," *Annales E.S.C.* 27 (1972). On the complex problem of forced entrance in convents, see Angela Tarabotti, *La semplicit ingannata* (Leida [but Venice], 1654), pp. 33–34: "If you cannot lead your daughters to rich and noble marriage which would increase your fame, marry them in less high and more modest marriages. Divide among them without partiality the lands, and your riches, because God so desires; you do not want to raise one to the summit of worldly greatness, precipitating the others in a *Chaos* of miseries, in an abyss of damnation. Moderate the lust of the males and remember that the females are still your flesh: you do not want to bind those feelings, which God has left free to each one." I plan to write further on Tarabotti: see for the time being E. Zanette, *Suor Archangela, monaca del seicento veneziano* (Venice, 1960).

103. Archivio pii istituti educativi (Bologna); I examined the institutions of the Baraccano and Santa Croce.

104. Letter from Father Biffi, who rejoiced in the forthcoming investiture. Unfortunately, the registers containing the names, surnames, and amounts of the dowries of the Ursulines for this period are nowhere to be found. A list of this type, undated, fixed at 300 scudi "the dowry which serves as patrimony and anticipates besides expenses of investiture equal to L. 43/12." The dowries around 1730 are very different: they go from 200 to 2000 L. There is also a bit of information on the nineteenth

century. In a sheet that bears the date 1825, the aspiring Ursuline is warned that "presenting herself to the Lady Prioress without a dowry of L. 1500, she will be accepted neither by the Lady Prioress nor by the Canon" (Archivio Arcivescovile di Bologna (hereafter AAB), Orsoline, carton 3, Miscellanee 1–20, 0–377).

105. The Company of Saint Ursula was founded in Brescia on 25 November 1535 by Angela Merici. The first secular female institute, it was approved by the bishop of Brescia, Msgr. Cornaro, on 8 August 1536. Paul II approved it on 9 June 1544. Carlo Borromeo obtained its confirmation by Gregory XIII on 24 October 1582. It was reserved for virgins and widows.

106. AAB, Orsoline, Istromenti dall'anno 1614 all'anno 1763, "Inventory of property found in the house of Diamante Guarmani, a poor Ursuline, found dead on 8 July 1731. The value of this property and the investment of that money."

107. "On every regular religious festival each one teaches the Christian doctrine in the schools of their districts, in accordance with their ordination." Boncampagni, *Regole della Compagnia*, p. 22.

108. "The most eminent pastor, then, to whom is recommended the state of virginity particularly by the Sacred Council of Trent, should see how much utility and edification are the virgins of this Company in our own houses, attending to the Christian doctrine and pledged to other pious acts." Ibid., p. 36.

109. Ibid., p. 33.

110. Ibid., pp. 15–17. Concerning unmarried women and women who are not nuns, it would be very interesting to study their living according to a measure defined by clothes: it is, in short, the habit that makes the nun, the prostitute, the Ursuline, the old maid.

111. Fol. 492v.

112. Boncampagni, *Regole della Compagnia*, p. 35, subdivision 5.

113. In fact, the request for acceptance in the Company was often also motivated by difficult economic situations. One example among others: "Castel Guelfo, 13 October 1828, To my most Illustrious reverend Lord, a certain Maria Rambaldi, sixty-six years old, my fellow parishioner, unmarried, of pious conduct has received the vocation to become an Ursuline to unite herself more and more with God, but also with the scope of procuring for herself more secure means of subsistence in the last years of her life, removing from the Monte del Matrimonio [a dowry fund] two dowries deposited for many years in her favor."

114. Boncampagni, *Regole della Compagnia*, pp. 11–12.

115. Ibid., pp. 20, 38.

116. Fols. 529–530r.

117. Michelangeli, *Vita della serva di Dio*, pp. 14–15.

118. Ibid., p. 73.

119. Ibid., pp. 53–54.

120. AAB, Orsoline, congregazioni, fasc. no. 5, 1705–1835. I believe that the undated sheet refers to the period between 1707 and 1717. By Christmas 1701, in fact, the rent of Ursuline Angela Scaffi was paid and in the same list Angela also appears as having died. Angiola Angiolina appears there as well; her death certificate is dated 25 October 1717. Finally, Diamante Guarmani appears in the same list; as we have seen, she died in 1731.

# 7 Mothers-in-law, Daughters-in-law, and Sisters-in-law at the Beginning of the Twentieth Century in P. of Friuli

*by Flaviana Zanolla*

This article considers the meaning that childbirth assumed in a community of the Lower Friulian plain at the beginning of the twentieth century as a way of examining the conflicts among women within the extended families of tenant farmers.

Between 1976 and 1979, fifty-five biographies of women were collected. Many, born between 1895 and 1900, were still residents of P. (a province of Udine) in 1976. Almost all of them came from families of tenant farmers. Some were wives of small artisans (cobblers, tailors, carpenters, etc.), others of ex-tenant farmers or manual laborers who became factory workers. Nevertheless, in drafting this study, only the biographies that reflected the general pattern of rural married life, that is, of women married to tenant farmers, have been used. Given their similarity in age, the recollections of these women come from the first years of the twentieth century, when P. had about eleven hundred inhabitants.

The village is spread out; it has developed along a principal road and outward from there. The vineyards extend beyond the residential area and are interrupted by barren fields. Rows of vines twined about live trees (poplars, mulberries, willows) cross fields usually sown with grain. The landscape is, in general, quite poor: swamps, marshy areas, an intricate maze of ditches, with grinding mills scattered here and there along the small irrigation canals.

Excluding priests, civil servants, and nobles, the rest of the population earn their living in the rural economy, working the land or hav-

"Suocere, nuore, e cognate nel primo '900 a P. nel Friuli," *Quaderni Storici*, no. 44 (1980): 429–50. Translated by Margaret A. Gallucci.

> ing it worked. . . . Subtracting from the total population the half that are priests, civil servants, industrialists, nobles, the disabled, old people, and children; there remains the other half of this commune's population: the male and female workers. . . . Landowners, for the most part, live in the built-up areas; their principal concern consists in collecting from tenant farmers, in person or preferably through their agents or administrators, the payment of rents at the harvest time and in overseeing the making and subsequent division of the wine. . . . The cultivation of the fields is thus almost entirely left to tenant farmers who, although they work with considerable diligence and are not simple temporary renters, are still always uncertain about whether or not they will actually enjoy the fruits of their labors. Such circumstances certainly weigh against any improvement of the rural situation.[1]

At the end of the nineteenth century in P., noble possessions comprised 76.23 percent of the commune's territory and were primarily estates of more than two hundred hectares. The property of the corporate bodies was somewhat limited: religious ones (including parochial benefices and Church property) made up 4.85 percent and communal ones 0.41 percent of the area. Nonnoble and noncorporate property accounted for 18.51 percent of the total.[2]

In this community, the privileges of noble birth appear to have been taken for granted and fundamentally accepted. What was not so widely accepted was the landlord's "assured profit."[3] More odious yet in the eyes of the tenant farmers were the nonnoble proprietors. They possessed an authority that was founded on their access to liquid capital and on their decisive influence on the determination of market prices. They participated personally in collecting rents and dividing harvests, and, because of their peasant origins, they knew well how to recognize peasant thievery. The tenant farmers, ranked according to the amount of land leased to them, constituted the most numerous social group. The *vaciarui* (very small proprietors) were few in number. Below them, on the lowest rung of the social scale, fell the day laborers—the *sottani.*[4] "The estates are owned directly by the landowners and are worked generally by tenant farmers, obliged through temporary agreements to meet annually the terms of a lease requiring a fixed quantity of grain or of other crops and one-half of the wine, the quarter, the tenth, the gratuities for the landowner, a few fowl and the transport of commodities within the district."[5]

In P. at the beginning of the twentieth century, living arrangements in the community were strictly organized around males: when a woman married, she moved into her husband's house. An extended family (father and mother with sons, daughters-in-law, and nieces and nephews) lived there, which was organized as a unit of production and consumption.

The organization of work was directly linked to the production of subsistence goods: the necessity of cooperation, which the cycle of agricultural work imposed, led to the establishment of durable and permanent relationships, characterized by interdependence among the members of the group. The rigid division of labor, which was especially to be found in large families, was always accompanied by some flexibility within the group, made possible by the nonspecialized character of the tasks to be carried out. It was this flexibility that permitted the overcoming of difficult economic moments, assuring the continuity of the group's existence above and beyond the risks of illness, misfortune, and bad harvests.[6]

For the families that worked the rented land, the contract of tenancy was given, by custom orally, to the oldest male of the family. It was then passed on with the consent of the landlord to one of the sons, normally to the firstborn or to the son with the most offspring. The only thing of value (*bene*) which a son could inherit, then, was the right to pass on the contract to work the land. For the daughters, who had been given to their husband's family, the value of their formal dowry was minimal. They brought with them few things: some lengths of cloth, a little linen, and sometimes mattresses. Their real dowry was their capacity to produce and reproduce.

Entering the husband's family, these young brides shared the space and times of their daily life with other women: sisters-in-law (daughters or daughters-in-law like themselves) and the mother-in-law. A web of internal conflicts existed among these women, which is interesting whether considered at a given point in time or over time. First, I examine the new wife's position as she entered the family and how her pregnancy and childbirth brought to light the tensions that surrounded her. Second, I consider the history of conflict across the whole span of the women's lives as changing functions within the family modified the strategies of conflict.

❧ How did the distribution of power in the husband's family present itself to the young bride? There existed a dynamic of conflict that passed vertically through the familial group and was realized between the two old parents and the group of male children and their families, and horizontally between the latter. The vertical axis provided the principle of authority: there was the legitimated authority of the father-in-law and that of the mother-in-law, which involved profoundly different competencies and spheres of influence.

The quality and quantity of the powers of the senior male parent rested, above all, in managing the agricultural production of the family (its division into shares for new planting, food, supplies, etc.), all of which acquired greater significance in the context of the economic function of the familial organization. For the family was not so much a victim of external market conditions as the place where relations between production and consumption were defined, as well as the place where certain compensatory mechanisms were found to counter the imbalances of agricultural production.

The authority of the senior male parent began to diminish when other familial nuclei took shape—couples made up of a son and daughter-in-law with children; these engendered conflicts with him and between couples over the satisfaction of their separate needs. The former, nevertheless, retained authority, but it was largely symbolic. The very role of the patriarch contained the premises of his demise: the continuity, endurance, and solidarity of his family had always been the foundations of the old man's honor, but it was these characteristics that in the end endangered his power.

In the interviews with the women, the figure of the father-in-law was hardly remembered: he had become the symbol of unattainable authority with which one rarely established a relationship. In fact, the relationship between a father-in-law and a daughter-in-law was nonexistent; each moved in and occupied different spheres. For the young wife, the fundamental reference point was her husband, who in turn had a relationship with his father, although not directly but through the mediation of his mother. For the old man, in fact, the relationship of particular value was with his wife. But she, precisely because of her alliance with the children, extended the boundaries of her own power and progressively corroded the authority of her husband. The remaining authority of the old man was public and concerned a sphere of male relationships; in the house, the feminine balancing of familial equilibriums escaped him and yet revolved around him against his will.

"With the father-in-law there was less to suffer. We didn't speak to him and that was that. But with the mother-in-law—what can I say—one had to stay by her, side by side for life. Every once in a while there were girls who didn't understand these things, the mother-in-law knew that it was better to leave [her husband] alone."[7]

What might be interpreted as "remaining above the factions" was in reality an attitude compelled and dictated by the patriarch's being outside the decisive relationships within the family. When he was a young man, he stayed outside of the house from sunrise to sunset, working in the fields; grown old and his productive activity ended, he suffered from his permanent extraneousness. He remained apart; he focused on public male relationships. And he spent his time more and more at the local bar. Information about the state of family relationships was communicated to him by his wife.

This male figure was, so to speak, open to female influence: directly from the wife and indirectly from the daughters-in-law. The latter did not actually have any direct relationship with him; thus, they worked on their husbands, who in their turn, either directly or indirectly, actively or passively, as sons or as maternal pawns, acted on the authority of the old man. But actually it was the old woman's (*vecia*) or mother-in-law's power that directly concerned the family's future:

> But you know what I'll tell you, we women were servants, but also respected—my mother-in-law above all. I remember that when we were at my father-in-law's house and someone came to buy or sell something, a cow, or to divide up something, to do any business at all in other words, there were his sons all around him, but in a corner there was always the old woman, apart. We daughters-in-law could not stay. And there sat this old woman who was sewing socks or sewing something else or embroidering and she always kept silent. She never said anything and if she said something, the *padrone* [her master/husband] immediately said to her, "Let me work. Why are you talking?" But afterwards when there was something to sign the *padrone* looked at his wife, and the sons could say nothing and it was enough for the old woman to say, "OK, it seems all right to me." Then he would sign. But if the old woman remained silent or cleared her throat or she said something against what they were doing, the old man said: "Well, Toni or Giacomo, we'll see tomorrow, we'll do it, we'll do it." But later he never did anything. . . .
>
> And it's true that when it was just us women, it was worse; the mother-in-law ruled over our husbands more than us. Then, I re-

> member that after the land was divided among the brothers and every evening the accounts were settled, we were all together then and one could say something, but things were done more by them than us. . . . Afterwards the old men were wont to say that the old women had a nose to smell those who wanted to cheat or take advantage. . . . I remember that there was one [old woman] opposite our house who had the farm manager thrown out. I don't remember whose manager it was, but I think it was one who worked for the counts of R. And she had him thrown out of the house.[8]

The mother-in-law's authority derived from the realization of her reproductive potential, from her children: this authority was exercised first through her sons and then on their families. The group of male children functioned as the mediator of authority in relationships between the old woman and the daughters-in-law, but the mother's alliance with and authority over the sons became the fundamental weapon for the isolation of the patriarch and the affirmation of her own power. Since neither the mother-in-law nor the new wife enjoyed autonomous authority, they had to work through the son or the husband; thus, the latter became the center of the conflict between mother-in-law and daughter-in-law. For the mother-in-law as for the new wife, in order to hold authority, having influence over the son/husband was crucial.

Louise Lamphere, in observing relations among women in the same familial group and using the data of Michaelson and Goldschmidt, noted that, in cases where authority within the patriarchal family is hierarchical and in the hands of men, women enter the husband's home as strangers and make their presence legitimate only by having children.[9] Margery Wolf, on the other hand, in her work on Taiwanese family life, advanced the hypothesis that each woman tends to construct her own biological family by bonding with her children and excluding her husband, in order to overcome her isolation and assure herself of a good measure of security in her old age. But this objective, which each young bride sets before entering her husband's family, interferes with similar efforts that the other women—and the mother-in-law in particular—have been making for some time to the same end and will continue to make. The daughter-in-law represents a danger to the mother-in-law's strategies and, to a degree, to those of the other sisters-in-law; the son is caught in the middle of the conflicts that arise between his wife and the family into which he was born.[10]

The other line of conflict that developed among the various familial nuclei in P. was also an area of female competition. It was a constant effort to persuade one's own husband; a continuous struggle to increase the range of the power and the decision-making ability of each nucleus.[11] Even the relationships a woman cultivated outside the family group, with women of the neighborhood, could be a factor in the competitions and alliances that existed among the women of the familial group. These relationships could provide power: they offered the possibility of making "a man lose face" by means of manipulating public information.

In defining the development of this network of alliances and the internal and external conflicts among women, it is necessary to keep in mind that the changing nature of relationships was a given. A woman's male ally was never defined once and for all. Not only did her role shift with changes in age—first as a young woman, then as a wife, a mother, and finally as an old woman—but she was always redefining herself in a dynamic relationship with males. It was different, in fact, to be a girl, a wife, and a mother, but it was also different to be a mother of males or of females, of many or a few children. The story of these peasant women's strategies does not allow simplifications or grand generalizations; rather, one is limited to identifying certain tendencies in goals sought and methods used. But what were the objectives that these peasant women set for themselves?

In the biographies of these women there were precise recollections of the small battles waged by means of the figure of the husband for a portion of *polenta* (cornmeal mush), an extra sack of flour, or a slice of salami for one's own children. There were also significant victories against other familial nuclei, such as attaining the transfer of the lease to one's own husband rather than to another brother. But these were cited as moments and stages of a journey in the construction of authority and of a much broader, complex power.

Whatever the area of actual dispute, all the battles accompanying the growth of female authority were fought in the context of creating more favorable conditions for one's own children. The father's power was exercised *on* the children, the mother's power *through* the children. The progressive autonomy of the children was the basis of the loss of the father's power, while the mother's power increased. The father's power was inversely proportional to the children's; that of the mother, directly proportional. Each small victory, in and of itself insignificant, acquired relevance in a long-drawn-out strategy, where the objective was a general improvement of one's own power, projected onto the future of the children.

The young wife, then, her relationship with her natal family cut off (it disappeared at the moment of marriage from the biographies of all the women interviewed), found herself alone with her mother-in-law and her numerous sisters-in-law. The new couple, permanently joined (and especially the newly acquired woman), lived in a climate of isolation, in a situation of suspension, of liminality.

The new wife's pregnancy marked the moment when it was necessary to face the barriers that in fact existed between the various groups within the family. At that moment, the biological transformation of the wife, the visible enlargement of her stomach, energized a series of mechanisms of conflict that forced a definition of stable and permanent boundaries between this new nucleus and the rest of the familial group. This grew out of not only the birth of another child but also the emergence of a new woman who was becoming a mother. Internal relationships were being rearranged and had to find a different organization for the order and the organic relationships that constituted the group.

The roles and the statuses of the man: son/husband/father, and of the woman: daughter-in-law/wife/mother, were modified, upsetting the internal divisions of familial authority. The woman's original isolation became a potential source of conflict, as there was the possibility that she might isolate in her camp the figure of the son/husband.

For the entire group, a new pregnancy constituted a moment of crisis. On the one hand, it was a sign that the process of the son/husband's separation from the mother/mother-in-law, already begun with the marriage, was being fulfilled. On the other hand, it promised the beginning of the formation of a new order of relationships, since now a new figure would enter the game—a woman with child.

> When a woman was pregnant—not that one told everyone, even if we others learned about it anyway—then one would tell one's husband first and afterwards he would go to tell his mother and the others. . . . One didn't talk about these things much in the family. One heard about it in that manner. And after, nothing, the sisters-in-law didn't speak to you even to ask you how you were feeling, absolutely nothing. With the first child, nothing. They didn't explain anything, absolutely nothing. They didn't let you know anything and when one gave birth they didn't say anything. When I

myself gave birth to my son I was alone. No one was at home. I would say it was that way on purpose. . . . My mother never told me anything . . . but it seemed to me that they felt, I don't know how to say it, but as we used to say—a kind of envy. . . . Think about it—with so many children [literally, "with children to sell"] to feel envy. But they also felt resentment. They were afraid that perhaps [yours] would be preferred after it was born. . . .

After so many children, one right after another, we even began to sympathize with each other. But for the first child it was that way . . . in all families, not only in mine. . . . After there were even too many and we did it without even noticing . . . but the first child was difficult. . . . There were also many miscarriages because one worked all the same, no precautions . . . but it was in the family that they didn't pay attention; not even to the *voie* that one had. [Editor's note: *Voie* were the pregnant woman's desires for special foods or other things that if not fulfilled could supposedly damage the baby or endanger the pregnancy. Birthmarks to this day are often half-seriously referred to as a result of unfulfilled *voie*.] They said that one had to work like the others and hard. . . .

I'll always remember that when I had the first child, my mother-in-law was very upset [literally, "had a devil in her hair"] and I didn't understand why. Then one day when she was outside in the court-yard and I had to speak to her—one couldn't go for days and days without speaking. I had to ask her about things as one does in a family, and then I got fed up and I said to her that she should tell me what she had against me. And she, without even looking at me, went to chat with a sister-in-law who was nearby and, speaking to her, she answered me. . . . You can see what malice, she didn't even face me to speak to me. Instead she answered me by going around chatting with this other woman to tell me that it was time to quit complaining and that I thought that I was someone now that I was pregnant, but that I was just like the others. . . . But you can imagine—I was always mistreated. You can understand—if I had the courage to say something . . . but no; it was because she was like that that I could no longer control my nerves. But I think that it was my sisters-in-law too who put her against me even more than she already was, because they went to her to tell her tales [about me] that weren't true.[12]

My mother-in-law always told me how I was like a sow with this great stomach hanging out, that it was time to get it over with. . . . But she had a way of doing things, I don't know myself what she

> was thinking of at times. . . . But she always wanted to rule over everyone and everything and it didn't sit well with her, for example, that the child would be mine. After she told me that I had tricked my husband; that he was too good for me; that I had taken advantage of him; that she knew how things would end up; that she had already seen it happen with the other sisters-in-law, that after they had children, they became difficult and bold.[13]

For mother-in-law and sisters-in-law, the dangers of female management of this new familial nucleus were forcefully delineated. The pregnant wife was no longer alone, and "in the name of the child" she would have the ability to *inzingarar* (trick) the husband.[14] For the mother-in-law, this meant one more woman who could plot against her. The attitude of the sisters-in-law showed diffidence, fear; in sum, it was not clear how things would work out. There was now one more mother, another woman like themselves, who could undermine the daily routine in search of enlarging her own authority and influence, through the power of the husband, in the complex dynamic of group relationships.

Fears, diffidence, and hostility surrounded the pregnant woman:

> When I was pregnant, I was always alone, more alone than before. Everyone was against me. I knew even before that I could not expect any help from my mother-in-law, but when the time came I didn't know what to do.
>
> Q.: But what did she have against you?
>
> A.: But imagine, they looked at me so nastily, my sisters-in-law were like that. I remember that the first time I was pregnant it was awful; the first times I even hid my stomach—it seemed to me that it bothered them. My mother-in-law was there; she called me a cow, one couldn't say a word. Even before it was bad, but then, especially with the first child, it was awful. Even my husband [said] not a word. But afterwards they all got their due. She was right, that woman whom I told about these troubles, when she said to me: "Don't be upset—let it pass—and later you will settle accounts with everyone. Don't let it get on your nerves now, and afterwards with a child you too will begin to give your own evil looks."[15]

In these female biographies, mothers-in-law and sisters-in-law were always remembered when pregnancy was mentioned: they were the direct protagonists of such moments. Men did not enter directly into these memories, or if they did, it was because they provided the official word on the wife's state to their mother and then to the other members of the family.

The woman's strategies to obtain her objectives and pursue her aims developed fundamentally out of (without necessarily being resolved by) "tricking" the husband, by "working through men," whether husbands or sons. The major strength that the woman could use in her relationship with a man and with the group was the certainty of her irreplaceable reproductive role and her exercise both of her influence and of a more efficacious authority in the name of her son.

There was no diminution in the work asked of the pregnant woman;[16] no special attention was given her by any member of the family. In fact, the wife quickly realized the hostility that her state of pregnancy provoked around her and recognized the reasons.

> We weren't treated decently. If one was ill, one worked all the same. Night and day, suffer and be still; suffer and work and all was well. . . . One endured it because after with a child it would be different. . . . One hoped so—I don't know how to explain—one would have more respect, one could say something more, even if my husband was not able to say and do what he wanted. Now he had a child and he had to toe the line. We laughed—I'll tell you—and afterwards the oldsters had to pay attention to the fact that I was no longer the wretch who asked for a few extra crumbs [literally, "a few extra leaves of wild greens"]. I had to bring up a child. . . . And later on—well, I'll tell you, when you're old, you need children.[17]

The very moment of childbirth was distinguished by the suffering and isolation of the woman giving birth. She gave birth in her husband's house; the midwife, if she was called, was called so late that when she arrived the baby was already born. More often the sole help was some neighbor; it was a significant fact that neither her mother nor her sisters intervened, nor were they informed.[18]

Upon marriage, the woman was transferred entirely to the husband's family.

> Q.: But who was a woman with when she gave birth?
>
> A.: With? No one. If there was a midwife around, she came into the room, and that was it. No one was allowed to enter. What could they do? Watch her suffer? Afterwards there were a few women; if it went well, there were good sisters-in-law. If not, not even them.

The mother-in-law would not stay, not even to talk. They cared only for their daughters . . . they didn't even look in.

Q.: But your mother?

A.: My mother, what could she do? Come to watch her daughter who was suffering, and that was all. It was better that she stayed home, so at least she didn't have to witness the spectacle. In the end one could not use her as an intermediary with the mother-in-law, even if she treated one badly. She [one's mother] had no role any longer.[19]

In regard to her first birth, she continued:

I was alone, without anyone because even my mother, who had a little experience in these things, was not there. I kept myself on the bed and that's all. And then the baby came out dead; a shame too because it was even a boy. The second time, instead, I kept it to myself. But it didn't work out. I was in my seventh month and I hid the pregnancy under an apron. When the pains came, a neighborhood women was sent to call the midwife. This time, they were two old women, one called R. T. and the other R.C . There was also one from C. If one had a horse or a buggy, she sent for her, because she was not a witch like the others. How many died at the hands of those two, who had no other help.[20]

We worked, after we were married, even more. After the children were born, we had more respect, even if we worked as much. But in all the families about half of the children died and the women died, too, because when they gave birth, so many times even the midwife didn't come. Even though you had to pay her, she often didn't arrive until after the child was born. There were women who knew a little about these things, but if there was a hemorrhage, there was nothing to be done. There was not even anyone from the women of the family to keep you company—we are not speaking of the daughters of the mother-in-law—but not even the other women of the family. . . . In the end, when a woman was expecting, it was never the case that one was wished well; there was always some rancor in the family.[21]

What do you want—we all had these children, some were born even in the field. Perhaps if all went well they stayed healthy, but if not, if there were no doctors, nothing. . . . When one of us felt the pains, they sent for the midwife to come, or maybe not even that and one

> gave birth with no one near, not even one's mother came, especially if the families were on bad terms. Or a mother would say, "I do not want to go see my daughter who is suffering so much." And as a result one stayed there alone like a dog.[22]

> "Money for a midwife, money for a whore," they used to say, and they were right. They came when it was all over. Many times they didn't even tie the umbilical cord well and so the child died. And those women who suffered, my God there's nothing to say. It was natural, there were those hours of suffering and that was it. But to at least have someone nearby—my mother was very good; she always came when the midwife did not come. Because then they [the midwives] visited around and usually did not come immediately, because they thought that labor pains would last who knows how long! And then my mother would go to call among the houses so that they come to aid in the birth.[23]

But more than the suffering, which, after all, it was natural to refer to in remembering such moments, what was recalled was the climate of isolation from the other female figures of the acquired family and from the husband as well, who was almost always absent.

Childbirth was remembered as a traumatic moment, when the woman ran a great number of risks, from the physical to the emotional, with the aggressive behavior of the mother-in-law and the sisters-in-law.

> I remember when one of my sisters-in-law was pregnant. She was in her last months. She was making *polenta*—the kind that you stir by hand with a wooden spoon. She was working very hard to stir it and as a result the pains began and then the baby started to come out. She was alone in the house, so she bent to pull up her clothes, which at that time were worn long, and holding them up underneath her so that the baby would not fall she ran upstairs. It was a good thing that she had the bed ready because she had been expecting the birth any day. So she went to bed. My mother-in-law, who was also hers, had gone out—you see how those old women used to go out in those days when they could. When she came home, she saw that woman in bed in the throes of giving birth. She did not have anything better to say to her than, "But why did you leave the *polenta* half-made?" Yes, it was like that at one time. She did not ask her how she was or if she needed something; no, nothing, since she had left the *polenta* half-made.[24]

During childbirth, the specific attitudes of the mother-in-law and the sisters-in-law, which had already begun to come into focus during the pregnancy, became completely clear. There was no reason to give special attention to the woman giving birth: childbirth was a fact that directly concerned her alone. Having children was a natural event, which all these women, starting with the mother-in-law, had already demonstrated that they knew how to face. There was no personal merit involved. The pregnant woman was left alone because childbirth was also a test: a wife must pass it, confronting all the possible risks involved. In turn, that violent and open moment of pain was barely tolerated by the mother-in-law; she completely refused, no matter how distant she was, to accept the reduction of her own sphere of influence.

The way in which the women interviewed explained the reasons they chose to become pregnant raises questions about how the decision was made. There apparently was a deeply rooted perception that children were an instrument for advancing the status of women in the domestic group. "One had children because when they were grown up they helped and one was better off": this is the affirmation that, with different nuances, one finds most often in female biographies.

> It was one thing to be alone, another to have children . . . . What can I tell you—the children always stayed by the mother; even my husband aligned with his mother, and it would be that way with my son. Things would be better . . . whoever didn't have children, it was bad. Even my sister-in-law who didn't have children—do you think she was happy? She couldn't say anything. If she said one word, they said to her, "But what are you talking about? Why are you complaining, once you have eaten?" . . . And so she could not say anything.[25]

> My mother always said to me, "After the second child, I cried." But she wanted children all the same. Perhaps one remained unhappy immediately after the birth because no one helped. But afterwards it was different—what can I say, with a husband, he comes in through one door and goes right out the other—with children, it's different. They are always there. And when you grow old, if you don't have children, what can you do?[26]

> We daughters-in-law could never say anything. A little bit of *radicchio* from the fields to eat and be quiet—and still they made you feel as if they had given you a gift. But when the children began to be

> born, it was not just me who worked like an animal maybe without even eating. There were children who were yours as well . . . and so only then they [the family] understood that things had to change.[27]

During pregnancy, feelings of pride and strength from the wife, of repulsion and annoyance from the mother-in-law, of fear and competition from the sisters-in-law, of extraneousness from the male figures, were interwoven into the emotional fabric of the family. The pregnant woman was a woman constructing her own power; she too was becoming an old woman (*vecia*). In this regard, it seems important to note that the greatest tension in the relationships among mother-in-law, wife, and sisters-in-law arose during the first pregnancy, while the conflict disappeared when a woman reached her fourth or fifth pregnancy. This is significant because it reveals that in later pregnancies, the burden of too many children replaced the importance of a change in status. The advantages deriving from becoming a mother had already been realized; other children offered little beyond an added burden for the entire family. Many women recalled, in fact, how the birth of the fourth or fifth child provoked feelings of uncertainty and fear because of the difficulties it placed on the distribution of food resources.

> When a child was born where there were already so many, it was worse than a funeral. Then one cried. After so many they said, "Good, another one is born." But no one was really happy. Sure, a hen was killed, but there was another mouth to feed, and do you know what it means to have one more mouth to feed? . . . I remember that here in P. there was a family of sixteen who were our neighbors. You can imagine, what misery. And the old woman, the mother-in-law, always said to me, "Look at that, those people have a well nearby, without a fence around it and no one falls in, what bad luck!" Think about that—in those days one thought that way. To have one die was almost a good thing, when there were already so many born. So many tiny little coffins I saw. . . . God, for a little baby I remember that one paid nothing for a funeral, after so many one did not even bother with one.[28]

❧ Often it is said that in female biographies marriage is remembered as the decisive moment of life. Even in P., women reserved a very important place for weddings, yet they didn't talk of them as much in terms of gaining a husband as in terms of themselves and the change in life circumstances that marriage brought. The husband, the ceremony, the celebration, were irrelevant in their accounts of the marriage.

> We got to know each other because he came to my house to get the milk for his relatives. He worked at the mill. At first I did not like him at all, not at all. But he kept on trying, coming to call and this and that, and finally we were married. . . .
>
> Q.: Why, when you didn't want to?
>
> A.: I don't know; really, I did not like him at all.[29]

The lack of specific aspirations with regard to family life and to the choice of a spouse is significant, because it was motivated by the inaccessibility of the processes of formation and division of familial nuclei: "Sooner or later, in sum, one got married." The girl's inertia in the choice of a spouse was linked to the meaning that marriage assumed for women: it was fundamentally a passage from one social group to another. In brief, it involved a change of *padrone,* and in this transition a woman's room for action was very narrow—so much so that in the narrations, meeting her future husband was attributed to fortune, to destiny.

Women seemed to have been considered something worth having only during courtship. The young bachelors tried to "conquer" the girls, and in this phase they identified importance, value, and merit with the capacity to bring children into the world. Immediately after the marriage, the man began a kind of reconfiguring of the importance of the woman's procreative function. In an attempt to limit the damage that could derive from a woman's consciousness of her own importance, being able to bear children became merely a natural attribute, common to all women. The effort to reduce the woman's reproductive potential to a "natural fact" generated a potential alliance between the husband and the mother-in-law. The pregnant woman was rebuked for assuming an attitude of pride that the mother-in-law and the husband deemed unjustified and out of place. The mother-in-law, in short, tried to communicate to the daughter-in-law that she was not deceived; many children had been born within the family, and yet she was still the "old woman." The husband, reducing pregnancy and childbirth to "natural" phenomena, denied all merit and recognition to his wife.

The negotiations for marriage were conducted between familial groups. From having been the protagonist during courtship, a woman was reduced to her capacity to avoid unsuitable unions. The emotional component seemed to occupy an extremely reduced space: it was fortunate if it occurred, but its presence or absence did not affect agreement on a marriage contract. "Even if we did not like each other, we married all the same . . . Why? Because with him or with another it was the same."

Sooner or later, the web of social relationships controlled by men brought one to marriage: the meshing of individual personalities, the desire to live together, loving one another, were elements that perhaps could be envisioned for an indefinite future. But they did not constitute in and of themselves a necessary condition for contracting marriage.

"They were going to F. to find another girl. They passed in front of my house. I was at the window and I heard them saying to each other: 'Is that one there married? No. OK, Let's stay here; tomorrow we can go visit that other one.' And I too stayed here [married to one of them]."[30]

Even if one translates into visual images these recollections of the customs and moments of the meetings between couples, one sees the same portrait of a relationship. The woman, during the meetings, was always still or framed by an activity: standing in front of a window or busy in domestic or farm work, she was an element of the landscape. It was always the individual man or the group of men who wandered about the village, moving around in order to allow the names of available women to circulate literally in their group. It was the man who entered the house, who was the protagonist of the action.

The man's choice having been made, nothing remained to the woman but to wait for the two families to create the necessary conditions for her transfer. And these conditions were realized with the exit of a female member from the man's natal family, which created a vacancy that needed filling; or else by the marriage of one of the woman's brothers, which created an imbalance in her family by adding another female mouth to feed and thus fueling the desire that she leave. It was crucial to maintain an equilibrium within the rigid roles of the family; thus, the harvest, financial gain, the expiration of agricultural contracts, pig killing, and religious rules all determined the times for marriage.

One may observe that in this first, fundamental attempt at community organization, which turned on the exchange of women on the basis of their reproductive capacities, males determined the group's organization. Living with the male's family, the extraneousness of the bride in the new family until the birth of the first child, the marginalization of her opportunities to decide and to matter, were enough to affirm an essential female passivity. The stories of men and women proved to be extremely coherent from this perspective; the "agent" was clearly the man. It was he who was organized, who went to the woman's home, who married her, who brought her back home, and so on. The interviews are characterized by a repetitiveness and monotony—all of them seem to confirm the image of a group of enterprising men, violent and active, and of a group of women, quiet and passive.

The girl worked at first in her natal family, then was transferred to another family along with her capacity to work and reproduce. Work guaranteed her maintenance, but she had neither a dowry nor any wealth and lacked as well the affective ties she had had in her family. Until the birth of her first child, the wife lived moments of great social weakness. This explains the importance that the memory of a good husband assumed in the women's interviews. For the rest, as we have seen, until her children reached adulthood, the women had to invest great effort in "forming" the husband. The "clay" from which a "good" husband was formed was one that was predisposed to be molded:

"He is so good that I do what I want with him."[31]

"It was up to me to always stay at home, to clean, to make things to eat, to go into the woods and carry wood into the house . . . but my husband was a good man—I would not have been able to find another companion equal to him."[32]

"He was really so good, I really was lucky, he was really good."[33]

The high value placed upon a "good" man was common to all the women interviewed: it was a piece of advice one gave to young women of marriageable age. The memory of a really good husband had all the flavor of a victory.

For the woman who got married, the nature of authority in her life was transformed, and, if one had to live under someone else's authority, it was best to try to choose the least burdensome:

"My mother always said to me: 'Who is lucky if not you and me, my daughter; you because you are married, me because I found a good man.' "[34]

Even if these affirmations were colored by the desire to remember one's own life as beautiful, this did not exhaust the meaning and importance assumed by the figure of a "good" husband in female strategies: he provided the guarantee of an ally as well. But in the end a husband was that much better the less he existed; ideally, a truly "good" husband was equal to no husband at all.

❧ The different aspects of the female and of her authority may be culled from and discovered in the very structure and details of the interviews' narrative development.

In the first interviews, when I did not know the women of P. well, the structure of the autobiographical account was rather stereotypical. The implicit message of these first versions of a woman's biography offered an image of a woman oppressed by the weight of events. It was evident that a female prototype existed: a model of woman that one could refer to in the narration of one's own life, the image of a woman who "works and suffers." The constant elements in these first autobiographies were resignation in facing the ineluctability of life—the cycle that poses ever anew the same contradictions, difficulties, and tensions—a woman's own story of being a mother, and the stories of the others, of the husband, of the children; stories of work and of war; and the story that is history and imposes its own time, that recalls a woman to her role. And the paths traversed in the reconstruction of these female stories were those accepted and shared by the community.

In these first meetings, it was not only the woman interviewed who decided what to narrate: the code of behavior of the good Friulian peasant suggested discriminating between what could be told and what must be kept quiet. What one could tell of one's own life was the labor, the continuous toil, the serving, one's own subordination, the submission, all the essential qualifications for being accepted from the outside; what was clearly absent was any hint of reaction or rebellion against this code of behavior. The story of an honest and serious female peasant from Friuli had to recount work, marriage, and then children, the natural death of some of them, a husband to appreciate only because he chose her.

The woman would be married inasmuch as she was a good woman (*donna brava*), capable of supplying an infinite series of services to the husband and his family, and the description the woman furnished of herself was the same as what males held to be significant and defined as making a woman *brava*. The woman's emphasis on being just this way, her working and her suffering in silence, might suggest that there had been an interiorization of the model of feminine behavior, just as requested by the husband.

The woman's public aspect was that of being a function of the man. But what relationship was there between the proposed image, the apparently accepted model, and the perception that women in fact had of their own identity? Was this model accepted equally by girl, wife, mother, and mother-in-law? An attentive reading of the autobiographical data offers some answers to these questions.

Comparing the first interviews with successive ones, I realized that as the relationship between myself and the women of P. gradually became deeper and more at ease, the tone and contents of the account changed. The reconstruction of the stages of life was accompanied by a growing awareness of the narrator's own past importance. And as the narration took off and acquired life, the woman interviewed seemed progressively more convinced of having been necessary to the family that she had married into and expanded with her children. On the other hand, there also emerged the realization that her attainment of authority was a process that had taken a very long time—built little by little in a continuous effort of adaptation, assimilation, and redefinition of the boundaries of her power. The ineluctable acceptance of suffering and exhaustion might be defined as the dominant model in the organization of the memory of these women; the conflictual, rebellious aspects of power were submerged in that stereotypical, rigid model.

Taking the analysis deeper, we find in the biographies a stratum of unarticulated models on the narrative level in opposition to the dominant one. This provides, in sum, a typology of female behaviors not codifiable in the axiom of "work and suffer." These behaviors reveal a series of widespread tactics that varied according to the relationships to power, the objectives to be sought, and the tenacity of the resistance and the opposition. These were moments in which the structure of the story told was not rigid; rather, it was presented like a novel. The woman interviewed, using the first person singular, recited the story of an authority that was never defined once and for all, that accompanied the biological and social maturation of her own life with growing contradictions, presenting areas of retreat, resistance, attack, and defense.[35] In other words, from this second level of the autobiographical accounts emerged those characteristics of conflict between the old woman, the wife, and the sisters-in-law that I have considered in this essay.

The majority of previous studies by anthropologists considering the domestic sphere have focused on understanding the structure of power held by men and the way in which women saw and lived this power; few efforts have been made to try to analyze how women moved within it.[36] Instead, as we have seen, an extremely complex dynamic of authority existed within the family: it was rearranged from time to time by new mixes of both the roles and the status of each member and group of the family. Its formation was never defined; instead, it was dictated by recurrent but unforeseen combinations of alliances, conflicts, and competitions. The distribution of domestic power was characterized by extreme precariousness and mobility and by a continuous formation and reformation of strategies, objectives, and aims.

From these female memories emerges the story of perennial conflict: on one side, the man's continual effort to re-create internally, in his relationship with his wife, rules and norms, ends and legitimations, for female submission; on the other, the woman's deeds and actions, stemming from her awareness of the strength derived from her "natural" function.

This knowledge provided for the woman (and her children) an image of herself as "necessary" and undermined the husband's certainties. Part of the man's power was to dominate his wife, while part of the woman's power was to dominate her children. The woman as wife fell once again under the man's hegemony; as mother, she escaped it. The reality of the maternal figure clashed with the patriarch's (*vecio*'s) need to safeguard his prestige as head of the family, and created his need to receive, through female silence, ever new confirmations of his own power. This was, in fact, the deeper meaning of the stereotypes found in the narratives of these women.

## Notes

1. Archivio di Stato di Gorizia (hereafter cited as ASG), Catasti, sec. 19, Operato estimo catastale della Commune di P., busta P.

2. ASG, Catasti, secs. 18, 19, Mappe ed Elaborati, busta P., no. 427, Protocol of the land registry from extracts of all real estate situated in the commune of P. and in the division of S. Rinschaltungsbagen Gruneparzellen Protokolle. Archivio Curia Archevescovile di Gorzia, Chiesa di P. e A. tutela capitali, fasc. no. 200, V/4, 64; Chiesa

di S. tutela capitali, fasc. no. 201, V/4, 65; Benefici ecclesiastici, fasc. no. 293, V/9, 1, V/9, 2; Libro e Giornale contabile della Parrochia di P., busta no. 34.

3. See P. Bois, *Contadini dell'Ovest* (Turin, 1975), pp. 144–62.

4. See R. Salvadori, "Nota introduttiva," in R. Salvadori, ed., *Inchiesta Romilli* (Turin, 1979).

5. ASG, Catasti, sec. 19, Operato.

6. See E. Wolf, "Tipi di comunità latino-americano," in *L'antropologia economica,* ed. E. Grendi (Turin, 1972), and A. V. Chayanov, *The Theory of Peasant Economy* (Homewood, Ill., 1966).

7. Interview 9A. These symbols correspond to the catalogue numbers given to all interviews.

8. Interview 14A.

9. See L. Lamphere, "Strategies, Cooperation, and Conflict among Women in Domestic Groups," pp. 103–4 in *Woman, Culture, and Society,* ed. M. Z. Rosaldo and L. Lamphere (Stanford, 1974).

10. M. Wolf, *Women and the Family in Rural Taiwan* (Stanford, 1972), pp. 191–205.

11. When I refer to the relationships among sisters-in-law, I am referring exclusively to those that occurred between women acquired by the familial group and thus among the wives of brothers.

12. Interview 25A.

13. Interview 29A.

14. *Inzingarar* is dialect for *imposturare, ingannare* (to trick); see S. Domini, A. Fulizio, A. Miniussi, and G. Vittori, *Dizionario fraseologico del bisiac* (forthcoming). The etymological root of the term *inzingar* derives from *zingaro,* or gypsy.

15. Interview 10A.

16. During pregnancy, hygienic/sanitary measures were nonexistent; the woman never left work, she did not even escape the most strenuous tasks. This perhaps was also because of the lack of medical knowledge, but was above all due to a particular attitude in the face of infant mortality. "There were six, even seven children, and at times there were even those who had thirteen, fourteen. But at that time so many children died; hardly like now, now there is more assistance, more doctors. Now also if women don't have milk, they get it. Once there weren't things like this, we never even saw doctors. . . . It was bad; because as you know, without help they all would die. But it was also a good, now they all grow up, even those who are underweight, and those who are retarded—they let them grow up all the same" (interview 8B).

"Eh, once it was like this, some were born rich, some poor, some healthy, some sick" (interview 4C).

17. Interview 30A.

18. The absence, during childbirth, of women with whom the woman in labor had some bonds of consanguinity was even more significant if one realizes that in this community matrimonial strategies were characterized by a high rate of endogamy. From an analysis of the *Liber Matrimoniorum* of this parish it appears that up until the second half of the twentieth century marriages were primarily among the young people of the village. Beyond examining the complex problem of matrimonial strategies, I am interested in emphasizing the rupture that occurred after marriage between the new bride and her natal family. Although mothers and sisters lived near the bride's residence, they very rarely intervened in the details of her matrimonial life.

19. Interview 3C.

20. Interview 3C.

21. Interview 23A.

22. Interview 4C.
23. Interview 3C.
24. Interview 3C.
25. Interview 29A.
26. Interview 32A.
27. Interview 35A.
28. Interview 4B.
29. Interview 9A.
30. Interview 18A.
31. Interview 9A.
32. Interview 18A.
33. Interview 3C.
34. Interview 4A.
35. Even the tone of voice of those interviewed was somewhat repetitive and in part reinforces what has been said up to this point on the narrative development of the biographies. For readers it will undoubtedly be difficult to perceive this, but to a sensitive observer it seemed quite evident. Even if the following examples do not work entirely for those who must read them, what is immediately perceptible when one watches a woman being interviewed is how much she conveys on the plane of gesture, action, the rhythm of the account, tone, nuances, and the logic of selection, aggregation, and grouping of the elements of the recollection. I would like to report some rather typical moments that reveal stereotypes:

"Oh, miss, good afternoon, how did you get here? By car? Do you want me to tell you something? . . . Eh, I told you, work and suffer, only work and that's it; now I'm going to mass" (interview 32A).

"I'm tired, I was keeping a sister company . . . I told you, miss, work and suffer; it's good that you come into the house because it's cold outside" (interview 30A).

"Eh, what do you want me to tell you . . . you were to the other old women as well? Always that same thing . . . work and keep working, suffer and keep quiet, resign yourself to have to go on. You fall back if you couldn't go on, right?" (interview 29A).

36. See M. Fortes, *The Dynamics of Clanship among the Tallensi* (London, 1945).

# 8 ❧ Women in the Factory: Women's Networks and Social Life in America (1900–1915)

*by Giulia Calvi*

The central concern of this essay is the relationship between women and industrial work at the beginning of the twentieth century. Closely related issues include the ways in which this relationship was lived by the women involved, their perception of their new identity as workers, and their use of time, money, and the space in which they worked—the factory. To examine these phenomena I have used three different types of sources: (1) official, primarily quantitative documentation from government sources; (2) the first histories of female work written by sociologists; and (3) three autobiographical accounts written by women who directly experienced life as factory workers, even though their experiences were different. The silences, errors in record keeping, and the disparity between regulation and reality, on the one hand, and the triumphantly emancipatory (and, in a way, compensatory) dimension, on the other, have required beginning with official sources of a historical-sociological nature and then switching to subjective ones. The field of analysis thus shifts, focusing first on the New York factories crowded with female immigrant labor and later on the individual stories that were born there. Thus, from the history of female work in the factory, I have moved on to the stories of the women who worked there—moving, as a result, from the problematic of condition to that of experience.

In the concluding section I consider the complex intertextuality that these autobiographical accounts convey and their links to the quantitative sources. One preliminary observation seems in order:

"Donna in fabbrica: Communità femminile e socialità del lavoro in America (1900–1915)," *Quaderni Storici*, no. 51 (1982): 817–52. Translated by Margaret A. Gallucci.

from the comparison between these different types of documentation an underlying reality of work and life emerges, which, although veiled by moralistic condemnation, was completely absent from official sources—the reality of the social ties of female life in the factory. The community of coetaneous women, their very being together, was the first and fundamental discovery that work in a factory offered to young women workers: in the space of the factory, an autonomous female social life grew up that provided women with their first experience of a collective relationship free from any conditioning discipline, whether scholastic or familial.

This social life, however, was also shaped by models transmitted through fashion, reading, music, and films and packaged by a cultural industry that increasingly equated the feminization of cultural goods and mass behavior and consumption. The social life of women in the factory was, in this sense, conservative, both with respect to attempts at trade-union organizing of female labor and to the drive for emancipation and the contemporary campaign for suffrage. Nevertheless, it revealed an apparently elementary demand for liberty fixed at the limits of the body and its modernization. And this demand, at least embryonically, opened vistas well beyond the constrictive codes of the broader culture to which these women workers belonged.

## The Place and the Time

The ninth volume of the impressive inquiry ordered by the United States Congress on the conditions of women and children in industry focused on the history of women in factories. It opens with this statement: "The story of women's work in gainful employment is a story . . . of underbidding, of strike breaking, of the lowering of standards for men breadwinners."[1] It was 1911, and very little was known about women who worked—particularly in factories—because women "were not considered the important part of the labor force, and were frequently ignored in the discussions," as was maintained in the second volume of the same study.[2] We know, from the introduction, that while men were breadwinners, women, even if they were workers, continued to be dependents. This explains the limited consideration given to the work of women, whose placement in the productive universe remained ambiguous and whose "sphere" was regularly subject to redefinition. In the United States, the term had a long history, as the investigator who drew up the final report for the Senate recalled:

"The proper sphere of women has long been a subject of discussion. At least as early as 1829 opinions on the subject were divided along practically the same lines as to-day."[3] This stressed that beyond any small disagreements, the opinion shared by everyone, including the first union vanguards, was that women had to be identified with the domestic sphere. This was true to such an extent that the first workers' struggles for salary increases had as an objective giving male workers the ability to keep women at home.

The centrality of the house as the place that gave women their identity did not restore, however, the oppressively Victorian accents, which, in other contexts, were positing anew the image of the virtuous, asexual, domestic woman-mother. In this study the home emerged as the space of female work—of woman's skill—in opposition to the factory, which drew instead upon a woman's degraded surplus labor. Two issues were central—both harking back to the preceding stage of the traditional domestic factory—in reproposing the home as the place of the original, happy, organically integrated relationship between women and work, professional ability, and productive efficiency:

> The condition of the great majority of working women, indeed, as regards skill and efficiency, is probably worse now than that of their grandmothers who were not wage-earners. Before the introduction of machinery women were probably, on the whole, as compared with men workers, more skillful and efficient than they are to-day. The occupations taught them then were theirs for life. . . . Gradually, however, as girls have been forced on the one hand by machinery . . . and on the other by divisions of labor . . . to undertake tasks which have no direct interest to them as prospective wives and mothers, there has grown up a class of women workers in whose lives there is contradiction and internal discord. Their work has become merely a means of furnishing food, shelter, and clothing during a waiting period which has, meanwhile, gradually lengthened out as the average age of marriage has increased. Their work no longer fits in with their ideals and has lost its charm.[4]

An analogous vision, centered on the progressive elimination of female jobs by an industrial sector managed and controlled by men, was also shared by intellectuals more actively involved in these problems. Both Alice Henry, editor of the *Life and Labor* monthly of the Womens' Trade Union League, and Edith Abbott, author of the first systematic work on female labor in the United States,[5] saw the definitive break between domestic and factory work as dating from the original rupture of the unity of the home as the place of production, which went hand in hand with the rupture of personal relationships and affections in the home. The last step of this process of degradation was seen as occurring in the present, where women were limited (for the most part) to finishing work in the plant: the home was transformed from the seat of productivity and skilled work into a mere appendage of the factory.[6] The problem with industrial work for women rested (according to this vision), then, in the destruction of a spatial-temporal unity that had stressed the integrated rhythm of a communal existence where the unchanging nature of female biological destiny followed the rhythms of a working economy into which it was functionally integrated.

At the beginning of the twentieth century, this golden age of female work mythologized by Henry and Abbott still existed in the most remote areas of the United States. There the traditional relationship between production and nuclear family still survived, and the lives of women workers had not yet been divided into a "before" and an "after," and individual expectations regarding marriage had not yet been redrawn. Girls, Henry observed, continued to do the same jobs in the husband's home that they had done in the paternal one, with impressive artistic and productive results.[7]

The emerging social awareness of the brutality of working conditions in the plant carried with it an element of nostalgia for the frontier, the direct democracy of the town, work as art, and the family as the place of integrated roles. And this was true even if, as Henry herself recognized, "intellectual and emotional life must often have been a silent tragedy of repression."[8] Focusing on the "worthy" components of work in domestic manufacture functioned like the other threads of the great nostalgia of industrial America for the nineteenth century—as a memory that legitimated the reality of the present rather than subverting it. The insistent recollection of the home as the place that ennobled female work was used to reinforce the aspirations of the present and thus legitimate a life no longer defined solely by the limits of domestic walls.

"Women have always worked" was, in short, the message of the reformers. This irrefutable fact justified—above all, in the polemic with the American Federation of Labor—the female presence in the industrial universe. The reformers and the union organizers, in fact, knew that they had to face the sense of unworthiness that workers had by now internalized. Even intelligent women, having entered the world of the factory, accepted the idea of male superiority and were content with their role as second-class citizens. Sophonisba Breckenridge, the noted sociologist from Chicago, observed in 1906 that "one difficulty in securing advancement for girls is that they acquiesce in the general judgment as to their inferiority. Young women who are most contemptuous regarding the ability of certain young men still feel themselves disqualified in some mysterious way from entering the profession the young men have successfully entered. . . . Employers take girl-workers because they are more easily satisfied: 'They don't ask for a raise.'"[9]

In reality, from the beginning of industrialization profoundly different views explained the social inferiority of male and female factory workers. The factory was male in terms of what made one individually or collectively skilled. And even if only theoretically, the possibility of progressing up the ladder of skills was recognized for the male worker. Yet it was generally denied to women. In other words, male identity coincided in large part with a man's working role, while the female role was not socially legitimate in any but the domestic sphere. "My mother"—Elisabeth Hasanovitz wrote in her autobiography—"could not tolerate the idea that I might become a working-girl. The tradition of a respectable family in our town, no matter how poor, was to keep their daughters at home. The only occupation for girls was either dressmaking or domestic service—the latter being very degrading."[10]

The disastrous results of attempts throughout the nineteenth century to organize female labor in factories is, in fact, largely attributable to the presumed irreconcilability of women with work, or better, to the inability of delineating for women a model of social identity as workers.

In the second half of the nineteenth century, we witness a radical transformation in the status of women from both the middle and lower classes: the entry into the factory of the latter was accompanied by an accentuated confinement of the former in the by now solely sentimental universe of the home. This process was not painless and brought with it a gradual redefinition of the concept of female work itself. The comprehensive devaluation to which this was subject was not limited to factory jobs, for it penetrated the domestic walls as well and resulted in a general "de-monetarization" of domestic work.

Popular female narrative constructed its stories around the housewife who—mysteriously—never spent money, who was surrounded by consumer goods whose monetary value she did not know, and whose world, populated by petulant servants and governed by infantile caprices, sterilely mimicked the lost communal universe by now reduced to the sphere of bourgeois privacy.[11] Middle-class women had to ignore money and, consequently, paid work: "A true lady"—we read in *Ladies' Home Journal*—"even if needy, must always pretend to not work, or at least to do it only for her own enjoyment."[12] The 1890s were marked by the spread of Women's Exchanges, which had as their objective addressing the needs of poor women. They encouraged these women to do small jobs for neighbors, so that they might preserve the appearance of bourgeois decorum, cautioning them to deliver merchandise in the evening and not to rent out rooms to anyone.[13]

To work for monetary compensation was, then, equivalent to admitting one's own misfortune publicly. The academic vision of the importance of the market economy for industrial and financial development was ignored in the domestic sphere because the economic value of female work was rejected: women had to be kept ignorant of the violence of the laws (both economic and social) that regulated profit and accumulation. What was central was that women perceived their own (devalued) working experience in an atomized way, as reintegrated in the private dimension of a female universe, and not as part of a collective one involving productivity and social utility. Thus, even if the bourgeois woman experienced confinement and domestic isolation, the female worker was the one who was considered to have suffered internal "contradiction and conflict." The study cited above concluded that the "broken up" life was hers. As Alice Henry wrote: "Her life during her first fourteen years is utterly unrelated to the next period which she spends in the factory. . . . When they [her factory years] are ended, and married life entered upon, we are again struck by the absence of any relation between either of these two life-periods and the stage preceding . . . this means an utter dislocation between successive stages of a woman's life."[14]

## The Factory and The Modernization of Behavior

Asocial behavior by women in the factory was a result of the temporary nature of the work experience, which usually ended with marriage; the sense of social inferiority which surrounded that experience;

the continued qualification of such work as secondary to domestic activities; and the inherent contradictions in the woman's first relationship with salaried labor. Numerous reports document the submissiveness and minimal drive to organize; the nontraditional and freer relationships with men; the tendency to work too much and for subsistence wages; and the absence of apprenticeship and professional development.[15] Union organizers were responsible for some of this, since they were well aware of the influence of female stereotypes (the acceptance of sacrifice, obedience, submission), which had always been obstacles to emancipation. The leaders of the American Federation of Labor even used the existence of such stereotypes to justify statutory clauses that—in a vicious circle—barred women workers from the union.[16]

In sum, work, especially factory work, was not adapted to the female sex: this was the common opinion, which, along with social divisions, contributed to defining a profile of a mythical woman/mother immune to the dangers of the new extradomestic socialization and which in turn shaped the progressive ideology of educated motherhood.[17] Motherhood became the female profession *par excellence.* This viewpoint grew in the context of increased emphasis on both domestic productivity and scientific child-rearing. Extradomestic work was gradually reconceptualized on this model, so that the occupations into which women were channeled (e.g., teacher, nurse) were defined as natural extensions of domestic labor.[18] Factory work was the only area that resisted assimilation and, therefore, was considered unworthy and dangerous for women. It was so characterized because it had the potential to emancipate women workers—not so much because it used trade union and political consciousness as models, but because it presupposed attitudes, behaviors, life styles, and social life once solely reserved for males.

Such a transformation was more threatening the more a strong and nonconventional sensibility was attributed to women of the lower classes. In a popular novel of 1901, *The Portion of Labor,*[19] for the first time there appeared as protagonist a woman who liberated herself from her double subordination (female and worker) by organizing her fellow plant workers during a victorious strike. The analytic care that the author dedicated to the formation of the exemplary character of Ellen, the protagonist, created a forceful model of female uniqueness. Ellen, in contrast to her milieu, was endowed with great self-control:

the passions and conflicts that drove her family did not leave a trace in her personality. Constantly capable of self-examination, she was different both from her social class and from her group of contemporaries; she had a logical intelligence beyond the intuitive, and, as she grew up, she differentiated herself more and more clearly from her "parent stock." Ellen triumphed because she was able to emancipate herself from both social and sexual subordination, avoiding those psychological-cultural characteristics that the industrial universe attributed to a premodern and therefore historically vanishing world.

In spite of the nature of factory work, emancipation did occur. Sociologist Robert Woods, in a study of two thousand workers in Chicago, affirmed that "the level of accuracy required in the crudest form of employment calls for a certain moral accomplishment; the general experience gained often makes the girl more liberal in her ideas, offers her a wider basis of comparison, and affords wholesome human competition."[20] On the negative side, however, factory work brought about sexual promiscuity, loss of "ideals," and a general lowering of morals; as a result, such work served as a focus for concerns about the degeneration of the race due to the diffusion of venereal diseases among workers.[21]

The magnitude and complexity of values expressed by this web of questions and answers, which contemporaries proposed on the issue of women who worked in industry at the beginning of the twentieth century, require a closer examination—above all, of the protagonists. Who were the workers? Where did they work? How and why did they go to the factory? How were they able to leave it?

## The Ambiguous Numbers

Until 1908, published materials about this problem were scarce and diverse in form: articles in weekly and monthly journals attentive to "social ills" (*Atlantic Monthly, The Survey, Century Magazine, Harper's Magazine*, etc.); novels; denunciations by the first reporters (the term *reporter* was conceived in this period); and some inquiries on the conditions of factory work in the major metropolises.[22] These were the years when a group of probing journalists, the muckrakers, discovered the corruption of trusts and political interest groups. And it was also the time when those who examined the social realm proposed solutions that were aimed at guaranteeing a scientific amelioration of the morbid degeneration that afflicted society.

In 1908, the lead was taken by the first great social survey, *The Pittsburgh Survey,* which meticulously studied the mining community.[23] The national interest in the results of the inquiry, accentuated by a large and bloody strike some years earlier, was considerable.[24] The six-volume survey consisted of a collection of studies from both inside and outside the industry; its authors claimed that it was the first factual study and one that captured the consciousness of a community. Soon the social survey would become, therefore, not only a denunciation and diagnosis of the problem but the central moment of self-revelation of the human group. The shattering of subjective experience (for miners, for women) was transcended by a new collective understanding of the functional bonds within the community. An entire volume, *Homestead: The Households of a Mill Town,* compiled by Margaret Byington, registered, quantified, and revealed what Robert Parker had grasped as the central point of the social survey—the extensive world of the phenomena hidden in the folds of the everyday. With an attentive eye Byington measured the acquisitions, free time, and mortality of the female population: the language, despite the statistical tables, retains the airy and impressionistic quality of journalists and novelists. Caught between science and literature, the volume is marked by the nervous bourgeois curiosity of women who, in studying the community, discovered a quasi-unknown throng of other women.

This was not the case for the second systematic inquiry extended to more representative centers of the nation and contained in the nineteen volumes of the 1911 *Report on the Condition of Woman and Child Wage-Earners in the United States.* Here the dense succession of data and tables was limited to translating facts into spatial relationships. The monotonous repetitiveness of the vocabulary, which guaranteed the typicality of the phenomena, intentionally annulled any tendency to subjectivity. The obligation to be neutral kept researchers from drawing conclusions from the figures and offered a text impenetrable to analysis.[25] Normality and the attempt to register it blocked every opening for the expression of individuality as an object of study: room, board, salary, and living and working conditions were quantified because they were concretely reformable. And yet, positivist science had to come to terms with individuals: the interaction of women and men with the questions of the investigators was obvious and unavoidable. Through the limited give and take of questions and answers, one sees the inquiry's degree of allegiance to the very social reality that its authors sought to know and control.

The fifth volume of the *Report on the Condition of Woman and Child Wage-Earners,* entitled *Wage-earning Women in Stores and Factories,* focused on six major urban centers: New York, Boston, Chicago, Philadelphia, St. Louis, and Minneapolis-St. Paul. Women workers were divided into those with a family (that is, those who were dependents) and those who were "adrift" (that is, without family ties). These latter were of special interest to the investigators, who immediately introduced the central question: how many women without a home were there in the great cities? And, more importantly, precisely at what moment in the process of the breakdown of the home could a woman define herself as adrift?[26] This question abandoned the pretext of objectivity and made clear the semantic-ideological potential that the term *home* entailed: this latter disappeared when the family no longer existed as the transmitter of "influence" on the woman. The domestic sphere, it was further specified, had a double function, "to sustain her in time of need" and "to restrain her in time of temptation."[27] Along with the single girl, most often of non-American origin, the abandoned woman would then be labeled "adrift," as would the widow with children, the woman who lived in a boardinghouse, and the woman for whom "those so-called homes have become only impeding wreckage."[28]

On this point it was necessary to establish the number of women workers in both categories. To quantify such artificial categories was not easy, bearing in mind, among other things, the low quality of the statistics previously gathered.[29] "To discover from the great army of wage-earning women the number that were adrift was in itself not an easy task," the investigators warned as they made explicit the methodological criteria adopted: the compilation of lists of factory workers and store clerks on the basis of the names and addresses furnished by their employers; the casual selection of some names; the rearranging of the same names on the basis of districts of residency.[30] A preliminary attempt at verification revealed that a vast majority of the addresses collected were apparently false: "There was strong evidence in some cases of a desire on the part of the girls to give the numbers of houses of better appearance," in part due to the fact that "a girl endeavoring to secure a position and finding herself rejected because she has no home in the city is under strong temptation, when she finds another vacancy, to say that she is living with an aunt or a cousin or even with her parents when she is really dependent on the boarding or lodging houses. She quickly learns, too, to give an address in the home district, rather than in the boarding-house sections."[31]

This type of experience was imprinted in the memory of many factory workers: in Dorothy Richardson's, for example, who entered a factory after the death of her parents. "'Where do you live?'" the head of the department asked her when she began work. "'Over in East Fourteenth Street. . . .' 'Home?' 'No, I room,' then reading only too quickly an unpleasant interpretation in the uplifted eyebrows, a disagreeable curiosity mirrored in the brown eyes beneath, I added hastily, 'I have no home. My folks are dead.'"[32]

The painful secrecy that enveloped the whole issue of living arrangements accentuated, conversely, the socializing functions of the street and the place of work. Richardson herself, struck by the sudden illness of a companion, decided to go visit her, but immediately realized that "I had never even heard the name of the street. I knew it was somewhere on the East Side; that was all. In all our weeks of acquaintanceship no occasion had arisen whereby Bessie should mention where she lived."[33]

At the same time, it was not only fellow workers who were ignorant of each other's addresses, but business management itself. In fact, the investigators declared that the lists of names furnished by the employers in many cases were not up-to-date, were perhaps even two or three years old: "In one instance out of a list of 146 names, 131, or nearly 90 per cent, were of no avail in the investigation."[34] The plethora of unskilled and low-paid workers rendered registration superfluous, but the condition of marginality itself—complicated by the daily strategies for eluding its effects—undercut the precision of the official data. If female identity was defined by the domestic sphere, to acknowledge one's condition as adrift was the same as accepting one's difference from the norm, which was both uncomfortable and subject to the disciplining attention of welldoers and social workers. The difference from the corresponding male is revealing: not belonging and mobility were in part joined in the negative image of the hobo or at least in the image of the marginal man who refused to adapt and was unwilling to work. In contrast, women had no other option beyond a certain firm resistance to the questions of superiors, department heads, employers, and investigators, in order to deny their own independence while in private protecting it.

The relationship of the data to social reality was further undercut by the varied forms of the productive structure, their degree of modernity, and the sectors examined. The amount of error increased with increasing proximity to the metropolis: while the data regarding textile industries in New England, for example, appeared largely homogeneous and were more readily available,[35] for New York, the clothing sector—which employed the largest number of female workers—posed very different survey problems, fragmented as it was by the coexistence of the sweatshop with the small and medium-sized unionized factory. The investigators had to admit that the general disorganization of the sector had impeded the collection of available data on salaries and hours, but they concluded that "as to wages . . . and as to hours there is practically no limit, except the endurance of the employee."[36]

The presence of women in this sector also escaped meaningful quantification because the factors that conditioned it were too numerous: the new technology of electric sewing machines, the nationalization of the market, the constant flux of the female immigrant work force, the improvement of working conditions, and the gradual disappearance of the contractor and the sweatshop. "Whether the effect of these changes has been to increase the number of women employed, can not, however, be affirmed." In fact, the investigators stated that "these influences, according to the testimony of employers, have served to reduce, rather than augment, the proportion of women employed in the industry."[37]

What portrait, then, do the official sources paint of female workers? We know that they were very young, even if there is no consensus on their number: in 1908, the Department of Commerce and Labor calculated that 75 percent of the workers in the six urban centers already cited were younger than twenty-five years of age. We are informed that the vast majority (between 75 and 87 percent) lived with their families (but we have seen how difficult it was to obtain this information); that a minority—between 13 and 25 percent—was "adrift." We know how much they earned: between three and four dollars per week if they were apprenticed, up to a maximum of twenty to twenty-four if they were skilled.[38] We know how much, on the average, they spent to live,[39] what their lodgings and the places in which they worked were like, and what portion of their salary they turned over to their families. The data also recorded how many joined union organizations (prevalently the skilled) and how many instead slid toward immoral or criminal occupations.[40]

We do not know, however (and such sources can reveal nothing to us on the subject), how all these things came together to form individual experience, stirred by values and questions, by compromise, resistance, conflict. How did people bridge the deep gulf between the "before" of life and the "after" of work about which Alice Henry wrote? What did it mean—as we read in the government study—that work had lost every attraction for these young women? What was this broken life, the life of one who had left home and knew the discipline of the factory?

## Three Biographies: Dorothy, Elisabeth, Bessie

Some deeper understanding of such questions can be drawn from a different kind of text. Here I use *The Woman Who Toils*, a journalistic account written in the first person by a social worker of bourgeois origin, Bessie Von Vorst, who, in 1903, went to work in a factory for awhile, and two autobiographical narratives that are limited to the working experience of the protagonists: *The Long Day*, by Dorothy Richardson (1905), and *One of Them: Chapters from a Passionate Autobiography*, by Elisabeth Hasanovitz (1918).[41]

Dorothy Richardson came from a lower-middle-class Pennsylvania family. After a period of factory work in New York, following the death of her parents, she became a journalist and a militant member of the American Socialist party of Eugene Debs. Before she began working in the factory, she had taught for a period of time in a rural school.

In the city, Dorothy moved within the milieu of the Women's Trade Union League, an organization founded in 1903 on the initiative of a group of women workers and bourgeois women who were active both in the union and in the suffrage movement. The League's objective was improving working conditions in the factory by favoring the admission of women workers into the American Federation of Labor; to this end they used intensive propaganda and backed the first labor struggles. But the politics of organization was divided internally by opposition between its bourgeois members, more sensitive to feminist themes, and its workers, more attuned to union goals. In the end, the hegemony of the bourgeois women brought with it the progressive assimilation of factory workers into suffragist models and life styles typical of the well-to-do reformists. Nancy S. Dye, a historian of the organization, wrote:

> The more a worker dedicated herself to the League the more her difference from bourgeois women vanished. Both groups of women were a-typical in American society at the beginning of the century: the majority were not married at an age in which the majority of other women were; they were proud of being independent and of supporting themselves on their own; they lived in a purely female milieu in which their most intimate friends, their colleagues at work, their sources of emotion, were women.[42]

*The Long Day* reflected these issues firsthand and elicited broad support from the outset—above all, among those committed to progressive reforms. Some social workers pressed for its distribution among young workers, emphasizing its accuracy and social commitment,[43] even if the success of the volume (three editions were published in four months) was accompanied by strong disagreements, which further intensified the differences within the League. Leonora O'Reilly, one of the union leaders, resigned from the organization in order to emphasize her dissent with the book's contents. The workers Dorothy wrote about were not—according to O'Reilly—those who crowded the New York factories. In particular, it was feared that the explicit mention of prostitution would favor the prejudices and tastes of a bourgeois public and would degrade and mask the real life of workers.[44]

The Richardson-O'Reilly polemic established the orthodox vision that continues to dominate the histories written by feminists, which tend to lose the complexity of real suffering by adopting a moral perspective geared to the ends of the movement. The workers we read about in the works of the last decade appear to us through the filter of a fundamental economic reductionism: they are women who endured hard work and poverty and who liberated themselves through conflict in the industrial setting and admission to the union. The interpretive scheme and the journey to redemption from subordination mirror essentially those of the male workers' movement. In contrast, *The Long Day, One of Them,* and even *The Woman Who Toils,* although agreeing on women's ultimate goals, allowed a very different female reality to show through, even if it has been forgotten. Dorothy's workers were above all girls who experienced their work in the factory as the discovery of an autonomous female social life. The group of coetaneous women emerged as the primary and fundamental experience; all other experiences were subordinated to it. This strong level of solidarity was, however, also interwoven with a gravely weakened female culture, and this regressive element very probably eased the process of abstraction that has guaranteed the survival of "progressive" elements in the historiography of women workers while ignoring the specificity and conditions of female life in the factory.

*One of Them: Chapters of a Passionate Autobiography,* by Elisabeth Hasanovitz, was also conceived within a milieu close to the League. It described the union situation and provided a more circumscribed vision of the dynamic within the factory. Elisabeth was a Russian immigrant who arrived alone in New York at the beginning of the century and earned her living working in the clothing sector. She was Jewish and a socialist and had known from infancy the harshness of social marginalization and political persecution in her homeland. Having grown up in a village, the daughter of an elementary schoolteacher, Elisabeth brought with her to America an enduring communal and religious memory: family, her father's school, nature, and religious ceremonies recur incessantly in her work to emphasize the break created by the experience of emigration. Elisabeth would later become a union organizer. Both Richardson and Hasanovitz attained a brief moment of notoriety because of their autobiographies, but the rest of their lives is lost in silence.

## ❧ Identity and Writing

In reality, the two works are more than autobiographies: they are *tranches de vie,* autobiographical accounts centered on a unique phase of life—their arrival in New York and the initial experience of industrial work. In this sense they are close to Bessie Von Vorst's journalistic account, *The Woman Who Toils,* which examined, however, different milieus and places: Chicago, the heartland, the South. Three women, working among women, then wrote about it, and the diversity of their works complemented the survey movement, with its broadly drawn and diagnostic interest in the social realm. Their writing reflected the unresolved fluidity of a language that was becoming scientific, although still attuned to other echoes: the realistic novel of the day, militant journalism, and progressive reformism which had preceded and outflanked the socialist reform movement. In the process of "community introspection"[45] begun in these years, the still ill-defined analytical structures left space open for their impressionistic use of language. Lacking a scientific terminology, their language gained meaning precisely in terms of individual stories.[46]

The autobiographies of Dorothy and Elisabeth reflected the unchronicled experiences of the majority of young women who, from Europe, the heartland, or the countryside, came to the city and the factory for the first time. Each reiterated the strong polarization between a past self and a present self, which was the central element in the relationship between traditional female identity and industrial work. This dialectic, which shattered time and identity, was also common in the immigrant experience. There the self of the Old World was opposed to the self of the New, and the impact of modernity was understood as the breakdown of the original cultural context—as the symbolic death of the past self. An exemplary work in this sense, capable of registering the multiple fragmentation of time-space-identity, is the autobiography of Mary Antin, who emigrated to America from Russia at the beginning of the century:

> I was born, I have lived, and I have been made over. Is it not time to write my life's history? I am just as much out of the way as if I were dead, for I am absolutely other than the person whose story I have to tell. . . . My life I have still to live; her life ended when mine began. . . . *A proper autobiography is a death-bed confession.* . . . I am not yet thirty, counting in years, and I am writing my life history. . . . I have not accomplished anything, I have not discovered anything, not even by accident, as Columbus discovered America. My life has been unusual, but by no means unique. And this is the very core of the matter. It is because I understand my history, in its larger outlines, to be typical of many, that I consider it worth recording. *My life is a concrete illustration of a multitude of statistical facts.* . . . I began life in the Middle Ages, as I shall prove, and here am I still, your contemporary in the twentieth century, thrilling with your latest thought.[47]

In this sense, the working experience was seen as one that initiated a conversion in the context of the violent rupture of time and the subjective consciousness associated with migration. It was not by chance that this type of individual development was expressed especially well by autobiography: as a genre, in fact, it gained meaning from the contrast between the narrating self, who was also the present self, and the past self, whose transformation it explained. The legitimacy and exemplary nature of the present self lay entirely in the break, in the transformation/negation of the past self and the possibility of communicating this to produce similar reactions in the reader.

The double break in time and identity, common to young workers and immigrants, was resolved in the two autobiographies with a positive catharsis. Both Dorothy and Elisabeth were able, in fact, to leave the factory in order to describe it, abandoning the doubly subordinate work of a female factory worker. The present self was reintegrated with the past self through writing. "I want you to start, as soon as you are ready, to write about your experiences from your first shop and steadily on," is the proposal that Mr. Valentine, a reformer associated with the *Labor Board*, made to Elizabeth. "I want all the details, interesting or otherwise. Write of the work as it begins in the morning and ends in the evening. Write of the surroundings, the treatment, the relations between one worker and another, and between worker and employer. Write of their homes, their lives, their recreations, how it affected you and others."[48]

Emancipation from factory work was accomplished through autobiography, the narration of the self, at the very moment when a woman perceived her development as exemplary: when the individual broke away from the collectivity in order to explain it, revealing its connections and internal relationships. Significantly, Elisabeth titled her autobiography *One of Them* in order to redeem from anonymity, through narration, an experience that was exemplary.

"Part of the horror and loathing of that unhappy period of servitude fell away from me"—wrote Dorothy—"the sordid suffering, the hurt to pride, the ineffaceable scar on heart and soul I felt had not been in vain."[49] Her autobiographical account had slid into the form of the *epistola calamitarum* of the Protestant and Anglo-Saxon tradition, where a negative chain of events had the function of exalting, by contrast, the individual determination to overcome. From the victorious encounter with adversity there emerged a model for life.

## ❧ Past and Present

Dorothy Richardson was one of the innumerable country schoolteachers who left a village or small town to find work in the city:[50] "Why in the name of all common sense, had I ever come to New

York?" she asked herself; "Why was I not content to remain a country school-ma'am, in a place where a country school-ma'am was looked up to as something of a personage?"[51] Bessie Von Vorst also noted, immediately after she entered the factory, the refusal of young women factory workers to take jobs connected with traditional female roles, such as teaching and domestic service. After speaking with a one-time rural teacher who had just arrived, she observed, "She could not say why school-teaching was uncongenial to her, except that the children 'made her nervous' and she wanted to try factory work."[52] In the context of advanced industrialization, the backward and inadequate preparation of a country schoolteacher accentuated the sense of futility and isolation that a job so underpaid already implied. The tendency to desert school teaching was confirmed in a report by the Industrial Commission on Immigration and Education at the beginning of the century: "New England is being educated by 11,000 women teachers, who can not and never should be held responsible for the technical education of her industrial population. Ten per cent of them abandon the profession every year for matrimony, and show their good sense in so doing."[53]

Fiction echoed the same vision: teachers who appeared in contemporary novels were characters who were negative, old, repressive, and bigoted, or else bored and filled with frustrations.[54] Una Golden, protagonist of Sinclair Lewis's novel *The Job*, had taught for "two miserable terms . . . in the small white district school, four miles out on the Bethlehem Road. She hated the drive out and back, the airless room . . . the shy, stupid, staring children."[55]

In the same way, young women refused domestic service: the efforts of social workers to redirect girls who had just come to the factory to such service failed completely. Even Dorothy was approached by "a stately middle-aged woman" who suggested to her that she become a maid. With Dorothy's firm refusal, the woman moved away, looking at her with "mingled disappointment and disgust."[56] If for many social workers domestic work seemed ideally suited to the "sensitive" nature of young workers, the refusal of this option, which many reports document, revealed that entry into the factory was a choice of a role and job that was modern and preferred over such archaically female ones as seamstress, maid, and teacher. It was not by chance that the *Ladies' Home Journal*, which in 1903 sold one million copies, was preoccupied with encouraging American women not to abandon the more traditional and less skilled occupations to immigrant women, "given that you can no longer find anyone who knows how to do them."[57]

In the same magazine, Commissioner of Labor Carroll D. Wright observed that a majority of young women preferred the factory to "comfortable quarters and healthful surroundings in some family," perhaps because the long hours and toil that characterized industry were compensated for by independence: "So the term 'domestic servant' offends her. It degrades her in a social sense. . . . Her social relations are practically destroyed, not only through the designation of 'servant,' but also by the habit of employers of considering her engaged in menial employment. . . . So the woman in domestic service is lonely."[58]

The traditional domestic role and its isolation were in fact tied to that inevitable biological point of departure (marriage and maternity), which many young women seemed to want to postpone, if not redefine. The attraction that the factory and the city had for them expressed, more than anything else, a desire for a social life different from both that of their family and that of their original ethnic community. This implied a desire to place themselves as individuals at the center of a network of modern relationships, defined no longer by consanguinity but by historical factors focused on the necessity of earning a living. In this sense, home, as the place of origin, became a memory dominated by a feeling of loss mixed with rebellion against the predictable oppressiveness of daily life and familial control. Elisabeth Hasanovitz, attempting to force her father to let her leave, refused to eat for two days: "I shall go to America," she affirmed in front of her whole family; "I do not want to waste my life. I want to be free." Yet at the moment of separation the old bonds made themselves felt: "All I left behind me with regret and yet with no regret."[59]

## Rites of Passage

The unnerving fascination of New York was the first point of contact: "a giant city that hung splendid on the purple night," wrote Dorothy Richardson; "turret upon turret, and tower upon tower . . . a city such as prophets saw in visions, a city such as dreamy childhood conjures up in the muster of summer clouds at sunset."[60] The same city, criss-crossed in the frenetic search for work, became by day the place where the past was lost and familial (and even religious) traditions were broken. After an afternoon spent in the vain search for a job, Dorothy set out to buy some food—potatoes, milk, a little butter—realizing too late that it was Saturday: "Never in my life before had I bought anything on the Sabbath day, and never before had I seen a place of business open for trade on that day. My people had not been sternly religious people, and theoretically, I didn't think I was doing anything wicked; yet I felt, as I gave my order to the grocery man, as though I were violating every sacred tradition of birth and breeding."[61]

The break between the past and the present had been forcefully realized: the conflict would be repeated and would be once again of an ethical nature. This time it signaled the betrayal of communal solidarity. Having obtained an initial promise of work, Dorothy ran to the factory; at the corner of the street she saw the house of a friend in flames: "I stopped at the corner, strongly tempted by my innate sense of decency to the memory of the dead. But only for a moment: the law of life—self-preservation—again asserted itself."[62]

In her autobiographical account, these two betrayals of the past prefigured and prepared her entry into the factory. The violence of her encounter with the building, the noise, and the crowd, and the effort necessary to overcome it assumed the characteristics of a veritable initiation: her present self was born. The individuality lost in the metropolis was reborn in a communal microcosm—that of work.

"The instant impression was one of repulsion, and the impulse was to run away. But there was fascination, too, in the hag-like visage of those grim brick walls, checkered with innumerable dirty windows. . . . It was the fascination of the mysterious and of evil; and, repulsive and forbidding as was its general aspect, nothing could now have induced me to turn back."[63]

Before taking on a completely new identity as a factory worker, it was necessary to go one last step in the annulment of the earlier self. The loss of one's name severed the last tie with the past: "We were called by numbers in most of the shops," Elisabeth recalled, and Dorothy noted: "The foreman made quick work of us. Thirty-two girls . . . [he] addressed each one as 'Sally.'" Bessie Von Vorst had the same experience: it was literally two days before anyone called her by her own name.[64] It was her fellow workers who gave Dorothy a new identity, rebaptizing her—as was the common practice—with a fictitious name, taken from one of their favorite novels.

While for young male workers the factory was the world of their fathers, for women entry into the factory created their first group relationships with coetaneous women outside of the family and school.[65] For boys, the plant was the place where they learned a trade, and deference to older men was both felt and of value: for girls, the social life of work hardly included older people. Their milieu was made up primarily of others of their age: department heads, the spokesmen for business interests, were excluded from all group activities and did not offer a model of adult life to the female workers. Having broken the ties that bound them to the past, these women lived only in the present, in conflict with the maternal image, of which they were ashamed—especially if they were immigrants.[66] In the absence of other places (the street, the salon) in which to gather, the workplace was the one location that, during the day, replaced other social spaces reserved for male contemporaries. As a result, the workplace provided the locus of group dynamics and group social life for women: there, solidarity of sex prevailed momentarily over that of class and ethnicity.

The absence of older workers, on the other hand, accentuated the separation of the group from the real experiences of nonworking life, fomenting a lively exchange of daydreams, readings, stories, songs, and so forth. Aware that the factory experience would last only for a brief period in their life, the majority of young women workers strengthened, by means of the group, a female subculture whose unanimous support of emancipation nevertheless concealed a traditional content. The greater freedom won within the family, thanks to their new condition as salaried employees, was connected to the growth of a working community paradoxically cemented by the romantic mythification of the future. They dreamed of love and marriage, but they were to be free from the tutelage of parents and the unconditioned expression of "passion." Because of its brevity, working experience was perceived as a liminal moment with respect to the complex parabola of life: social life with other women was a slight pause before encountering what remained *outside* the factory. In this sense, being together coincided with a phase of relative suspension of normality.

According to Victor Turner, the condition of liminality was the basis for the rise of communal relationships. These were characterized by a sense of equality and by the development of rules through which symbols of communication took forms that were distinct and pertained to the experience of the transition shared by the group. This simplification of the social fabric was accompanied by a complication of the cultural one: the reciprocal giving of romantic names, taken from popular novels, was an indication of this symbolic break in identity, which had grown out of the interpersonal relationships of the group of women.

One encounters here a total redrawing of self-perceptions heavily conditioned by female role models created by a nascent mass culture industry and diffused through magazines, popular novels, and songs: in this sense, the young women workers strengthened their bonds through group forms of language and perception shot through with conventional content. As Bessie Von Vorst noted: "Above the incessant roar and burring din they called gaily to each other, gossiping, chatting, telling stories. What did they talk about? Everything except domestic cares. The management of an interior, housekeeping, cooking were things I never once heard mentioned. What were their favorite topics, those returned to most frequently and with surest interest? Dress and men."[67]

Dorothy Richardson followed the story of friendships and hostilities within her work group with particular interest; her previous experience as a teacher had sharpened her perception of language, accents, and intonations, in addition to having given her a special interest in written culture. Phoebe, "a girl with tortoise earrings and paper rollers in her hair," introduced her to her colleagues; she had the job of initiating her into her duties. The "greenhands," without experience in factory work, immediately became the object of contention and rivalry among the more skilled workers. Training the new workers, in fact, increased the piecework of the instructor, who received the money earned by the apprentice. Suspicions of favoritism by the heads of the department and diffidence toward the greenhand helped increase tensions: Phoebe introduced Dorothy to her job, but above all she mediated the relationship between the group and the new arrival. "They are capable of playing the most senseless tricks on a new worker's clothes," Phoebe told Dorothy, taking her overcoat under her protection and reminding her that the first duty toward others was to not behave "oddly." In practice, the only freedom was "to do as the other girls do"; the punishment was ostracism.[68]

Entry into the community of women was, then, sanctioned by a precise and permanent ritual, "the cast iron code," as Dorothy called it.[69] The rules on which the group was founded were essentially meta-individual, given that the extreme mobility of labor and the seasonal nature of this type of production did not guarantee continuity or the emergence of leaders. The punishment of deviants assured the consensual functioning of the group, whose survival was guaranteed only by the maintenance of a prudent middle road: diversity was not tolerated, just as the imposition of managerial discipline, which threatened unity, was resisted.

David Montgomery's studies of the dynamic within male groups in the factory and of the means by which the unskilled were assimilated into the group of skilled workers offers a male version of an analogous process. Permanent employment and the possibility of advancement, which typified the working experience of men, however, provided the very dynamics that threatened the horizontal cohesion and solidarity characteristic of female groups.[70]

## Writing and Language

Aware of the new rules of the community, Dorothy began the refinishing work that was assigned to her, surrounded by companions whose "tongues flew as fast as their fingers."[71] At noon they took a snack break, sitting in the center of the tables with the paper wrappings open on their laps. "The girls lunched in groups of ten and twelve. . . . By an unwritten law I was included among those who rallied around Phoebe, most of whom she had 'learned' at some time or other."[72] They exchanged candies and cucumbers, and the youngest distributed tea: after a few minutes, many would "steal away to a sequestered bower among the boxes" to read a novel voraciously. The half-hour went by in this way, with the "less literary" chatting about dances, clothes, daily scandals, and fires. A fire, Dorothy observed, was feared by a person who did this type of work, enclosed as she was in the suffocating space of the shop, which evaded all health and safety regulations.[73] At the same time, her attention was fixed on the lunchtime readers, who returned to work enraptured and told their companions stories of "bankers and mill-owners who in fiction have wooed and won and honorably wedded just such poor toilers as they themselves."[74]

The history of the literary tastes of working women explains in great part the conservative nature of the social life of these groups. Together with songs and the products of the nascent film industry, serials, novels, and women's magazines promoted the model of an adult femininity no longer mediated by the traditional channels of family and school.[75] The content of these publications was for the most part transmitted orally, and Dorothy learned about them from her companions' accounts of the romantic plots of this genre.

Young workers were avid consumers of this type of female mass literature, which began to appear in America around the middle of the nineteenth century. Written by women for women, these stories introduced a sentimental theme into the literary culture of the time, which was imbued with a debased form of Victorian sentiment. The literary "feminization" of these years marks the birth of a new consumerism of books, sustained by a public of women attracted by the intense emotional content.[76] These novels are marked by the transfer of areas of conflict from the socio-economic to the moral, sexual, generational, and geographical; in the process, the significance of class was replaced by environmental and psychological factors. The events narrated turned on good people and bad people, women and men, young and old, and Northerners and Southerners, while the differences between poor and rich were invariably overcome by means of disinterested love and domestic virtue.[77]

Already present in the popular female narratives of the second half of the nineteenth century, this pattern was again found in the plots that Dorothy—astonished and entertained—heard from her companions, and in the serials of the *Ladies' Home Journal,* the most successful female monthly in America. Here a vast number of love stories, preferably with a historical background, were published. While the historically progressive tone of the story was guaranteed by the pre-chosen context—the Civil War or the Revolution—the parable of the protagonist's individual redemption was nevertheless ahistorically always the same: a woman, generally poor, obedient, and naive, married a noble/rich/brave man, but only if she was beautiful. For women there was no historical redemption from subordination, but only an individual, private one through the uniqueness of body and sentiment.[78] Defined by her own nature, a woman, in this vision, was indifferent to time and culture: whether aristocratic Southerners, democratic country girls during the Revolution, or sensible contemporary ladies, their destinies were marked by an identical biological determinism.

The characteristics of a "language of women" marked a revealing division between forms of writing: the male learned one of politics and history; the female, a "natural" (sentimental) one of literature. From the beginning of the nineteenth century, militant New England women reformers opted for a "virile" model of writing. Both Elizabeth Cady Stanton, a leader of the suffragist movement, and Elizabeth Blackwell, the first woman doctor in America, appropriated scientific and political language in order to denounce the historical subordination of women, accepting as a *fait accompli* the sentimental-narrative confinement of female expressive codes in popular literature. Reform and engagement took up the "language of men," which was already identified with high literature. The path was one way only: the woman who emancipated herself had to emerge from the immobility of nature to become a man.

Dorothy Richardson, Elisabeth Hasanovitz, and Bessie Von Vorst proposed male models of language and consciousness to their fellow workers. Dorothy chose the area most congenial to her, literary culture, seeking "to purify the tradition concerning romance through the spread of the great novels."[79]

"I replied with the names of a dozen or more of the simple, everyday classics," Dorothy wrote; "They had never heard of *David Copperfield* or of Dickens. Nor had they ever heard of Gulliver's Travels, nor of *The Vicar of Wakefield*. They had heard the name of Robinson Crusoe, but they did not know it was the name of an entrancing romance."[80] She illustrated the value and meaning of *Little Women* and *Les Miserables* to her colleagues, provoking a complex range of questions. But her interest in the *Bildungsroman* was not, in the end, shared by her colleagues, who unanimously protested, "That's no story—that's just everyday happenings."[81] The "masculine" realism of the nineteenth century had to give way to the sentimental novel: the degradation of work, Dorothy reflected, was followed by the degradation of culture. It was useless to try to limit the diffusion of "yellowbacks" with Shakespeare and Ruskin, as reformers and social workers tried to do with obtuse austerity. After a hard day of labor, workers wanted to enjoy themselves, and the solution lay in "cater[ing] to the very primitive feminine liking for identity" in order to put forth models capable of stirring positive and mimetically liberating emotions.[82]

Insensitive to the mediated paths that link the reader to the text, Dorothy found the source of a "degradation" of behavior in a "degraded" literature; leaving out the role of interpretation, she equated reading with a smooth assimilation of the model that "must cater to the very primitive feminine liking for identity." The possibilities were limited: if reform were to occur through education, it would be actuated by writing and reading, and Dorothy placed herself at the center of the exemplary autobiographical schema, in the place of the female heroine of popular literature. The first step was the woman who thought, who knew how to control her emotions. Dorothy, Elisabeth, and Bessie never talked about love: their experience was collective, never private. It was rage against exploitation, suffering, hunger, and poverty, and the desire for redemption. These were sentiments that ignored a female subculture that defined the body as an ornament and depicted an individual, liberating, emancipating space that surrounded the body. They, in contrast, experienced the body as undergoing suffering, aging, and mutilation.

Dorothy and Elisabeth were part of the nineteenth-century tradition of the "literary operative": the literate and learned worker who was given high literature from the circulating libraries of the first manufacturing centers by an even more illuminated patron. This tradition originated in Lowell, Massachusetts, utopia of the textile industry in New England in the early nineteenth century. Here the figure of the skilled and "worthy" factory worker was conceived, later to become the model for progressive culture. Its founder was Lucy Larcom, a textile worker who later became the director of the local working women's newspaper. In her memoirs we find the following:

> A near relative of mine, who had a taste for rather abstruse studies, used to keep a mathematical problem or two pinned up on a post of her dressing frame, which she and her companions solved as they paced up and down, mending the broken threads of the warp. It has already been said that books were prohibited in the mills, but no objection was made to bits of printed paper; and this same young girl, not wishing to break a rule, took to pieces her half-worn copy of Locke on the *Understanding*, and carried the leaves about with her at work, until she had fixed the contents of the whole connectedly in her mind. . . . It was a common thing for a girl to have a page or two of the Bible beside her thus, committing its verses to memory while her hands went on with their mechanical occupation. Sometimes it was the fragment of a dilapidated hymn-book, from which she learned a hymn to sing to herself, unheard within the deep solitude of unceasing sound."[83]

Already in 1847, then, the group of literary operatives warned their colleagues against the dangers of the sentimental penchant of

*Godey's Lady's Book,* a women's magazine read more than "the works of Gibbon, or Bancroft, or Goldsmith."[84]

Beginning in the mid-nineteenth century, then, the image of a feminine, subordinate woman worker was opposed to that of a colleague who "never spends her evenings . . . in the reading of fictitious works" or goes out dancing but who, in solitude, studies "history, or the biography of some distinguished individual"—who, in short, is "possessed of morals and [an] intellectual mind."[85] In the New York Public Library, in contact with modern classics, Elisabeth Hasanovitz found "my coveted America."[86]

Even in the metaphorical language of good literature, we glimpse an analogous symbolic vision. Ellen, the previously mentioned heroine of *The Portion of Labor,* constantly risked taking the solitary path offered to her by the body, enjoying only with "the rich" the privileged relationship that her beauty guaranteed her and excluding her female peers. Only her intellect and rationality secured the reentry of Ellen into her class and into solidarity with the workers in struggle.

## ❧ The Boundaries of the Body

Like men, Dorothy and Elisabeth were "adrift"—that is, they did not live with their families but were single women who supported themselves. They were breadwinners; they did not turn over all or part of their wages to their families. Unequivocally driven by the necessity of working in order to survive, these women were the only ones who garnered the support of reformers. Dependent girls also worked to survive by contributing to the meager familial budget. Yet they were considered by employers, and often by reformers as well, as women drawn to work by frivolous and consumerist motives. They were not working for wages but for spending money, to be independent.

"The women were divided into two groups"—Bessie Von Vorst wrote—"those who work because they needed to earn their living and those who came to the factories to be more independent than at home, to exercise their coquetry and amuse themselves, to make pin money for luxuries."[87] For them, in short, the problem of wages was not vital; in this sense, along with their inferior physical strength, they were different from men. "What should we think of a class of masculine clerks and employees who spend all their money on clothes?"[88]

At five o'clock on Saturday afternoons, Bessie observed, the streets of Perry, the small industrial center where she worked, swarmed with people. Everyone bought, and the shops were crowded. At dinner each girl showed the others the purchases she had just made: "stockings, fine lace, fancy buckles, velvet ribbons, elaborate hairpins. . . . 'I am not working to save' was the claim of one girl for all. 'I'm working for pleasure.'"[89]

Certainly, the "sensible" have always imputed the absence of saving to the "moral baseness" of the lower classes and never to their wages, which barely provided the money necessary to live. The expenditures of the young factory workers nevertheless engendered lively debate. Along with censure, there was also some rethinking of the working and union positions. The congressional report itself recognized that women workers had little margin for buying themselves frivolities, given their wages and the fact that they generally bought clothes by saving on food or moving out of expensive lodgings.[90] Elisabeth recalled how, during the slow time of year, the girls passed the time by making clothes for themselves out of scraps: "It made one wonder to watch with what endeavor they tried to piece out waists of the smallest remnants, copying the styles from our shop."[91] The situation of young women living with their families was not much different: they turned over the majority of their wages to the household (88.1 percent of it in New York). But that percentage decreased with increased age: from the maximum turned over at about sixteen years of age, it had dropped by at least half at twenty-five.[92]

Beyond these disparities, however, the heart of the problem was centered in the new aesthetic aggressively attributed to money by the young women factory workers. Paradoxically, however, it also concerned the naive carelessness that accompanied being used to not having any money.[93] For these women, the body was their primary concern—it was the filter of a modernization that was posited as an expanded need, the focus of necessities and desires that were perpetually growing and being redefined. As the boundary of consumption and the center of individual identity, it was the body that the family claimed to protect. And it was clothes that distinguished the scholar from the girl who worked, the child from the woman. It was clothes that, from the very beginning, instructed women in the journey toward adulthood and entry into the world. "For those working-class girls who remained in school after most of their friends had taken jobs," a New York investigator commented in 1911, "the dresses of their employed friends are constant sources of envy."[94]

Around the body, made uniform for the masses by American aesthetic canons created by the culture industry, were intertwined forms of an elementary social identity fixed at the boundaries of gender, but not limited by the more archaic ethnicity. These were the ways (seen as so dangerous by Dorothy, Elisabeth, and Bessie) of being women.

"Here again I met"—Elisabeth wrote—"the queens of imitation. . . . In the evening, as soon as the power stopped, powder-puffs were extracted from stockings, faces were smeared again, the aprons changed for the latest style of short hobble-skirts, and off they went to pace Grand Street."[95] With sympathy, if not with pity, Elisabeth judged the cheapness of their world and the backward forms of association that restrained the unionization of female workers. Union consciousness had for Elisabeth the same valence that high culture assumed for Dorothy: both values were diametrically opposed to the female focus on the body and the sentimentality that in no way could be assimilated. The subculture of female groups had to be destroyed, like the immorality of the subproletariat and the primitivism of the Indians. During a strike in a small manufacturing plant Elisabeth met Lena, a Russian emigrant who told her about her conversion to politics. Lena had a past that was common to many: she left school because "it was too monotonous" and began to work.[96] She enjoyed prostituting herself on the street corner and spent everything she earned so that she could go dancing and have a good time. "The prince of her dreams" was a boxer she had met in a dance hall. Suddenly Lena had given all that up: she realized that the true heroes were not the ones who climbed into the ring but "George Washington and Lincoln . . . some one who does something for the people . . . [even some one who] make[s] waists to clothe the women who cannot sew for themselves."[97] Her consciousness was not of exploitation, but of the superiority of the rational and bourgeois culture to an ethnic and popular one: "A prize fighter is like a thief or a murderer—Lena said emphatically—and the people who enjoy such sports are like Indians who dance around the fire where they burn white men alive."[98]

The contrast focused on two lists of attributes: (1) national hero, white man, worker; (2) popular hero, Indian, subproletariat. Political consciousness and union organization were conquests which belonged by nature to the first. After she heard Lena's story, Elisabeth reflected:

> Lena had had an opportunity to finish school. Why did she not? Why did she enjoy flirting on the street corners and prefer the dance-halls and ice-cream parlors? And as I walked on, nearer and nearer to the tumult, into the hot boiler steaming with trashy humanity, where all sorts of vices can find a splendid hiding-place, as I made my way through the multitude of children that crowded the sidewalks and thoroughfares, through the masses of suspicious, eagle-eyed young men, lurking about and trying to entice the children for criminal purposes, an answer rang in a loud, poignant voice. Lena was a child of those streets—to quote her own words: "the streets were always so lively, but school was too monotonous, they make you memorize, memorize and that's all. . . ." On questioning her as to her mother's indifference, she answered: ". . . To me, as to many, my mother was a 'greenhorn,' a foreigner, and, of course, inferior to me, an American girl.—So you see, my mother had no influence over me." "Not being controlled by their elders, being little taken care of in the schools, and living in dirty slums, what becomes of them?" I thought.[99]

Lena changed after she met Sonia, a unionized worker with a long history of struggle. "How many Sonias did we need to convert all the Lenas?" Elisabeth asked in conclusion. For Bessie, Dorothy, and Elisabeth, then, the female form of reality was to be totally censured, without further analysis. Rouged, bodies adorned with flashy clothes, young women workers focused on novels, songs, chats, and "superstitions of all kinds: to sneeze on Saturday means the arrival of a beau on Sunday; a big or little tea leaf means a tall or short caller, and so on. There is a book of dreams kept on a table in the mill, and the girls consult it to find the interpretation of their nocturnal reveries."[100] It did not matter that some of these practices were the same as their mothers'; for the three women they had only one meaning: their subordination to men and to History. Their writings all concluded in the same way, stressing the centrality of skilled work and its ethics.

Women worked without a method and without discipline, Dorothy observed, and because of this they did not reach the skill levels that would have permitted them to guarantee themselves a better future. And because of this they did not love their work. To overcome this, Bessie concluded, it was necessary to reform the educational system, which would require the establishment of female industrial schools that would offer the professional training that was lacking. Also an attachment to work, independent of marriage, would develop from a process of discipline acquired earlier through domestic work and school. Since their childhood, her colleagues at work, Dorothy reflected, had not known "the delight of sitting in a little red chair in a great circle of other little red chairs filled with other little girls, each and all learning the rudimentary principles of work under the blissful delusion that they were at play."[101] In Taylor's America, the free kindergarten movement began preparing the disciplined and methodical workers of the future from a very young age.

The austerity of these judgments obscures, however, the confused enthusiasm with which young workers still expressed a strong demand for freedom. The subculture of the group, through the plant, the dance hall, and the nickelodeon (even if marked by the mass forms of the nascent industrial culture) crucially reinforced a feeling of solidarity among these girls and broke the vertical links of paternal and managerial authoritarianism. The support of colleagues in tragic moments, which so frequently marked the life of small factories, was conceived in terms of work; the subversive happiness, which all the observers noted, was the first sign of a horizontal linkage that set these women against a tradition of resigned and subordinate meekness. "The contrast between the ordered world of school, where the model of success was a decorous female authority figure, and the explosive sociability of the factory was real," wrote Leslie Tentler.[102] Bessie Von Vorst concluded that the contrast between "natural duties" owed to the family and "fictitious duties" in the new female groups (clubs, committees, groups, professions) was dangerous.[103]

Being together was the great discovery, the most fertile stimulus that grew directly from the factory experience. Only personal experience and the present mattered: "Their conversation is vulgar and prosaic; there is nothing in the language they use that suggests an ideal or any conception of the abstract. They make jokes, state facts about work, tease each other, but in all they say there is not a word of value—nothing that would interest if repeated out of its class."[104]

These observations recall those of a noted critic, Thornstein Veblen; he also observed—in 1904—the disappearance of any reference to the culture of the bourgeoisie in that of nonskilled workers; the weakening of the ideological pillars on which bourgeois culture had been constructed (natural liberty, natural rights, and property), and the complex decline of "norms of validity that rest on usage and on the conventional standards handed down by usage."[105] The consolidation of new values, in the context of working experience, isolated that world by means of diverse and specific languages, alienating "whoever belongs to another class." The rupture of both communication and its traditional structures followed the break with old forms of female belonging: it separated much as the environment in which it took shape was separated. Female social life in the factory, which occupied so much space in autobiographies, was passed by in silence in official sources. It was an intermediary reality—not yet the expression of political and union consciousness, but no longer the reflection of premodern and preindustrial tradition. It was an elusive reality, potentially capable of inspiring liberation still profoundly marked by elements of conservatism and stasis. It was, however, a new reality, which must be traced beyond the boundaries of the workplace in order to determine its grip and its capacity to modify the spaces and times of the lives of women and men.

## Notes

1. U.S. Congress, Senate, *Report on the Condition of Woman and Child Wage-Earners in the United States,* S. Doc. 645, 61st Cong., 2d sess. (Washington, D.C., 1911), vol. 9, *History of Women in Industry in the United States,* p. 11.
2. Ibid., vol. 2, *Men's Ready Made Clothing,* p. 504.
3. Ibid., vol. 9, *History of Women in Industry,* p. 13.
4. Ibid., p. 31.
5. A. Henry, *The Trade Union Woman* (New York, 1917); E. Abbott, *Women in Industry* (New York, 1919 [1909]).
6. Abbott, *Women in Industry,* Introduction.
7. Henry, *Trade Union Woman,* p. 218ff.
8. Ibid., p. 221.
9. L. W. Tentler, *Wage-earning Women: Industrial Work and Family Life in the United States (1900–1930)* (New York, 1979), pp. 76–77.
10. E. Hasanovitz, *One of Them: Chapters from a Passionate Autobiography* (Boston, 1918), p. 10.
11. A. Douglas, *The Feminization of American Culture* (New York, 1979), p. 56.
12. See, for example, the columns "Pin-Money Made with the Needle" and "How 32 Girls Made Pin Money," *Ladies' Home Journal,* January 1904, pp. 22–23. Even the stories that have women social workers as protagonists never touch on their relationship with institutions: the philanthropic theater is always the home. Douglas, *Feminization of American Culture,* pp. 157–58.
13. Cited in S. M. Rothman, *Woman's Proper Place* (New York, 1978), p. 86.
14. Henry, *Trade Union Woman,* p. 222.
15. On all these points, see R. S. Woods and A. J. Kennedy, eds., *Young Working Girls: A Summary of Evidence from Two Thousand Social Workers* (Boston, 1913), p. 25.
16. P. S. Foner, *Women and the American Labor Movement* (New York, 1979), p. 250; Henry, *Trade Union Woman,* p. 158.
17. Rothman, *Woman's Proper Place,* p. 82. In 1870 the sale of contraceptives was prohibited by law and abortion became a criminal act. These two principles became

the cardinal points of the so-called crusade for purity, which found in two prominent women, physician Elizabeth Blackwell and temperance reformer Frances Willard, its strongest supporters. This legislation remained in effect through the 1920s, helping to widen the gap between the role of wife and that of mother by privileging the latter.

18. Ibid., p. 153; see also *Ladies' Home Journal* for the years 1902 and 1903.

19. Mary E. Wilkins [Freeman], *The Portion of Labor* (New York, 1901).

20. Woods and Kennedy, *Young Working Girls*, p. 31.

21. Ibid., p. 84ff.

22. C. C. Taylor, *The Social Survey: Its History and Methods* (Columbia, Mo., 1919), p. 30ff.; A. H. Baton and S. M. Harrison, *A Bibliography of Social Surveys: Reports of Fact Finding Studies Made as a Basis for Social Action* (New York, 1930).

23. *The Pittsburgh Survey*, ed. P. V. Kellogg, 6 vols. (New York, 1909–14).

24. Taylor, *Social Survey*, pp. 10–12.

25. On these problems, see the introduction by Raffaele Romanelli, "La Nuova Italia e la misurazione dei fatti sociali: Una permessa," *Quaderni Storici*, no. 45 (1980).

26. *Report on Woman and Child Wage-Earners*, vol. 5, *Wage-earning Women in Stores and Factories*, p. 9.

27. Ibid., p. 12.

28. Ibid.

29. The figures are those of the *State Census of Manufactures:* for 1905, these sources calculated that, in the six cities in question, working women numbered 400,000. Those without a home varied from 3,000 to 25,000 and constituted about 16 percent (65,000) of the total workers.

30. *Report on Woman and Child Wage-Earners*, vol. 5, p. 12.

31. Ibid., p. 13.

32. *The Long Day: The Story of a New York Working Girl as Told by Herself* (New York, 1911 [1905]), p. 64.

33. Ibid., p. 225.

34. *Report on Woman and Child Wage-Earners*, vol. 5, p. 13. These are data relative to the number of "adrift" female workers and to those residing with their families:

| | Boston | Chicago | Minne-apolis/ St. Paul | New York | Phila-delphia | St. Louis |
|---|---|---|---|---|---|---|
| Home | 544/74.7% | 326/83.6% | 181/81.5% | 1686/87.0% | 855/82.0% | 543/78.4% |
| Adrift | 184/24.3% | 64/16.4% | 41/18.5% | 252/13.0% | 188/18.0% | 150/21.6% |

35. *Report on Woman and Child Wage-Earners*, vol. 1, *Cotton Textile Industry*, pp. 37, 469. In 1905, of a total of 142,063 workers in the New England textile industry, 45.4 percent were women, compared to 48.6 percent men. Of a sample group of 1,017 female workers, 16.1 percent were 16 years old. The percentage progressively decreased with age (3.6 were 23 years old), then rose again to 3.7 percent (24) and to 7.2 percent (from 25 to 29) and declined slowly to 6.0 percent for workers aged 30 or older. Female workers from 16 to 19 years old constituted the majority of the sample, accounting for 57.9 percent of the total. The average number of years spent in the plant was 2.3 for girls aged 16 and 22.5 for those 30 and older.

36. Ibid., vol. 2, p. 502ff.

37. Ibid., pp. 511–12.

38. Ibid., vol. 5, p. 47ff.

39. Ibid., p. 17ff.

40. Ibid., p. 142ff.; vol. 10, *The History of Women in Trade Unions;* vol. 15, *The Relation between Occupation and Criminality of Women*, pp. 75–77ff.

41. John (Mrs.) and Mary Von Vorst, *The Woman Who Toils: Being the Experiences of Two Gentlewomen as Factory Girls* (New York, 1903), with an introduction by the president of the United States, Theodore Roosevelt; Richardson, *The Long Day;* Hasanovitz, *One of Them.* On Mrs. Von Vorst, see Robert W. Smuts, *Women and Work in America* (New York, 1971), pp. 40–42.

42. Nancy S. Dye, "La solidarietà difficile: Femminismo e lotta classe nella New York della Women's Trade Union League (1903–1914)," in *Donna Woman Femme,* nos. 10–11 (1979): 40; Foner, *Women and the American Labor Movement,* p. 244ff.

43. Woods and Kennedy, *Young Working Girls,* p. 63. Woods refers to the habitual practice among club leaders in immigrant and working communities of distributing "good literature"—for example, *The Long Day.*

44. Foner, *Women and the American Labor Movement,* p. 310.

45. Taylor, *Social Survey,* p. 11.

46. On these themes, see Gianna Pomata, "Madri illegittime fra Ottocento e Novecento: Storie cliniche e storie di vita," *Quaderni Storici* 15, no. 44 (1980): 530.

47. Mary Antin, *The Promised Land* (London, 1912), pp. xi-xiii (emphasis added).

48. Hasanovitz, *One of Them,* pp. 320–21.

49. Richardson, *The Long Day,* p. 273.

50. Ibid., p. 76.

51. Ibid., p. 55.

52. Von Vorst, *The Woman Who Toils,* p. 78.

53. U.S. Industrial Commission, *Report of the Industrial Commission on Immigration and Education* (Washington, D.C., 1901), p. 67; see also Rothman, *Woman's Proper Place,* p. 76ff.

54. Dorothy Deegan, *The Stereotype of the Single Woman in American Novels* (New York, 1951), p. 90.

55. Sinclair Lewis, *Le donne lavorano* (Milan, 1955), p. 15 (*The Job, An American Novel* [New York, 1917], p. 9).

56. Richardson, *The Long Day,* p. 57.

57. *Ladies' Home Journal,* March 1904, p. 22.

58. Ibid.

59. Hasanovitz, *One of Them,* pp. 9–12.

60. Richardson, *The Long Day,* p. 4.

61. Ibid., p. 33.

62. Ibid., p. 59.

63. Ibid., pp. 59–60.

64. Hasanovitz, *One of Them,* p. 204; Richardson, *The Long Day,* p. 231; Von Vorst, *The Woman Who Toils,* pp. 21–22.

65. Tentler, *Wage-earning Women,* p. 50.

66. Woods and Kennedy, *Young Working Girls,* p. 50.

67. Von Vorst, *The Woman Who Toils,* p. 73. See also *Report on Woman and Child Wage-Earners,* vol. 1, pp. 540–42: in a sample of 969 female workers in New England textile factories, 60.1 percent stated that they did not perform any domestic work, either because their husband was unemployed or because it was done by an elderly relative or a dependent. Female workers interviewed "in most cases . . . claimed that their being at work had no effect at all, or at least no bad effect" (p. 541). On the concept of liminality and its formation in the anthropological field, see Arnold Van Gennep, *I riti di passaggio* (Turin, 1981), and Victor W. Turner, "Passages, Margins, and Poverty: Religious Symbols of Communities," in *Dramas, Fields, and Metaphors: Symbolic Action in Human Society* (Ithaca, 1974).

68. Richardson, *The Long Day,* pp. 66–68.

69. Ibid., p. 68.

70. David Montgomery, *Rapporti di classe nell'America del primo Novecento* (Turin, 1980), pp. 29–50. On the subject of prevalently male processes of socialization, see Jürgen Schlumbohm, "'Traditional' Collectivity and Modern Individuality: Some Questions and Suggestions for the Historical Study of Socialization. The Examples of the German Lower and Upper Bourgeoisie around 1800," *Social History* 5, no. 1 (1980): 71–103.

71. Richardson, *The Long Day,* p. 70.

72. Ibid., p. 72.

73. Ibid., p. 73.

74. Ibid., p. 74.

75. On this subject, see Elisabeth Ewen, "City Lights: Immigrant Women and the Rise of the Movies," *Signs* 5, no. 3 (1980): 45–65; Sandra Perry, "Sex and Sentiment in America," *Journal of Popular Culture* 6, no. 1 (1972): 32–48; John S. Haller, "From Maidenhood to Menopause," ibid., pp. 49–69.

76. Douglas, *Feminization of American Culture,* p. 6.

77. Ibid., p. 300.

78. See, for example, the comments published in *Ladies' Home Journal,* July 1902, p. 7.

79. Woods and Kennedy, *Young Working Girls,* p. 98.

80. Richardson, *The Long Day,* p. 85.

81. Ibid., p. 86.

82. Ibid., p. 301.

83. P. S. Foner, ed., *The Factory Girls* (Urbana, Ill., 1977), pp. 22–23; L. Larcom, *A New England Girlhood* (Boston, 1889).

84. Foner, *Factory Girls,* p. 93.

85. Ibid., pp. 119–20.

86. Hasanovitz, *One of Them,* p. 162.

87. Von Vorst, *The Woman Who Toils,* p. 160. Yet, dependent girls were deliberately taken on first, and their wage levels determined the wage scale for all. See *Report on Woman and Child Wage-Earners,* vol. 5, p. 22.

88. Von Vorst, *The Woman Who Toils,* pp. 113–14.

89. Ibid., p. 83.

90. *Report on Woman and Child Wage-Earners,* vol. 5, p. 17.

91. Hasanovitz, *One of Them,* p. 227.

92. *Report on Woman and Child Wage-Earners,* vol. 5, pp. 19–20.

93. Woods and Kennedy, *Young Working Girls,* pp. 51–52.

94. Cited in Tentler, *Wage-earning Women,* p. 97.

95. Hasanovitz, *One of Them,* pp. 92–93.

96. Ibid., pp. 73–74.

97. Ibid., pp. 73–77.

98. Ibid., p. 77.

99. Ibid., pp. 80–82.

100. Von Vorst, *The Woman Who Toils,* p. 92.

101. Richardson, *The Long Day,* p. 92.

102. Tentler, *Wage-earning Women,* p. 67.

103. Von Vorst, *The Woman Who Toils,* p. 80.

104. Ibid., p. 38.

105. T. Veblen, *The Theory of Business Enterprise* (New York, 1932 [1904]), p. 310.

Designed by Martha Farlow
Composed by G&S Typesetters, Inc., in Stempel Garamond
Printed by The Maple Press Company, Inc., on 50-lb. Glatfelter Eggshell Cream